BLUE FIRES

BLUE FIRES

The Lost Secrets of
Nazi Technology

Gary Hyland

HEADLINE

First published in 2001
by HEADLINE BOOK PUBLISHING

10 9 8 7 6 5 4 3 2 1

British Library Cataloguing in Publication Data

Hyland, Gary, 1940–
Blue fires: the lost secrets of Nazi technology
1. Strategic weapons systems – Germany – History 2. Defense
information, Classified – United States 3. Unidentified flying
objects – Sightings and encounters – New Mexico – Roswell
4. Conspiracies – United States
I. Title
909.8'25

ISBN 0 7472 7146 1

Illustrations copyright © Mat Edwards

Typeset by Avon Dataset Ltd, Bidford-on-Avon, Warks
(www.avondataset.com)

Printed and bound in Great Britain by
Mackays of Chatham PLC, Chatham, Kent

HEADLINE BOOK PUBLISHING
A division of Hodder Headline
338 Euston Road
London NW1 3BH

www.headline.co.uk
www.hodderheadline.com

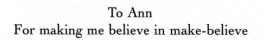

To Ann
For making me believe in make-believe

acknowledgements

A big thank you to all those who helped in some way with this book. In particular, Dan Johnson at LUFT46.COM, Alexandra Bruce, Justo Miranda and those contributors and sources who must remain anonymous. Also, to the team at Headline and anyone else I've not mentioned – I thank you all.

contents

introduction

A little over fifty years ago, something crash-landed in the desert scrub of New Mexico, an event that, like a stone cast into a still pond, has been sending out influential ripples ever since. What *really* happened at Roswell in the summer of 1947 will probably never be known for certain, but over the years the legends and urban myths that have sprung up in its wake have 'informed' the world's population (or at least those who've cared to listen) that what crashed on to 'Mac' Brazel's ranch was an alien spacecraft and that one or two living crew members were subsequently taken into 'protective custody'. You can use your own take on the story to fill in the blanks – everyone with an interest has their own twist to offer.

The belief that 'flying saucers' have a distinctly 'alien' origin is now so pervasive that we seldom stop to question its provenance. For close on fifty years a succession of Hollywood blockbusters such as *Close Encounters* and *Independence Day*, together with a vast canon of science fiction literature and TV shows like *Star Trek* and sensationalist reports of UFO sightings in the media, have bombarded us with images and ideas that don't just promote the idea of life in outer space – but of life *that's visiting us*. Collectively, we seem to *need* to believe that this is the case.

1

Yet as a society, what hard evidence do we have to go on in reaching this judgement?

Put simply, there is none. We have forgotten that a UFO is simply an 'unidentified flying object'. Just because in most cases the easiest 'explanation' for a sighting of a craft is to deduce that it came from another world does not mean that it's the *right* deduction – merely the most convenient.

Since Roswell, of course, there have been countless reported sightings of UFOs the world over, some more lurid than others. Until recently, that is. The 1990s saw a perceived decline in the frequency of reports shown on TV or in print, compared with decades past. But why should that be? Have our cosmic brethren abandoned us, or have the brainwashing techniques used during human abductions now eliminated the risk of victims coming forward? As you will see during this book, I reject both scenarios and their like, in favour of something far more obvious.

Namely, that the UFO phenomenon has *always* been the public face of an incredibly secret, yet constantly evolving, military project dating from the Second World War, the origins of which – like so many others – began in Nazi Germany. Since then, the project has involved no more than the same three or four collaborating countries, and as time has passed the technologies used have improved to the point where such craft can no longer be accidentally seen by the public. In short, if we see them now *it's because we're supposed to*.

In order to arrive at such a conclusion, I wanted to show that behind the decades of official smoke and mirrors littering the topic of 'flying saucers', there *are* still areas of some importance waiting to be uncovered, historical developments that may or may not have relevance to the truth behind the UFO phenomenon. In setting them out here, I hope to inspire readers to revisit the subject afresh, to look again, while wading through this low tide of awareness and hysteria, with new eyes and clear heads, to see if fresh answers can be found to old sightings and phenomena.

How you'll view the subject by the end of the book is beyond my powers of persuasion, of course, but hopefully you'll realise that there is – and always has been – more to this story than meets the eye. Whichever side of the fence you prefer, the encouraging fact that you're holding this book in your hands shows that you're at least willing to learn something of the stories behind the stories, which may yet add up to the *actual* history of 'flying saucers'. And there is a lot to go through. Much of it, on the face of things, seems irrelevant but it is integral to the fabric of the emerging story. It may surprise many readers that in order to gain a foothold on the subject, we should begin by examining the origins of the semi-mystical religion of Theosophy and the many splinter groups it inspired. Many such 'secret societies' were based in Germany in the years leading up to and following the First World War; when one of them later spawned its own political party in the near-anarchy following Germany's defeat, Adolf Hitler was among its first members. Thus we can see the real roots of the pseudo-mysticism at the foundation of Nazism, the very influences that were warping Germany's educational and scientific establishment. When Hans Horbiger published his radical views on cosmology in a complex though resolutely cranky theory called 'Welteislehre' ('world of ice and fire'), it was seen as the apotheosis of this new Zeitgeist and woe betide its dissenters among the schools and colleges who were expected to teach such patent nonsense.

Necessity is said to be the mother of invention – and, in the case of the Third Reich during the Second World War, the statement is not entirely inaccurate. The Nazi-influenced education system and the new scientific establishment embraced the works of noted scientific figures working at the margins of acceptability, such as Nikola Tesla and the Austrian, Viktor Schauberger. While Tesla's ideas may have been useful in certain weaponry projects developed on both sides in the Second World War, Schauberger's led to the creation of a small flying device that apparently employed his discovery of a 'free energy' source. Such were the avenues of research now generally pursued by a scientific establishment idealistically remodelled and awash with military funding. Research that would ultimately perfect the liquid-fuelled rocket, the wire-guided missile, jet engines and helicopters and would one day gift the flying disc to the military, thanks to the efforts of individuals like Schauberger.

But characters such as one Dr Richard Miethe, and not Schauberger, are to be found at the heart of the 'real' disc projects, and in studying what is known of *their* wartime careers and achievements we get our first real glimpse of the two projects vying to produce the first practical flying discs. What little we know of the technologies is discussed, as are the likely milestones in flying disc development during the war. These range from crude prototypes built from converted conventional aircraft using circular wings, to comparatively sophisticated machines using bespoke jet engines mounted within circular airframes and reputedly capable of reaching levels of performance far beyond any aircraft then in service – and that includes the Luftwaffe's then-new Me 262 jet fighter-bomber.

But it seems as though their efforts were in vain, for it wasn't long before the Allies were picking over the bones of a ruined Germany in search of 'secret weapons' and the men who helped design, build and test the things – though, crucially, vital members of the SS (the last custodians of such projects) were already thousands of kilometres away. Many had fled to existing German communities in friendly countries across South America, though some are also believed to have reached a remote outpost, rumoured to have been sited in Antarctica, taking the last elements of the flying disc projects with them. We look at the evidence.

Meanwhile, back in post-war mainland Europe, the Allies were scooping up the multitudes of personnel and technologies that remained. The country most proactive at this – the USA – believed its secret Operation Paperclip to be the most efficient of all such recruitment drives, so we'll compare it with the efforts of the other Allies and look at its legacy of bizarre stories. But where the

Americans failed, I would suggest that the British succeeded. Somehow (and very much against the odds), it appears that Britain found itself the *very* lucky recipient of a complete set of blueprints for the German disc programme . . .

Whatever the truth behind this, two new strands then join the story. One takes us to British Columbia, on the back of stories suggesting that Britain and Canada began collaborating after the war to develop discs of their own based on these plans. The other has us looking once again at the Antarctic and in particular at a 1947 American expedition to the southern continent; an expedition long rumoured to have been sent to confront the newly established *Antarcticans* and their own salvaged (or new) discs – Operation High Jump.

Elsewhere that year, tensions between the Allies were growing. The rising military confidence of the USSR and its Eastern European satellites had begun to force wedges between Britain and the USA over the division of war spoils and material. I would suggest that it was a result of the frustrations felt on the British side that led to a decision to openly fly some of its new discs over mainland America. What is often overlooked is that Roswell was also home to America's only nuclear bomber unit, so overflights in the area were sure to antagonise: and all to prove to its main ally that Britain was still capable of 'punching above its weight' – something it still likes to think it can do today.

Which brings us to where we came in. Could it have been an Anglo-Canadian disc that crash-landed at Roswell? An event like this obviously has many ramifications, and these are discussed here, as are the arguments for and against the formation of an organisation, possibly established in the aftermath of Roswell, jointly to administer further disc development, between Britain, the USA and Canada.

Over fifty years have passed since the Second World War and Miethe's efforts. Disc technology as it stands today is almost certainly far, far removed from the first generation of craft seen then. One need only look at the progress made in conventional aircraft since the war to see how similar leaps in performance and engineering might have been made. The likely development of the electrogravitic propulsion system in the early 1960s would have revolutionised the project and given its three main member countries opportunities to reach out for the planets in our solar system ... For some, such talk is going one step too far into science fiction, which is why, after looking at some of the likely bases attached to this project, such as the famous Area 51 and others, we will end our story by looking at some of its more *reassuringly* offbeat facets.

With so much of the 'UFO/flying saucer' story now enmeshed in myth, it's sometimes difficult to know who or what we can take at more than face value. In the absence of any real official explanation or enlightenment, seekers of the truth often have to dig deep to find even the smallest crumb or lead, anything that might then take their studies and interest in another direction entirely. The subject is so vast and relatively uncharted that even the slightest deviation from the path can take years to unravel and decipher.

Before I started this project, I'd yet to find a convincing and all-encompassing explanation or theory that might support the 'official line' taken by our authorities over the UFO phenomenon. Even after reading countless books and watching many interviews with some of the world's most eminent ufologists – even witnessing a likely UFO for myself – my sceptical view of the accepted official 'truth' has remained largely intact.

It was for this reason, that I wrote *Blue Fires*. I wanted to find answers that *I* could find plausible, and by and large I think I've succeeded. In standing back and viewing the whole area like a Rorschach picture, I hoped that a hidden pattern might emerge. It did.

My hope is that you see it too . . .

Gary Hyland
August 2000

chapter one

'Theology is an attempt to explain a subject, by men who do not understand it. The intent is not to tell the truth, but to satisfy the questioner.'

Elbert Hubbard, *The Philistine*.

'What is objectionable, what is dangerous about extremists is not that they are extreme, but that they are intolerant. The evil is not what they say about their cause, but what they say about their opponents.'

Robert F. Kennedy, *The Pursuit of Justice*.

Before we look at the somewhat oxymoronic history of Germany's better-known 'secret societies' and their pivotal role in shaping German policy towards areas such as the flying discs, there is one whose very existence has been debated since the war and which, according to some observers, directed the very early development of the same flying disc craft we shall later study. This is the Vril Society, and its importance to the whole story is such that we should examine it first of all.

The source from which the society (and other individuals) took its inspiration can be traced to Lord Edward Bulwer-Lytton. An established British novelist of the nineteenth century, whose work inspired men such as Cecil Rhodes to later form the International Round Table organisation, his most enduring legacy as far as we are concerned is a novel entitled *Vril – The Power of the Coming Race*. In the novel, a long-lost race of 'supermen' called the 'Vril-Ya' emerge from their subterranean domains in the bowels of the earth, through portals in Tibet and elsewhere, to claim sovereignty over the surface with the help of a mysterious force called 'Vril', which causes mere surface-dwellers to submit to the Vril-Ya, when confronted by its awesome power.

But what exactly *is* Vril (or 'W-force' as it's sometimes known) supposed to be? Think of the 'force' in the *Star Wars* films and you'll get close to an explanation. Indeed, I wonder if the screen-writers had knowledge of Vril when they wrote the scripts, the parallels are so close. In short, Vril is an enormous energy field that surrounds everyone and everything at all times: 'the nerve centre of our potential divinity', as eloquently phrased by Pauwels and Bergier in their 1969 work *The Dawn of Magic*. Whoever becomes master of the Vril will become master of himself, of others and of the world – and final enlightenment should be the one goal in the life of anyone seeking this truth. The race of beings beneath our feet are adepts at harnessing this force and will use it when the time is right, to conquer us surface dwellers . . .

In reviewing material for this book, I have asked myself time and again if there might not be a grain of truth in what appears to be fanciful science fiction. On balance, I favour scepticism, but what *is* certain is that the first mention of such a society (also known as the Luminous Lodge or the Society of Truth) appeared in an American magazine article first published in 1947. Written by Dr Willy Ley, a prominent early rocket pioneer in Germany who escaped to the USA in 1933 after the Nazis took power, the article talks of a small group formed in Berlin during 1925, who were in touch with this shadowy race of 'supermen'. They were apparently working to create the conditions under which such 'supermen' might – with their Vril force – take over the world (presumably also with the help of the Nazis). Ley did raise one immediate question, in suggesting that the group began only in 1925, as this was long after Lytton's work had appeared and its contents assimilated by others: for example, the French consul in Calcutta and sometime adventurer/explorer, Louis Jacolliot, had borrowed heavily from Lytton in his own works and lectures. What Ley *doesn't* mention is that 1925 also saw the official dissolution of *another* group ('Thule'), from which members, such as the influential Karl Haushofer, could then have started Vril once free of its shadow. Both Thule and its own preceding group, the Germanenorden, were concentrating on acquiring knowledge of Aryan prehistory and its rituals, so to suddenly have them switch tack and examine mysterious Tibetan legends of Agharthi and Schambhallah (supposedly the Vril-Ya domains) would have been too much to ask of their membership. One therefore might conclude that the Vril Society was started in their wake, unfettered either by tradition or fear of the unknown and drawing on past work already carried out in secret by its new membership.

But what of the group's alleged connection with the discs? We have two options to follow here, depending on who you believe. One theory suggests that the Vril-Ya have bored out a series of tunnels that crisscross the world, along which they can move at tremendous speeds in flying disc craft built to their own design – and that the blueprints for the craft were passed to the Vril Society, in particular to one Dr W. O. Schumann, who constructed a craft using an electro-magnetic propulsion system built from more plans given to Hans Kohler, another member.

The second option asserts that the Vril-Ya are really extra-terrestrial beings (or 'EBEs' – 'Extraterrestrial Biological Entities', as they might be properly known), who have been visiting the earth for countless millennia, watching and monitoring mankind's spiritual development. With the rise of the Nazis, who saw themselves as an ordained race with a unique destiny and heritage to live up to, it's thought that these beings lent their flying saucer technology to the cause, but that when Hitler turned more and more to the 'dark side' of the Vril force, all help was withdrawn and may even have been redirected to the Allies. As mentioned, all this depends on who and what you might believe in – there are many shades of grey here. What is undeniably useful to understanding this early history of man-made flying discs, however, is that such stories even exist.

Before we draw a veil over the Vril myth, we should also examine a further point of interest that may have some relevance to the story. In the ruins of Berlin, as Soviet soldiers advanced towards Hitler's once-palatial Chancellery in the spring of 1945, they allegedly came across the bodies of a small colony of Tibetan monks dressed in their familiar orange robes; the apparent victims of ritual suicide. What were they doing there? On the face of it their presence seems absurd, yet when one remembers the pivotal role that Tibet and its mysteries had to the myth of Vril and the 'King of the World' the existence of the Tibetans makes some sense. If we consider their presence in the capital of the thousand-year Reich, they might simply have been maintaining links back to the Vril Tibetan Motherland – from the Aryan Fatherland. Hitler, right to the end it would seem, believed that his cause was just and that salvation was coming from the Far East.

Before talk of Vril carries our imaginations away, our story proper should begin in Victorian England, with the foundation in 1867 of the English Rosicrucian Society by one Robert Wentworth Little. A secret society with around 145 initiated members (most of whom already rumoured to be Freemasons), Little's group was the first British branch of an organisation established in mainland Europe in the fifteenth century and named after its founder, Christian Rosenkreuz. Its aim was the study and interpretation of arcane occultic lore, and this preoccupation dovetailed neatly with some of the more esoteric beliefs and ceremonials of the Masons. As with many societies, secret or otherwise, then as now, a core of leading members wished to forge links with similar groups abroad, and Little's Rosicrucians were no exception, having been in touch with similar groups in Germany almost since its foundation. One wonders why such contact was considered so desirable, if the organisation was professed to be 'secret', but it would be essential if the group were to keep abreast of the evolving rituals and routines of its order; the very fabric of its existence. The need for secrecy grows when one considers the turbulence that had affected the very existence of many societies in Germany towards the end of the eighteenth century. King Friedrich Wilhelm II of Prussia had them grouped together under the catchy title 'the Illuminati' before outlawing them amid fears they might foment revolution in his kingdom.

But even this established society was evidently too tame for some of Little's associates. In either 1886, 1887 or 1888 (the exact year is disputed), a splinter group was founded in London by a few ex-Rosicrucians. Ostentatiously called the Hermetic Order of the Golden Dawn, the members appear to have had little to do with the Rosicrucians hereafter, as their new group focused itself on the practising of ritual magic. The two main founders of this new group, Dr William Wynn Westcott and S. L. MacGregor-Mathers, drew in other noted personalities of the day, including the fantasy novelist Arthur Machen, Bulwer-Lytton himself, Aleister Crowley (who would later become notorious as a 'black magician' and was to be the group's last Grand Master), W. B. Yeats, the Nobel Prize-winning poet, and Bram Stoker, the author of *Dracula*. All told, the membership was almost entirely male but for one exception: Florence Farr, director of the Abbey Theatre in Dublin and companion of George Bernard Shaw.

Other spin-off groups had left Rosicrucianism in Germany by this time as well and were developing new rituals and powers – and sharing them with the Golden Dawn in the process. For example, the initiation ceremony to the Golden Dawn supposedly included a phrase spoken by the candidate in which he/she took a vow of silence 'under penalty of expulsion and death or *palsy from hostile current of will* [author's italics]'. This surely points to the fact that either the group possessed the secrets to harnessing these Vril-like powers or believed it did. Whatever the truth, successful candidates could be sure to keep silent on matters regarding the group; the perceived consequences for breaking this oath too abominable to comprehend. Mathers himself, writing the Golden Dawn's manifesto for 1896, speaks of being in sporadic contact with higher figures and of plainly being terrified of them and their potential for evil. Perhaps Lytton had a hand in creating these beliefs for the benefit of the leadership, but surely such a document, intended for the members, wouldn't have included such heady stuff without good reason? Perhaps we're missing the point somewhere – perhaps such threats were part of the mechanism used to keep the group's secrets and maintain the public silence of its members?

Whatever the truth, we should take into account the fact that here was an elite group of individuals, all serious players in their own fields, with enviable reputations, who wouldn't take kindly to their Grand Master behaving quite so melodramatically on such an issue without good reason. Remember, too, that all would most certainly have been aware of their colleague Lytton's work in exploring the Vril myths and its impact on their own area of study, so would have been able to question its accuracy if any doubts arose.

But while the appearance of the English Rosicrucians heralded a new resurgence in the movement, another, more potent and alluring group was gaining ascendance and would soon over-shadow them: the Theosophists.

There was a time, during the last years of the nineteenth century throughout all Western Europe, including Great Britain, when it seemed as though theosophy heralded a wholly new theology. A synthesis of many religions, it used the pitch of offering something for everyone to champion itself as the only doctrine to unite the world on the cusp of the third millennium, which was then only a century away. Against theosophy, existing Judaeo-Christian, Hindu, Muslim and other doctrines would be set aside, their limited scope found wanting. Theosophy offered an attractive and somewhat heady cocktail of 'esoteric Buddhism', the establishment of a universal 'brotherhood of man' and a hierarchy of 'secret masters', and when it was founded in 1875 it quickly spawned a number of associated groups throughout the world.

The early life of its joint founder, Madame Elena Blavatsky, in her Russian homeland was certainly colourful. She was married to an army general when aged only seventeen, but the union didn't last and Blavatsky left the country soon after to travel the mysterious East in search of some deeper spiritual meaning to her life, as so many before and since have done. After ten years away, she returned to Russia with highly developed mediumistic powers and an apparent skill in telekinesis – the ability to move objects with the power of the mind. While practising ritual magic, however, she suffered a near-fatal sword wound, which shook her self-belief and led her, once recovered, on another quest for enlightenment, this time to Cairo. While there, she founded a short-lived spiritual society, but after this collapsed under a welter of debt she moved to the USA, putting an ocean between herself and her creditors.

While in America, in 1873, she met and befriended one Colonel Olcott, in Vermont. Evidently, he shared her views on spiritual affairs, and they founded the successor to her Cairo group, the Theosophical Society, two years later. With two extra disciples (presumably supporting the society financially), the group transferred to Bombay, India, in 1878, settling on a riverside site at Adyar which it still occupies today. Before long, stories were reaching the West of the 'miracles' that the members – particularly Blavatsky – were performing there. These prompted the London-based Society for Psychical Research to dispatch a sceptical Dr Hodgson to Bombay to verify the wild claims reported in the newspapers. After studying the evidence at first hand, he reported back to London that he had found nothing but 'palpable fraud and extreme credulity' on the part of the Indian membership.

But Hodgson's was a lone voice amid the sea of hype and rumour growing around theosophy and did little to dissuade Blavatsky, who relished the chance to use the negative report in her favour – assuming, of course, that the good Dr Hodgson had informed her of his findings prior to his return to England. For after only a short while the main tenets of her and Olcott's beliefs were published in a work entitled *The Secret Doctrine*. Regarded by many writers on the occult as her masterpiece, Blavatsky used it to set out her stall on theosophy and to start the snowball rolling. A theosophical lodge had already opened successfully in Britain and was to prove the most influential of all the group's outposts in laying a course into the future. At this point in the Theosophical Society's history, we should mention one Annie Besant. The wife of a clergyman, Besant only joined the British lodge in 1889, but wielded such influence over the weak leadership in London that, on Blavatsky's death two years later, Besant was to move the emphasis of the lodge towards Hinduism and away from the more holistic approach favoured by Buddhism. This most unorthodox of English vicars' wives believed in the maintenance of the caste system, as a way of promulgating one's progression through karmic levels as well as the legacy Western civilisation owed to its supposed roots in the fabled Aryan-Hindu civilisation of ancient India.

Blavatsky herself hinted at this in one of her last works, *The Stanzas of Dzyan*. Supposedly lost for centuries in a Tibetan library, these stanzas were 'revealed' to her while entranced in 1888. The revelation centres on the last remnants of an advanced civilisation that once flourished in what is now the Gobi Desert; this civilisation abandoned the surface and descended into the ground to build two subterranean cities, Schambhallah and Agharthi. Whether or not Blavatsky drew on contemporary literary sources for her inspiration, such as the work of Bulwer-Lytton, or really *did* have a pipeline to more mystical sources we shall never know, but again we find references to a mysterious force that this hidden civilisation has harnessed over the millennia. With such rich and engaging material on tap, is it any wonder that under Besant's leadership the London Theosophical Society flourished? To an increasingly sophisticated audience forged during the unprecedented industrialisation of that time and looking for some new spiritual meaning and guidance in their lives, theosophy seemed ideal.

Following on from the success that Besant was having in promoting theosophy to the British, and given their richer history of societies, it is no surprise to learn that a German lodge soon opened. In fact, in Germany, theosophy spawned a number of different groups, which together later came to be regarded as 'ariosophy' – a motley ragbag of lodges, all busy tailoring themselves to emerging nationalistic sentiments, in direct contrast to the global aspirations of theosophy. Back in Britain, Besant's group, as well as the Golden Dawn, were to see membership slowly dwindle through general disenchantment at the waste and slaughter of the First World War. But in Germany, such groups were the very stuff of a population disgruntled with the Kaiser and the unexpected loss of the war. To find the roots of the catastrophe that was to engulf Europe once more a few decades later, we must look again at those groups that constituted ariosophy and which would soon leave their British equivalents in the shade. We also find in Germany at this time the first tenuous stirrings of an occultic movement linked to the development of flying discs.

In 1905 a lapsed Cistercian monk by the name of Adolf Josef Lanz (who had been expelled at the age of nineteen for transgressing the order's moral codes) assumed the imaginary though aristocratic-sounding title of Jörg Lanz von Liebenfels in an attempt to add both gravitas to his bearing and a degree of credibility for an anti-semitic journal he was planning to publish in Vienna. Named after the ancient Teutonic moon-goddess Ostara, whose name history has corrupted to 'Easter', *Ostara* was dedicated to the somewhat spurious explanation of ancient Aryan mythologies in terms understood by the ordinary Austro-German working man – the modern-day inheritor of the Aryan race. It also encouraged the ostracism of 'international Jewry' because it was behind Germany's (and the world's) various ills. One of the main thrusts behind the journal's articles was the idea of a universal psychic energy permeating the cosmos, which found its greatest clarity in the embodiment of a pure Aryan man: blond, blue-eyed etc. Those racial groups that didn't conform (Jews, Gypsies and so on) were to be 'purged' as offerings to the pagan gods who created and fostered the Aryans.

As well as publishing *Ostara* to a small but fervent readership, Liebenfels also found time to write a major book: *Theozoology*. It was one of the first attempts at establishing a framework within which one might better understand the emerging science of sociobiology and seek to reconcile race and class differences (between the Aryan race and others) on purely Darwinistic evolutionary grounds. Business must have been good, because two years later Liebenfels bought a small castle on a cliff overlooking the Danube. This was the place chosen to house his new project: a group of pliant disciples to the racist beliefs promoted by *Ostara* gathered together to form Ordo Novo Templi (Order of the New Templars). On Christmas Day 1907 Liebenfels raised the order's chosen flag from the battlements: it was a swastika. At the time, the symbol was in widespread use in its clockwise form as a potent good luck charm, but, not surprisingly, the order adopted the 'evil' anticlockwise version as later picked up by the Nazis. *Ostara* continued to be published, and in 1909 the castle was visited by a young Adolf Hitler, who was looking to purchase back issues. Heinrich Himmler, later to become head of the SS, was also said to be a subscriber. Many of the pseudo-mystical rituals performed by his Black Order stemmed from suggestions and routines outlined in *Ostara* – ironic since the Nazis, once in power, suppressed the journal because of its embarrassing mystical nature.

Another key figure in Germany at this time was Guido von List, a long-standing friend of Liebenfels, who, as a youth, was rapt with the works of the Roman scholar Tacitus, who described the ancient Germans as noble, blue-eyed, blond-haired warriors. He came to prominence in 1881 with the publication of his major work, *German Mythological Landscapes*, in which he sought to explain ancient monuments and ruins as evidence of a glorious Aryan past. With the emergence of theosophy in Germany, he was given a new focus and direction for his beliefs, and it seems inevitable that, when Liebenfels launched *Ostara*, List was to contribute articles and become a New Templar himself. In 1908, however, he broke away to form his own Guido von List Society with a small group of followers of his own, a few prominent theosophists among them. In practice List's society covered similar ground to Liebenfels', such as deciphering runes and the rituals of the ancient Wotanic priesthood. List was to die in Berlin in 1919 from a lung infection, aged 71, but his contribution to the spiritual rebirth of Aryanism was incalculable, for it was through yet another splinter group that the roots of the National Socialist Party – the Nazis – were to take hold.

In 1912, disenchanted members of List's own Berlin lodge broke away to form a new group, The Germanenorden ('the Germanic Order'). Although orchestrated by Philip Stauff, perhaps its most important member was Rudolf von Sebottendorff, who joined in 1916, for it was he who headed up a secret anti-semitic wing within its ranks, dedicated to combating 'the secret Jewish alliance'. Sebottendorff's real name was Adam Glauer, but he had followed others such as Lanz in adopting a spurious aristocratic title to add status. To attain rank-and-file membership, candidates were required to prove their Germanic ancestry back three generations and to have their skulls measured with calipers to 'prove' their Nordic Aryan roots. Under Stauff and Sebottendorff, the order took the original themes of theosophy and turned them on their head. Members believed that 'racial mixing' lay at the root of all miseries and that Germany should strive to create a super-race of Aryans to reclaim and rule the world. Moreover, the order claimed that its senior members were the instruments of the 'Secret Chiefs of Tibet' – descendants of Atlanteans, now living 'somewhere in the Himalayas' and ruled over by the 'King of Fear', or 'King of the World' as he was sometimes known to initiates. A mysterious figure, this 'king' was – or is – supposed to have the power of life or death over anyone on earth and was contactable through meditation and ESP. Members also used a special Tibetan tarot deck to contact him and, leaving nothing to chance, were supposedly also in possession of a special radio with which he could be reached. Given this hint as to the king's evident mortality, a number of possibilities have been suggested over the succeeding years as to who he might actually have been. One name crops up time and again: that of the Russian, George Ivanovitch Gurdjieff.

Gurdjieff had received spiritual instruction in Tibet before travelling through Europe and preaching to anyone who'd listen that he'd discovered that many people go through their lives 'asleep' to the reality of their existence – like so many living automata, barely aware of what was really happening to them and why. The only salvation for someone who believes himself to be in this situation is to undertake a series of mental and physical exercises to attain awareness. Hitler's later slogan, 'Deutschland Erwache!' ('Germany Awake!') and his references to the 'triumph of the will' are testament to his apparent belief in the same sentiments, though whether Hitler himself was ever in touch with the 'king' has been meat and drink to several speculative comment-ators since the war. By 1917, military conscription and the war in general was taking its toll on membership of other groups, yet the Germanenorden could still boast over a hundred lodges across the country (the Berlin lodge had so many members that it took to renting the ground floor of a town house for its meeting place and office).

The German trenches of the First World War were a fertile breeding ground for dissent on the part of the common enlisted man searching for some higher meaning to his life. Constantly surrounded by the filth and desperate conditions of the battlefield, some men took to sporting mythological symbols on their helmets as talismans to ward off British bullets. Much as American GIs sported peace symbols and slogans on their gear in Vietnam, so the Germans adopted superstitious beliefs in the trenches. And the most popular symbol? The swastika. To a post-Second World War generation, the swastika has obvious connotations; we associate it with the horrors of fascism and the atrocities of the concentration camps carried out under its banner. But before the First World War no such associations existed. In fact, the symbol has an ancient past, appearing in India at around the fourth century BC. It represents the infinite power of the divine wielded against its enemies: just what a cowering soldier in a trench is looking to believe in. While both sides of the conflict used the symbol, it was in Germany where the greatest interest lay as a result of its having been included in Blavatsky's *The Secret Doctrine*. Pre-war groups such as Ordo Novo Templi and publications such as *Ostara* adopted it as their logo and it slowly permeated the male-dominated 'warrior' culture of the trenches as members of such groups found themselves fighting for Germany – for their racial Fatherland, exactly as encouraged to do by the masters of their various lodges.

With the chaos that erupted in the country after the war was lost, it was inevitable that newly demobbed soldiers would turn to the societies once more for solace and guidance in such turbulent times. This movement was in tune with a country now acknowledging its ancient folk ('Völkisch') roots and becoming more inward-looking in its search for answers to the dilemma it now found itself in. Sebottendorff as well as anyone could see this pent-up demand at home in Munich and decided that his existing order was neither doing enough nor going as far as it might in order to satisfy the need for retribution on the part of the returning men. After all, the country had lost the war somewhat unexpectedly. The speed of defeat was a shock to both national pride and morale, and these men sought to make sense of it all – and of their place in the society that was emerging from the morass. Sebottendorff, as newly elected Grand Master of the Germanenorden's large Bavarian lodge, moved quickly to found a new society magazine. Entitled *Runen*, it first appeared in early 1918, reassuringly sporting a swastika on its masthead. Along with a new member, Walter Nauhaus, Sebottendorff saw *Runen* as an ideal focus for a renewed recruitment drive. From 200 members that spring, by the autumn there were over 1,500, largely recruited from returning soldiers among the educated professional class. Meetings were still held at his house in Munich, but soon the lodge began renting out club rooms in a hotel. The Germanenorden was about to take a leap into history.

Because of the extreme right-wing and anti-semitic nature of some of the speeches made by the members, in August 1918 Sebottendorff adopted the name of the Thule Society for his lodge, lest rival socialist and pro-republican elements tried to disrupt proceedings – and there was certainly a fear of that happening. The Weimar republican government was in the throes of being formed, and the country was divided politically as well as contending with organised militias of demobbed troops battling socialist forces. On 7 November 1918 Bavaria witnessed a bloodless coup in which anti-war socialists assumed power and declared the region an autonomous state. Two days later, Sebottendorff addressed a hastily assembled and stunned audience at the hotel, in which he passionately declared that the dream of a 'Fatherland' for which they had all worked so tirelessly had been snatched away and that if it was to be reclaimed they would now have to win the hearts and minds of the locals – as well as win battles against their enemies. From that day, the Thule Society was to become ever more militant and vocal as it struggled to unseat the socialists.

In taking the name 'Thule' (pronounced 'toolay') as the cover for his group, Sebottendorff was certainly tapping into a potent Aryan myth, for Thule was the reputed capital of the land of Hyperborea, also known as 'Ultima Thule'. This mysterious and legendary land to the far north, was supposedly the gateway to new worlds in other galaxies and dimensions, as well as to the 'inner world', that place so beloved by supporters of the 'hollow earth' theory, who would have us believe that the world is largely hollow and supporting another complete ecosystem. The original Hyperboreans were supposedly descendants from a crashed starship that had reached earth from an alien world decimated by a cataclysmic war. They settled in various areas around Europe, forming distinct racial groups such as the Basques, Bretons, Celts, Norse and also the Aryan race. The Thule Society's emblem had a dagger at its centre, its blade wreathed in symbolic oak leaves, with a curved swastika around its hilt emitting rays of divine Hyperborean light – all elements of the Nazi mythology later to evolve.

The two-pronged strategy that Sebottendorff and the Thule Society was to adopt, in fighting Munich's socialists, firstly involved developing a local newspaper, the *Beobachter*, which the group had already purchased, in July 1918, for 5,000 marks from the estate of its deceased proprietor. After changing its name to the *Münchener Beobachter und Sportblatt*, Sebottendorff shifted its previous editorial stance to create an overtly populist organ with extensive sports coverage mingling with reportage of events with nationalistic or anti-semitic overtones. In reinventing itself as a down-market tabloid, it was a great success. Until May 1919 its offices were part of the Thule premises in the hotel.

The second strand of the fight against the socialists and communists came in organising an armed struggle. No surprise there, as Sebottendorff had amassed a sizable cache of arms supplied, no doubt, by sympathetic ex-servicemen with access to armouries. In early December 1918 the group attempted to kidnap Bavaria's new chancellor, Eisner, at a rally, but this failed miserably, as did an attempt at establishing an antagonistic group of vigilantes, who were to disrupt socialist meetings and interfere with the local government. However, its third venture was to find success. Post-First World War Germany was witnessing a series of power vacuums throughout the country as the Weimar administration struggled to take root, and Bavaria was no exception. The socialists might have gained power, but the old provincial government was still meeting in Baumberg and held in virtual internal exile, yet it was this very group that the Thuleans realised they would have to return to power if the situation was to be resolved in their favour. Throughout the country, organised militias, made up of ex-servicemen, known as 'Freikorps' (literally, 'free corps') were being employed on an unofficial basis to keep the peace in conjunction with the police and the small standing army allowed by the Allies. It was a simple step for Thule to form its own Freikorps division ('Kampfbund Thule') as well as to support certain others emerging in the city, such as 'Wiking'. The following spring saw the government in exile order these various Freikorps to prepare for an uprising, and in May 1919 Kampfbund Thule succeeded in ousting the socialists after a four-day battle, alongside another Freikorps unit, the Bund Overland Group. Thanks to the *Beobachter's* successful 'hearts and minds' campaign, as well as publicity lauding those who had given their lives to the cause during the battle, public support in Bavaria for a return to the old government was immensely strong, and Thule received even more support as a result.

With the battle seemingly won, Sebottendorff now moved away from Munich to go travelling, leaving behind both Thule, the

Beobachter and a small political party, whose foundation he had fostered the year before, in September 1918.

Up to that point, the typical Thulean member was a middle-class white-collar professional, yet Sebottendorff knew that, in order to achieve any real influence at grass-roots level, it had to widen its appeal. Purchasing the *Beobachter* was one step in reaching the workers, but there was also a need for a political vehicle in which local blue-collar workers could get involved. So he asked fellow Thulean and occasional sports reporter for the *Beobachter*, Karl Harrer, if he would be interested in starting up a discussion group for workers to learn more of the foundations and beliefs of Thule. For Sebottendorff, this was probably seen as a way of broadening his church as much as learning the views of the masses, in order to produce a programme tailored more to their needs – just as any modern-day politician might use focus groups and spin doctors to shape policy. Harrer agreed and soon founded the *Deutscher Arbeiterverein* (*German Workers' Ring*), along with seven other members, of whom Anton Drexler (another Thulean) was the most proactive. While membership of the society grew steadily, Drexler urged them to take another step forward and formally enter the stage as a full political party. After constantly badgering the others, his views won out and on 5 January 1919 the Deutsche Arbeiterpartei (German Workers' Party) was formed with Drexler elected as its Chairman. With the socialists now defeated and Sebottendorff absent and unable to influence things, the new party soon 'acquired' the *Beobachter* from Thule. This caused tensions between the editorial staff, which were resolved only when the newspaper converted itself into a limited company and issued equal shares to the party and to Thule. However, by early 1921 all the shares were held by Drexler, who then passed them on to the party leader (by then Adolf Hitler). From then on, the *Beobachter* was to be the party's official mouthpiece.

At this stage one can only guess at Sebottendorff's opinion of this development, although I suspect that this popularisation of his beliefs, in an articulate political party, was one of his main hopes for the group. Indeed, even as this fledgling party grew, its leading lights were all ex-Thuleans, eventual Deputy Führer Rudolf Hess and Culture Minister Alfred Rosenberg among them. Another two members were to achieve a certain notoriety in subsequent histories of the origins of the Nazi party: Dietrich Eckart and Karl Haushofer.

It is also at this point that Adolf Hitler enters the story proper. After serving as a corporal during the war, Hitler had emerged with an Iron Cross for bravery and a racist mentality honed in the trenches, apparently to the boredom of his comrades, whom he would often lecture and belittle. After the war ended, Hitler returned to his adopted city of Munich where, in need of work, he was retained by a police intelligence unit to gather information on the various groups operating in the city. There can be no doubt that he was at least aware of the Thule Society, if not a member – after all, its tenets were right up his street and he *had* subscribed to *Ostara*. But no proof has ever emerged to this effect. Perhaps all traces were airbrushed out of history on his accession to power? But in September 1919 he certainly visited the fledgling German Workers' Party ('DAP') during one of its meetings in a Munich bierkeller, his police masters suspicious at its having the communist-sounding word 'workers' in its title. Finding the policies of the new party surprisingly to his liking, Hitler made a bland report back to his superiors before revisiting the party – and being successfully elected as committee member No. 7. Finding an oratory skill within himself, his impassioned rhetoric was to lead to his becoming elected as its chairman in place of Drexler on his eventual release from the army and police. Within a year, the party had changed its name to the National Socialist German Workers' Party ('NSDAP') – better known as the Nazi party – and Germany's fate was sealed.

By the time that Alfred Rosenberg was replaced as editor of the *Beobachter* by fellow Thulean Dietrich Eckart in 1921, the paper had been renamed again – this time to the *Völkischer Beobachter*, to reflect a folksy Aryan affinity and to take it back up-market, from popular tabloid to serious political broadsheet. Like Hitler, who had already been chairman of the NSDAP for just over a year, Eckart had been severely gassed in the war. Unlike Hitler, though, Eckart had suffered greater and had wound up a semi-demented alcoholic addicted to morphine to numb his constant pain. Yet even so, it was to Eckart that Hitler came for advice during these early years. Whether for tips on public speaking or effective speech-writing, this failed dramatist and poet had the answers. He also had contacts – for it was mostly through Eckart that Hitler was introduced to the Bavarian old-moneyed set, who donated generously to the new party. But as a Thulean, Eckart also had a grounding in the occult and was a keen student of the black arts and those who practised them, especially those rites and personalities originally from Tibet and the Orient. It is assumed by some that through these contacts and disciplines he was able to lend Hitler an animal magnetism trawled from some other dimension, but that merely disguises a lack of understanding in basic speech patterns and audience manipulation – something Eckart would certainly have known of and which Hitler used to full effect. A closet homosexual, like Ernst Röhm – leader of the SA, forerunner of Himmler's SS – Eckart was becoming increasingly concerned at the direction in which his protégé was taking the party; especially on Hitler's return from a decadent Berlin where the deep economic depression felt elsewhere in the country was being salved in a wave of unabashed hedonism. Hitler was deeply shocked at this discovery and vowed to rid the country of such decadence – bad news indeed for those such as Eckart, who could see that Hitler's tacit tolerance of minorities was evaporating. Yet before he died two years later, in 1923, Eckart was said to have prayed for the Thule Society and to remark:

Follow Hitler. He will dance, but it is I who have called the tune. I have initiated him into the secret doctrine, opened his centres of vision and given him means to communicate with the Powers. Do not mourn me, for I shall have influenced history more than any other German.

Perhaps more telling is the dedication Hitler himself makes to Eckart on the last page of *Mein Kampf*. After mentioning those fallen in the doomed Munich putsch, he goes on:

And among them, I want also to count that man, one of the best who devoted his life to the awakening of his, our people, in his writings and his thoughts and finally his deeds: Dietrich Eckart.

Some endorsement.

And of Karl Haushofer . . . what of this enigmatic figure? Born in 1869, Haushofer came from good German stock and, when appointed military attaché to Tokyo around the turn of the century, was lucky enough to indulge his love of the occult with frequent visits to Gurdjieff in Tibet when time allowed, between 1903 and 1908. It was as a result of his deep interest in ancient Eastern philosophies at this time, as well as new doctrines such as theosophy, that he came to believe the myth of the Aryan people having emerged from Central Asia – even Tibet itself. Such were his beliefs that on his return home and the outbreak of the First World War he joined the Aryan-fixated Germanenorden and, later, the Thule Society. Despite reaching the rank of general during the war, when it was over he forsook the army and instead took a teaching post at Munich University as Professor of Geopolitics – a post to which he undoubtedly brought his many years of diplomatic observations, as well as ideas on the occultic state of the world as he found it. So taken was he with his various ideas and theories that he even founded a journal, *The Geopolitic Review*, and wrote books on the subject. Rudolf Hess was one of his students at university and it was Haushofer who sponsored his candidature to join Thule, though whether or not either Hess or Haushofer later persuaded Hitler to join remains unrecorded. Certainly, Haushofer's influence on Hitler has been noted: for example, tracts of *Mein Kampf* covering geopolitics bear his stamp. Above all else – even above rumoured links to the Vril Society – Haushofer is remembered for believing passionately in the concept of 'blood and soil': to put it another way, that a race's very survival depends on its implementing a policy of winning Lebensraum (literally, 'living space') for itself. Such territorial expansion would be possible only through conquering inferior countries and races; by winning their land and having Aryan farmers settle there once the existing population was cleared – not a million miles away from the intentions of the Vril-Ya. Haushofer used to visit both Hitler and Hess regularly in Landsberg jail (where they served terms for their part in the failed Munich putsch, and where Hitler wrote *Mein Kampf*). Hitler was certainly won over by the concept of Lebensraum, which formed a central plank in the Nazi party manifesto.

Hess, too, needed little persuasion in accepting his mentor's view of society and the world. Years later, on the birth of his son, Hess ordered every Gauleiter (regional governor) to send him bags of soil from each Gau (district). The soil was then symbolically spread under a special cradle, so that the baby could begin its life proper, as a master of Germanic, Aryan soil. When Hess later defected to Britain, this unusual act was raked up by the tabloids and used in part to denounce him, yet when viewed from an occultic standpoint this is classic geomantic behaviour and closely mirrors accepted ceremonies in cultures from around the world. For example, at Douglas, on the Isle of Man, legend has it that Tynwald Hill is comprised of soil brought from all over the island and, given that the town is the administrative capital, this is said to preserve the dominion of the local government against outside control. The Second World War had seen Haushofer no nearer his goal, however – that of establishing an Aryan 'world government'. His only son, Albrecht, had been rounded up in the aftermath of the failed bomb plot against Hitler in the summer of 1944 and in the end died in Moabit concentration camp. Adolf Hitler was seen by many, including this old agitator, to have let the movement down and so, with little left to live for, Haushofer killed his wife on 14 March 1946 before taking cyanide. That his grave should have been unmarked and anonymous is perhaps wise. In the times in which we live, such beliefs as he fostered (Vril notwithstanding) might be viewed by some as highly potent talismans.

And what of the Thule Society and Germanenorden themselves? Membership began to leach away as the Nazis rose to prominence, offering them a greater future through political change and involvement, as opposed to a purely semi-mystical and closed secular group. Indeed, by 1925, when Thule closed its doors for the last time, the only common link between it and the Nazi party it had inadvertently spawned was the swastika. On the Nazis' accession to power, the SS and Gestapo sought to rid Germany of all the *flaky* groups and institutions which were now viewed as being incompatible with the new ideals of the NSDAP. Astrologers, fortune-tellers and any number of secret societies and groups were banned. Sebottendorff himself returned to Germany and tried to reopen the society in 1933, but the Nazis were by now in absolute power and had no need of such an embarrassing figure from their past, so deported him to Turkey, where he lived quietly until drowning himself on 9 May 1945, obviously at a loss to see the Reich he had helped create dissolve into the rubble of Berlin.

Only the established Christian Church remained – and this, only because Hitler wasn't yet in a position secure enough to remove it from everyday life. For millions of Germans, Rome as well as the Protestant faith remained an oasis of calm and sanity in their lives amid the tumult of economic decimation, rapid recovery and ongoing political suppression. Yet, for millions more, the Nazi party had created their substitute 'Reich Church'. Viewing film of the vast Nuremberg crowds chanting 'Sieg Heil' brings to mind an evangelical meeting, with its mesmerised audience or congregation brought to an ecstatic, feverish pitch by the preacher or Führer. And with the vast torchlit processions and columns of light orchestrated by Albert Speer and Propaganda Minister Goebbels, the impression of an ethereal cathedral in the sky is reinforced; something of mass and purpose, perhaps, rather than just a lightshow. It is an impressive display even today, and one can see why membership of such a group would impart such feelings of blind devotion in its leaders. In 1934 a Pastor, Herman Grüner, wrote:

The time is fulfilled for the German people in Hitler. It is because of Hitler that Christ . . . has become effective among us. Therefore, National Socialism is positive Christianity in action.

chapter two

'Why Antarctica? Because it's there . . .'
> BBC Radio 4 interview with a scientist
> from the British Antarctic Survey.

The previous chapter touched briefly on the importance of the Arctic region in Aryan myth and the legend of Hyperborea, with its mysterious underground civilisations. But it is Antarctica which assumes greater significance in the mythologies surrounding the Nazis, following on from their original roots in ariosophy and, later, the Thule Society. For an explanation as to what instigated this interest in the most lonely of continents we should first look not to the ancient legends but, instead, to the comparatively recent work of a Tyrolean steam engineer by the name of Hans Horbiger, whose work paved the way for a growing official obsession with the southernmost continent.

Born in Austria in 1860, Horbiger was a gifted engineer who found work, after finishing his degree, with the Budapest firm of LAND, which made steamrollers. While working there he patented a new type of steam valve which, once the design had been licensed to manufacturers around the world, made the young man very rich. So he left LAND and, using his new-found wealth to support himself, pursued a hitherto unrecognised interest in cosmology, an interest discovered while working amid the steam engines. Whereas most earnest young students with a similar interest might have acquired for themselves a telescope and studied orthodox astronomy, Horbiger was intent on explaining the cosmos through an entirely new, though somewhat unorthodox, theory of his own.

In time his new theory came to be known as 'Welteislehre' – 'world of ice and fire' – and eventually, after years of revision and with much dogged determination, in 1913 he published an 800-page tome entitled *The Glacial Cosmogeny of Horbiger*. The reception in Germany to the book was mixed, but, of those in favour, their conviction was total. After all, here was an almost believable explanation (after a fashion) for how the world, solar system and universe came to be, which also supported certain of the theories regarding the origins of Aryan man, Hyperborea and Thulean principles.

The essential principle of the book was to describe the universe as being in perpetual, eternal tension – between the forces of repulsion and attraction: fire and ice.

Imagine that somewhere in deep space was once a vast 'super-sun', millions of times larger than our own. Now imagine an equally large body of ice colliding with this sun and sinking deep within it. Nothing untoward happens for perhaps hundreds if not thousands of years, when suddenly, the steam pressure from the melting ice that has slowly built up erupts: the resultant cataclysmic explosion ejects huge quantities of matter out into space. Some smaller fragments are lost for ever as they're flung out into deep space. Others fall back into the original mass of the star, which is by now imploding back in on itself and sucking debris back in, to create our very own (and now smaller) sun, while large chunks are ejected out a second time into an 'intermediate band' to form the planets of our own solar system. According to Horbiger, the moon, Jupiter and Saturn are all made of ice, while the canals on the surface of Mars are merely visible cracks in the surface coating of ice that agglomerated around a rocky core. Only the earth, by dint of its closeness to the sun, isn't permanently icebound and suffers only from cold polar icecaps. The soil and rocks we see around us are the result of crashed meteorites and millions of years of flora and fauna – evolution.

Horbiger claimed that sunspots are actually blocks of ice falling out of their elliptical orbit around Jupiter (which they've been circling ever since the explosion). Given that Jupiter's perihelion comes around every eleven years and that sunspot activity, according to Horbiger 'coincides with this event', he therefore saw it as the most likely explanation for sunspots. In the inter-mediate band, the planetary bodies bow to two forces – firstly, the original outward thrust from the explosion, and, secondly, the force of gravity which attracts them to the nearest, larger mass: i.e. another planet. As the outward force weakens over time, so the force of gravity from other planets grows stronger, and the smaller bodies are drawn to the larger by decreasing the orbiting spiral they describe, until eventually these smaller planetary bodies crash into their larger neighbours. This repeats until the one immense agglomerated body of rock and ice remaining of our solar system is itself attracted to and falls within our sun to start the whole process again. As far as our earth is concerned, we should be most worried about our moon, which is, according to Horbiger, destined to fall gradually to the earth over a period stretching across several millennia. As the moon draws closer, Horbiger asserts that the force of gravity exerted on those still living on the earth should weaken, as it will be in conflict with that of the moon for longer and with more pronounced effect. The tidal reaches of our rivers and seas will grow ever higher and may even permanently flood many stretches of land, with effects similar to those expected as a result of global warming. All flora and fauna will feel the effects as earth's gravity weakens with untold side-effects, such as increased height and size of everything, from ants to trees to mankind, and as cosmic rays increase their penetration of our weakened atmosphere, genetic mutations would take place. Horbiger actually asserted that such human mutations might account for the past Aryan 'superman'.

Eventually, the moon itself might explode before actually reaching the earth; torn apart as a result of the conflicting forces acting on what is already a randomly compacted mass of material. Its debris would form a ring around the earth which, in turn, would rain down on what was left of our planet following the initial explosion. Horbiger would also have us believe that our moon is the fourth such body that earth has attracted to it and, as in the three earlier cases, will cause devastating effects when it finally breaks up. He was fond of citing the increasing size of dinosaurs of the past as evidence for the reduced gravity effects, their sudden disappearance put down to the third moon breaking up and crashing on to the earth's surface to create a new, even layer of aggregate material in which the bones of the dinosaurs were buried to become fossils. This might also explain the disappearance of the original Hyperboreans underground, though of course the two timelines don't tally with what we now understand really happened.

There is much more to the theory, but I think that's sufficient insight into Horbiger's unique, though warped doctrine. Many Germans, of course, scientists and ordinary citizens alike, naturally raised questions and doubts about the validity of such notions, rightfully dismissing them as so much nonsense. However, in the Germany of the 1920s and 1930s, such fanciful theories were finding favour in the highest circles, to the positive exclusion of rational science and such bigoted, official opinions merely added fuel to a movement known simply as 'Aryan physics'. This was a new scientific doctrine, which sought to displace 'Jewish scientific propaganda' as promoted by individuals, such as Einstein, in favour of a belief system in physics and science keyed in to the Aryan myths. Of course, this was rubbish – you can't change the laws of nature through political will. But for the massed rank and file it made no difference, once state schools and colleges began dropping established scientific curriculums for courses in the new movement. In 1925 Horbiger even sent out a challenging letter to all the main scientists and laboratories across Germany, suggesting that while Hitler was cleaning up German politics, only Horbiger himself was best placed to do the same for the 'bogus sciences', and that it would be in the best interests of German science if professors the length and breadth of the land join him in his purge of 'Jewish physics'. Behind the scenes, in the existing scientific circles at universities and labs throughout Germany, such patently ridiculous ideas were dismissed, and life – and science – continued as before. Yet this two-faced strategy was later to land noted professors, such as Werner Heisenberg, in trouble with the SS and Gestapo, as he and his team struggled with their efforts to build Germany's first atomic bomb, using officially discredited theories from 'Jewish physics' in the process. One can only imagine the reaction of his interrogators when Heisenberg pointed out that physical law is immutable and blind to politics or religion.

That this cranky amateur cosmologist was so influential is almost laughable nowadays, yet his theories on the origin of the Aryan race, emerging from under the frozen Arctic snow, having survived the last cataclysm with the third moon, found a receptive audience in Berlin. As soon as the Nazis reached absolute power, they were in a position to test some of Horbiger's theories for themselves. Hitler, himself, was such a fan that in plans for turning his home town of Linz into the cultural centre of the Danube, the new university to be built there would offer students courses on Copernicus, Ptolemy and, of course, Horbiger. It was also reported that whenever the two men met, it was usually Hitler who was shouted at, for interrupting the self-important Horbiger as he ranted on about his theories! Yet for all his bombast, this pseudoscientist *was* playing a useful role in the Reich, as his ideas were a convenient escape from the reality of the scientific world beyond its borders. There was no longer room in the country at large for rational scientific debate, and many professors were leaving their chosen vocations as a result. When serious scientific meetings and lectures became heckled regularly by Hitler Youth members and denounced for being against the spirit of Hitler's Aryan nation, it wasn't hard for many professors either to quit for new jobs or to emigrate. In fact, it was this subsequent 'brain drain', both of skilled teaching staff and university intake, which was to have an impact on the problems faced by Germany later in the war. There simply weren't enough highly qualified German scientists – chemists, physicists et al. – to go round in the various military projects; hence the over-reliance on 'guest workers' from occupied countries.

Horbiger, then, had sown the seed linking the Aryan legend to cosmology. He had synthesised a heady cocktail of beliefs perfectly tailored to the needs of the Nazi party, as it sought to establish a new national identity, and, while it may have been mostly bunkum, Horbiger was no dupe. Yes, he may have been misguided, but his doctrine none the less directly inspired Germany's renewed interest in polar exploration. In years past, though, German expeditions had set out for the poles with a more reasoned, *rational* standpoint. King Wilhelm I of Prussia, who was crowned German emperor in Versailles in 1871, knew that from a strategic standpoint, as well as merely on a matter of national prestige and morale, his new kingdom could only benefit from making exploratory ventures to both poles, and plans were quickly devised to achieve these goals. Two years later, the German steamship *Grönland* became the first powered vessel to visit Antarctica, under its British captain, Sir Eduard Dallman, on behalf of the newly founded German Society for Polar Research. During the next sixty years, four more elaborate expeditions were dispatched to the southern oceans, most notably in 1925 with the dedicated research vessel *Meteor* under the command of Dr Albert Merz. Since the first trip, little progress had been made on the idea of using Antarctica as a strategic base, as the expeditions had been of a predominantly civilian, scientific nature. But under Hitler this policy was set to change.

Along with many of his cronies, Hitler believed not only in Horbiger's Welteislehre theory but in other grand ideas, such as those proposed by Haushofer involving the importance to a nation of grabbing land for Lebensraum. Hitler believed that if the Third Reich were to play a part in shaping the new world order he envisaged, it had to be seen to be operating in strength on every continent. Before the war, Germany's presence in Europe, its friendly relations with Japan and other countries in the Far East and Asia, its relationships with tinpot though friendly regimes in South America and its colonial legacy in Africa, led Hitler to see Antarctica as a natural and obvious source of new territory. Since there was no military presence there to dissuade him or to dispute his claim on territory (unlike the Arctic Circle, favoured by Horbiger), events suggest that Hitler began drawing up plans for establishing some kind of forward operating base in that barren wilderness, as the war clouds gathered on the horizon. In so doing, he was putting the principle of Lebensraum into action, with elements of Welteislehre into the bargain; planning an icebound colony of pure Aryans, who would thrive in their isolation when all else succumbed.

But he had to do so covertly. The Western powers were already rearming by the time the project was begun in 1938, and Hitler obviously didn't wish to provoke them further, following the Anschluss of Austria and the coming invasion of Czechoslovakia, so the plan was drawn up as an overtly civilian effort, in partnership with the state airline Lufthansa. But with the Kriegsmarine (German navy) and the Reichsmarschall himself, Hermann Göring, throwing their support behind the venture, this was to be no ordinary civilian enterprise.

The command for the expedition was awarded to Captain Alfred

Ritscher, who could already boast of much experience in navigating polar waters. His ship was to be the MS *Schwabenland*. Named after the Swabian region of Germany, it was a one-time cargo vessel since converted to a crude aircraft carrier, with a pair of Dornier Wal ('Whale') flying boats which, since 1934, had been running a Lufthansa airmail service to the USA. Aircraft would leave the ship, from a short ramp built on to the rear half of her super-structure via a steam catapult, and fly on ahead, delivering mail and returning with mail for Europe, in a routine repeated closer to home waters. The Dornier Wal was a rugged and widely exported seaplane that first flew in 1922. With its open cockpit, it would prove an excellent observation platform in Antarctic waters – although not much fun for the frozen crew!

The ship was refitted especially for the voyage at a cost of over a million Reichsmarks – a not-inconsiderable sum – and the crew underwent special training at the hands of the German Society of Polar Research. As well as instruction on surviving out on the pack ice should things go wrong, the society had also invited Richard E. Byrd to Germany from the USA to give a lecture on what conditions might be like. He arrived at Hamburg in November 1938 and at a local cinema showed the crew and eighty-four invited guests a new documentary film of his about the Antarctic region. Byrd had already become well known for his various exploits at both polar regions (being the first man to fly over the South Pole in 1929, among other achievements), and his presence and advice were highly welcomed by the team. As we shall see in a later chapter, however, this might not have been the only time that Byrd would be in contact with German polar explorers.

Eventually, the MS *Schwabenland* left Hamburg on 17 December 1938 and reached her predetermined spot on the Antarctic coastline without undue incident a month later, on 19 January 1939, high summer on the continent. Over the next few weeks, both aircraft (named *Passat* and *Boreas*) flew more than a dozen wide-ranging sorties apiece, covering between 325 and 600,000 square kilometres. The reason for such a wide disparity is that while official records appear to confirm the lower figure, some subsequent commentators have sought to query them as not tallying with contemporary reports. They suggest that some sort of cover-up has gone on to disguise the true extent of the mission – which they estimate at the higher figure. What isn't disputed, however, is that at least 11,000 high-definition air-to-ground photographs were taken, and a few thousand swastika-capped metal marker-poles were dropped on to the territory. These poles had a weighted and pointed tip so that on landing, they'd stick upright in the snow – confirming the true nature of this expedition: simply to stake a claim on a piece of the permafrost which the team subsequently named Neu Schwabenland. But there was a problem.

The land claimed by the Germans already belonged to Norway. In fact, a Norwegian expedition had visited the area, known officially as Queen Maud Land, as recently as 1931 and had made extensive maps of the area – unashamedly used by Ritscher and his aircrews to navigate by. Certain other commentators, who come across as barely disguised Nazi sympathisers, have asserted that Norway paid only lip service to their claim and that their maps covered only the region close to the coastline; further, that it was left to the Germans to 'heroically' map the forbidding hinterland. Well, could it be that the Norwegians lacked aircraft on their expedition and so could only venture a short way inland? If they *had* been equipped with aircraft, they would then have had the same advantage, so it seems ridiculous that the German claim went virtually unopposed at the time.

After a month, and with the weather beginning to close in once more, Ritscher packed up and returned to Hamburg, arriving in April 1939. He was so pleased with the apparent success of the trip, that he immediately set to planning a return visit, this time with a number of Fieseler Fi 156 Storch light aircraft equipped with landing skis, which would allow ground reconnoitres.

However, the onset of the Second World War prevented these plans from ever materialising.

What we know of events regarding Nazi Germany's involvement in the southernmost oceans, concludes on a somewhat anticlimactic note with the exploits of three raiding vessels during the war that were given free rein to operate in and around Antarctica and the South Atlantic to attack Allied shipping. While the *Komet* and the *Atlantis* continued patrolling right up to the end of the war, their sister ship, the *Pinguin*, was chased down and sunk in 1941 by HMS *Cornwall* after she had sunk a small number of Allied vessels.

This escalation of conflict in such forbidding seas so far from home was somewhat unexpected: after all, no established trade route existed in the vicinity, save around the tip of South America at Cape Horn. Yet Britain was determined to nip in the bud these raids on shipping in the area, lest they got out of hand. With one eye on the post-war world, in 1943 the British government set up a listening post on Deception Island under the codename Operation Tabarin (which was actually named after a London nightclub to confuse German spies). Its mission was clear: watch for German shipping such as the *Komet* and *Atlantis* and report movements to Allied vessels in the area. It had another, hidden agenda too – to rattle the British sabre at the pro-German government in Argentina over its plans to establish control over the Drake Passage. The British operation was only publicly acknowledged and somewhat innocuously renamed after the war as the Falkland Islands Dependant Survey, which was to become abbreviated to 'Fids'. Even after the British Antarctic Survey was later established in its place, new recruits were still referred to as 'Fiddlers'.

So if that's the official history as accepted by most observers and historians, perhaps it's time for us to look at the alleged 'real history' – what might *really* have been behind Ritscher's expedition and subsequent events. Since the war there have been dozens of books and countless articles covering the secret Nazi expeditions to Antarctica, shipping movements and tales of secret bases and flying saucers. Yet in the two years of researching official records and accounts for this book, this author hasn't once come across a single report to either confirm or deny such stories. I'll present the 'evidence' as best I can, but leave you to make up your own mind – after all, when dealing with stories in the realm of legend, one can either take them with a pinch of salt or believe that a kernel of truth lies at the origin of the story.

After the Nazi hierarchy had dismissed its chances of establishing a major presence in the Arctic Circle, Antarctica was chosen as the spot for fulfilling the dreams of Horbiger, Hess and Hitler: a place where Aryan ideals could prosper and flourish, away from outside interference and from where the Aryan superman would one day re-emerge.

We know for sure that civil and military engineers numbered part of Ritscher's crew in 1938 and were there purely to evaluate the conditions in Neu Schwabenland for its suitability as a base station. There were also a number of marine biologists, botanists and cartographers on board, as well as a team of hydrographers whose job was to plot the sea bed as best they could, as the ship approached the region and subsequently moved around the coastline; the cartographers re-mapped the interior, from the data and photographs brought back by the seaplane pilots. The story goes that in the event the teams identified three suitable landing bays, each offering shelter and water deep enough for the ship. But the hydrographers were the first to hit pay-dirt when they discovered a deep trench, thought to have been formed as a result of underwater volcanic activity, which ran almost equidistantly between South America and Africa down to Antarctica (to Queen Maud Land) and actually straight under the continent. The trench was – is – almost totally comprised of immense stretches of pack ice floating on seawater. It was anyone's guess as to where this would eventually re-emerge, if at all, or what natural features might lie beneath the ice.

As the two seaplanes covered the continent, their crews were as amazed as the scientists to find large areas that resembled grassy Icelandic tundra, pockmarked with geothermically warmed pools of water. These were totally unexpected, and lent further weight to the feasibility of the proposed base station. With the locations all mapped, the expedition returned home; the apparent month's delay due to the ship off-loading several of the scientists in Argentina, from where they would plan a more covert return to their country's new territory. With such a successful mission behind them, Ritscher and his crew then began planning for a return in 1939, but the outbreak of war was to end such plans.

The rumours continue from that point with the apparent realisation by the project's sponsor, Reichsmarschall Göring and others, that not only would Germany *have* to return to Neu Schwabenland, but that it would now do so under wartime conditions. While German shipping, military or otherwise, was still relatively free to come and go during the first months of the war, it was obvious from the experiences of the First World War that this might not be so for much longer. So if the continuation of the project were to be assured, U-boats would have to be used. That this new dimension guaranteed a degree of secrecy to the operation was a bonus, so submarine crews began to train in the northern and eastern Baltic. These may have been Soviet waters, but at this stage the non-aggression pact between the two countries held, and German naval manoeuvres in the Baltic were tolerated. As U-boat production slowly increased, so more crews got to train in these subarctic waters until the time came for some to make the long voyage south. Packing these cramped and slow boats full of blueprints and scientific journals, as well as volunteer civilian colonists (selected as single, fervent Nazis willing to do their bit for their Führer and Fatherland), the first of the U-boats left Kiel or Hamburg sometime in 1940 bound for Argentina and a mid-voyage refuelling. There, they'd also meet up with their countrymen who had been busy working on the project since Ritscher had dropped them off two years earlier.

With the aid of the (mostly) pro-German Argentinian government, these scientists had, during their two years, designed and produced prefabricated buildings that could be erected on the tundra. These, together with stockpiled supplies, now sat in readiness to be shipped to Antarctica. The arrival of the submarines was obviously welcomed in the small port they had chosen to operate from (wishing to avoid British and American spies), and after loading one or more locally registered cargo vessels with some if not all of the material, a small convoy was formed and, with the U-boats as escort, sailed down to Neu Schwabenland to find it just as they had left it. On reaching one of the natural anchorages, a U-boat took her leave and, following the instructions of one of the original hydrographers, proceeded to track down the trench. As she made her way further under the ice pack, she apparently discovered several huge natural caverns that had formed under the ice from running meltwater, caused either by warming layers of algae or subterranean geothermic activity. Some of these were so vast (one was reportedly over fifty kilometres long) that the architects later changed their minds regarding building on the surface and elected to utilise these caverns instead, setting up their machine shops, hangars, barracks and numerous ancillary rooms within these spaces. After hollowing out areas into the ice walls of the caverns, away from the sea channels, such areas proved ideal.

Protected from the elements and insulated by the ice, access at first could be achieved only via submarine and later by well-concealed tunnels that opened out on to the surface, down which the bulky equipment could be brought in. With freshwater locked into the surrounding ice and with room for huge food and supply stockpiles in other caverns, colonists could survive here almost indefinitely and undisturbed. What's more, as the U-boats explored more of the trench, they found that it emerged on the far side of the pack ice, beyond the South Pole, and went on yet further – at least to the waters surrounding New Zealand. Their base now had two routes of entry.

The leaders back in Berlin were so delighted with what was going on that they christened their new base Neu Berlin – the capital of Neu Schwabenland – though its regular codename was the more prosaic Base 211. But what was Base 211 actually doing? Which organisation was running it and for what purpose? For the years up until 1943, no suggestions have been offered as to which government department was responsible, which appears odd when one considers that the Nazi government thrived on running a pervasive and invasive system, with an official department and office for absolutely everything. Perhaps in the case of Base 211, an exception was made and the project was being run under an innocuous cover, tucked into the brief of an obscure department: The Reichsbahn for instance (state railway system), or the Reichspost (state postal service). With their undoubted skill at administration, officials could easily have manufactured ways and means to keep a secret of the budget and mechanics involved in such an operation. To this day, no publicly available information has emerged that acknowledges the existence of the base, yet rumours of an umbrella project, codenamed Ultra, have surfaced, under which it is possible that the Neu Berlin project might have operated. However, the rumours run into confusion when one remembers that not only was Ultra the codename given to the British decoding of enciphered Enigma codes at Bletchley Park, but also subsequently the code mentioned by several UFO researchers as the cover for the USA's ongoing contact with EBEs. Of course, the simplest answer might be that Base 211 never existed – but then we'll never know . . . will we?

To return to the story, whatever the administrative headaches the operation was causing back in Germany, things were running smoothly at the base. U-boats were now arriving regularly, bringing new colonists, supplies and news from home straight to the door via the trench. Experience and techniques gained in Germany from constructing massive bomb shelters and converting old mine workings into underground factories, were employed in the base as it grew. Mining engineers tasked with burrowing out the ice to form new halls or caverns, were using equipment and plant brought in from Argentina or Chile, and, as new wings were opened up, so the remit of the base also changed. When first planned, it was probably intended merely to act as a listening post, the Reich's equivalent of the British base on Deception Island. If it could create a little ruckus in Allied shipping with its visiting U-boats into the bargain, all to the good. But as the war developed and the situation at home visibly deteriorated, even outwardly committed Nazis in Berlin and elsewhere were beginning to see the writing on the wall. Even if Germany's secret weapons had been developed earlier, there was little doubt that, against the irresistible tide of Allied troops from all sides, Germany would inevitably be squeezed into a bloody submission. Yet to the faithful, hard core of disciples to the Nazi creed, their faith in Hitler and his brand of politics remained unshakable, against the onrushing tide of communists from the East (whom Hitler had railed against in *Mein Kampf*) and the debauched and corrupt capitalists from the West. Base 211 – New Berlin – offered these people a means to escape and start the fight anew. They began planning their move towards the end of 1943. The catastrophic loss of Stalingrad proved the turning point in the war and, while still outwardly fanatical Nazis, these figures – some well placed and influential – were now committed more to self-preservation than to selfless immolation and needless sacrifice. They believed that pursuing the struggle would be more effective with them alive than dead – perhaps even that the struggle wasn't worth pursuing in some cases.

But what such an exodus required, though, if it were to be handled at all successfully this late in the war, was the involvement of the SS. This was the only group in 1943 that still had the ability to move mountains and get things done in the Reich. While weapon-production was being sorted out by Speer and his 'super-ministry', it was the SS who oiled the wheels behind the scenes with its forced labourers and increasing responsibility for secret weapons, as well as lining its own pockets for the inevitable. Himmler was no fool and could easily see what was coming; after all, this was why he had initiated secret peace overtures to the West – and to Stalin – at various times. He wanted to lead the Reich himself, through a time of transition to a post-war world in which *his* SS would be the power-brokers in any new adminis-tration. With all that he had achieved, Himmler, the great administrator, had too much to lose in the annihilation of the Aryan nation. Thus it was that sometime late in 1943, Himmler was approached to lend his active support to relocating key elements to Base 211, which one imagines he relished. After all, if events conspired to see him lose the Fatherland, then wouldn't an SS-controlled New Berlin elsewhere be an attractive, alternative option? As 1944 began, the SS were already organising a covert transfer of key personnel and materiel to Antarctica. The supreme commander of U-boats, Gröss Admiral Dönitz, was himself a fervent Nazi, so it wouldn't have been difficult for him to second boats and crews to Himmler's SS, if he thought they were engaged in such a patriotic mission – especially if the SS were supplying the fuel and supplies required. Many boats were reportedly lost during these last years of the war, so might it be possible that one or two might actually have relocated to Base 211? The official U-boat records show nothing of this, of course, but then again papers can easily be forged, lost or both.

Thus it was that from early 1944 to the end of the war, SS-sponsored U-boats visited Base 211. No one knows for sure about what their cargoes consisted of, but some form of military hardware was surely required. Stories of complete production lines for jet fighters, such as the Me 262 or Me 163, are off the mark; for a start, the necessary runway would have been visible to enemy aircraft, and the limited range of such aircraft would have made anything other than regular patrol flights of short duration impossible. In any case, the extensive production lines required to build such complicated aircraft, and the sheer amount of raw materials needed, would have been too much. However, as discussed in later chapters, building a flying disc might require less in the way of materiel, and its VTOL capability dispenses with the need for a runway; all that were needed were large silos with (camouflaged) sliding roofs. If entire laboratories were transported to Antarctica, together with a number of their workers, blueprints and small stockpiles of raw materials, production could commence, given time, of something smaller and simpler to build than a jet fighter. A flying disc craft would appear to fit the bill perfectly.

The personnel required for such an undertaking has been put by some at 100,000, though I would suggest that the true number would have been a tiny fraction of this. The larger figure was apparently comprised of boys from the Hitler Youth with no surviving family (or desire to see them again), slave workers of both sexes and SS NCOs and officers. This author would plump for somewhere around 100 or 50, which is still a sizable mass of humanity to have clinging to life in a frozen wilderness and, as the war dragged on through 1944 and into its last year, increasingly cut off from home. One wonders at the state of their collective morale at this time. Did they still believe in a surprise final victory, as so often heralded, or, in the final analysis, had they realised that they were on their own for better or for worse – and that they could never just surrender.

But one thing was certain: their Führer and the leading lights of his government and armed forces were virtually beyond help as spring 1945 neared. Hitler had placed his faith in the Western Allies eventually parting company with the Soviet Union. He envisaged the Americans and British then choosing to join forces with Germany and, thus united, fighting off the red horde together – the enemy he believed common to all sides and the one in whose best interests it would be to defeat. This was a myopic view of then-current world events, of course, but by this time, ever more confused and evidently suffering from Parkinson's disease, the ailing Führer was in no fit state to run his country, let alone the war. Increasingly, following the botched bomb plot of July 1944, senior army staff were muted in the face of the manipulative SS and other fanatical Nazis, and the voice of reason was becoming lost. The SS were now more in control of the war, and their grip could only get tighter as Hitler placed increasing levels of responsibility into their hands. As characters such as SS Gruppenführer Hans Kammler took to managing such vital projects as the V-1 flying bomb and V-2 rocket, more pragmatic SS and military officers were positioning themselves for the inevitable collapse. We've all heard stories about the countless art treasures and gold bars looted from banks, museums and collections across Europe, but this was only part of the SS plan to finance its own interests long after the dust settled. Base 211 now became the recipient of projects and resources that had hitherto been held in Europe: stockpiles of uranium and blueprints for machines capable of enriching it to weapons-grade material or, at best, creating fuel for power-generating reactors; more important – and relevant to the story – blueprints, working models and machine tools for building the first generation of flying discs; films and stills of the first disc prototypes in flight, to aid the test pilots and engineers evacuated to the base in their own reconstruction of these designs from the plans; new radar sets and electronic devices of all kinds. Whatever the base had been working on prior to 1945 was now either scrapped or integrated into the disc project – for this was to be its focus from that point on. In evacuating themselves to Antarctica, the colonists had vowed never to surrender – and to avenge their fallen dream of the Reich. The arrival of the disc project offered the best hope of doing just that.

Other aspects of this amazing story will be explored in further chapters, but finally let's give a thought to a member of Hitler's inner circle whose story might have some bearing on this whole myth. In his book *The Murder of Rudolf Hess*, Hugh Thomas casts doubt on the man who was locked up in Berlin's Spandau Prison for so long and offers fairly persuasive evidence that the figure held prisoner there was not the real Hess, but an imposter. Yet if that were the case – and the evidence is quite startling – why was he not executed at Nuremberg, as so many of his contemporaries were, or simply released as a harmless stooge, before his death there in 1981? Other characters served long prison sentences, such as Albert Speer, a civilian figure who might arguably have had a more heinous war record than Deputy Führer Hess, who, after all, absconded to Britain in 1941 before the war had taken a more serious turn for the worse. So why such a long sentence? It has been suggested that Hess was in some way connected to Base 211; perhaps in his role as Deputy Führer, he organised its initial development using his wide-reaching powers and the Allies kept him alive as some kind of 'bargaining chip' with the colonists. Or did the *real* Hess indeed abscond in 1941 to Base 211 itself, simultaneously using a loyal double, with instructions to fly to Scotland and thereafter take the brunt of ridicule and long incarceration? If so, Hess would have effectively disappeared to oversee the development of a fourth Reich in the southern hemisphere.

Whatever the truth, there is no doubt that the myth surrounding Base 211 is an extremely potent one and, for many misty-eyed dreamers, will always be regarded as fact. The heady mix of secret U-boat missions, vast ice caverns and flying saucers is something straight out of an *Indiana Jones* movie and will doubtless outlive this author's attempts at bringing it to heel, but it's all part of the wider picture. Along with the intricate history of the secret societies outlined in the previous chapter, the overall story of the development of flying discs in Germany is all the easier to accept when one looks at the background – be it legendary or otherwise. Like Base 211 itself, even the discs may yet turn out to be based on little more than rumoured conjecture, but on this last point I would prefer to keep my powder dry and opt for the argument that there's no smoke without fire.

chapter three

'They called me deranged. The hope is that they are right. It is of no greater or lesser import for another fool to wander the earth. But if I am right and science is wrong, then may the Lord God have mercy on mankind.'

Viktor Schauberger (1885–1958), a pioneer in the fields of 'natural energy' and water flow management who developed his own flying disc technologies during and after the Second World War.

In the preceding two chapters we saw how Germany was creating the conditions necessary for a radical sea change in its domestic sciences and politics, the Nazi party merely taking advantage of the brewing Zeitgeist to give form and direction to this coming change. Amid all the turmoil, scientists and engineers around the world at the turn of the twentieth century (and not just in Germany) appeared to believe that anything was possible. The Wright brothers had cheated gravity. The internal-combustion engine was promising to mobilise and liberate the masses, and although the First World War took some of the gloss off such achievements – the world could be said to have come of age during that war – it did at least propel and mature such technologies. We have already heard how the Vril Society might very well have had its own disc project in the 1920s and 1930s, and, regardless of how credible such stories might be, they do point out the fact that development doesn't occur in a vacuum. The idea of flying disc aircraft didn't materialise overnight in some shadowy office deep in a Berlin suburb, a lonely air-force base, close to nowhereville, New Mexico, or even a galaxy far, far away. Our story involves many individual figures who, while they may not have all been directly involved as far as we know, certainly contributed ideas and technologies through their work in various fields. The disc's designers, though highly skilled and insightful engineers themselves, would have had access to that corpus of work as they put together the first prototypes and models of the discs. But whose work might we examine in such a quest? Who are the likely suspects?

Perhaps the most obvious candidate should be one of the greatest inventors ever: Nikola Tesla.

Born in Croatia in 1856, by the time he was thirty Tesla's undoubted genius had taken him to America, where his subsequent research into electricity led him to work alongside the great Thomas Edison. But they disagreed on the relative merits of either Edison's then-dominant DC (direct current) or Tesla's own AC (alternating current), so Tesla left to develop AC (he later won the Edison Medal in 1917 for services to science, after having seen AC win out). After leaving Edison's lab and working to perfect several key elements of AC, Tesla then won backing for a new laboratory in Colorado Springs, in which he could pursue theories about how electrical power might be transmitted without wires. This obsession with the idea of the *wireless* transmission of electrical power was to be one of his greatest preoccupations throughout a long career, but back in 1899 he still believed himself to be on the brink of a major breakthrough.

When in that same year his artificial lightning generator succeeded in powering-up over two hundred fifty-watt lightbulbs at a distance of twenty-six miles, he must have thought the problem was solved.

Tesla came to realise that the earth is permanently surrounded by magnetic energy fields, resonating at a certain frequency (which was later proved to be 7.8 cycles per second) and that if you could somehow tap this wavelength it might offer a source of free energy. Like two adjacent and tuned violin strings, if one is plucked, the other next to it will pick up the harmonic vibrations and resonate at the same frequency, and Tesla saw parallels with the earth in this manner. He also looked at two distinct methods of transmitting this 'free' power from its collection point; either air transmission, as in his Colorado Springs experiment, or pumping electricity directly into the ground and allowing it to be carried along natural geomagnetic carrier lines – what we might now call ley lines. Such ground-breaking work was truly pioneering, yet little progress in this field seems to have been carried out in the years following his death. Odd rumours surrounded the eventual suppression of his work by the US government (supposedly to protect the emerging and influential coal-based generation of electricity and the oil-based auto industry), as much as the deliberate suppression by his financial backer at the time, J. P. Morgan, the famous banker who had already bankrolled Edison and who had much to lose if Tesla's theories worked – 'Free electricity, indeed!'.

Yet in Germany, perhaps unsurprisingly in light of what we've learned, Tesla's ideas were greeted warmly; the power transmission idea being seen by the influential Germanenorden and Thule Society as all but endorsing the existence of the universal energy of Vril – the W-force.

But aside from his work with electricity, Tesla was also busy in many other fields. For example, in 1897 he showed off a radio-controlled submarine at Madison Square Gardens, New York, which might be used as a platform for launching torpedoes against enemy shipping at anchor, at no danger to the (distant) operator. Little interest in the 'teleautomatics' system was shown by the shortsighted US navy, however, and even in 1915 an increasingly frustrated Tesla was writing to the US War Department to promote his boat and suggesting that they also consider:

My remotely piloted aerial machines, devoid of sustaining planes [wings], ailerons, propellers and other external attachments, which will be capable of immense speeds and are very likely to furnish powerful arguments for peace in the near future. Such a machine, sustained and propelled entirely by reaction [rocket] engines can be controlled either mechanically or by wireless [radio] energy.

Remember that this is seventeen years *after* demonstrating his teleautomatic submarine and that another thirty-odd years had to pass before the Germans brought their own 'advanced' technologies into service, and one begins to see just how ahead of his time Tesla was. Imagine the effect his inventions might have had on the battlefields of the First World War, if the powers that be had taken him up on his proposals. No wonder, then, that in 1920s Germany he was seen by some as offering the very tools needed to create the 'wonder weapons' Germany might need.

Tesla himself had no immediate love for Germany and would always offer his new developments to the Western Allies first, but, as his cash ran out in the 1920s and 1930s, he was willing to talk to anyone who'd listen – and more often than not that was the Third Reich. There is not enough space here to recount all of Tesla's achievements and inventions, but one has entered into lore as having links with the flying disc programme. Familiar to most sci-fi fans, the idea of a 'death ray' has triggered our imaginations for decades – yet Tesla claimed he had built one for real. On 1 July 1934, the seventy-eight-year-old inventor announced the creation of a weapon that he hoped would spell the end of all wars to come.

Although details were never revealed publicly, it was believed to involve a method of transmitting electrically charged particles through the air in concentrated beams of plasma energy, simulating ball lightning. Tesla flatly stated that any country that installed a perimeter ring of these defensive devices around its border would be impregnable. Invading ground forces, aircraft and the like would disintegrate under them, powerless against their attack. But no government was interested. Tesla offered his idea to several that year, but all turned him down – even Germany, apparently, but only because it had already started on a similar project of its own and presumably didn't want to pay Tesla royalties or offer him vindication. Working with high-voltage X-rays, Dr Schieboldt, the noted physicist, had begun work on a top-secret project, codenamed Hadubrand, to bring down aircraft using intersecting beams of concentrated X-rays. His idea ultimately proved unworkable, but apparently his studies led to one useful spin-off – the electron microscope. A derivative of Hadubrand was rumoured to have been fitted to some disc prototypes, however, and it seems as though it was further refined during the Second World War, but there is no evidence of its having been used operationally.

In 1936, on his eightieth birthday, the Croatian government founded the Tesla Institute in Belgrade and awarded him an annual pension of $7,200 in recognition of his contribution to science. The institute collected together all his many unpublished papers into a substantial archive, but when Germany invaded the region in 1941, the SS took control of the institute. No one knows the extent of what the SS found there – or of what they learned as a result. But Tesla himself was living in New York all the while, writing scientific papers and continuing to work. Even so, on his death in poverty-stricken obscurity in 1943, the FBI impounded all the material and handed it over to the the Office of Alien Property, where it was officially sealed until being handed over to the Yugoslavian-Croatian ambassador. But again no one knows for sure whether or not the FBI had already cherry-picked its way through the vast archive. Some commentators believe they would have been negligent in their duty if they had not, given the post-war climate of growing mistrust between the super-powers.

Another character whose work we should examine at this stage is one Robert L. Bartini. A committed member of the Italian Communist Party, Bartini became an aircraft designer of some note before moving to Russia in the late 1920s. Here he was to develop a series of exotic aircraft, the details of which even now, some seventy-five years on, are still classified and kept out of the public domain. For example, in 1935 the Russians test-flew an 'invisible aircraft' of Bartini's, made from a transparent material that couldn't be seen by the naked eye unless it was close by. This may have been similar to a Mylar-like material which the pioneering Horten brothers in Germany used in the 1930s to cover one of their early gliders (though it would be interesting to discover how the Russians had managed to disguise extra items, such as the engine, not found in a glider). Bartini was also a far-sighted pioneer in advanced aerodynamics. His thoughts on the subject might easily have found their way to German scientists working in the field at the time, especially to those pondering the benefits of adopting unorthodox shapes as the basis for a new approach to aerial craft.

In post-war years Bartini's main achievement seems to have been as the driving force behind the fabled 'Caspian Seamonster' – the first practical 'Ekranoplane' design, of which a few large examples were built, with smaller types being evaluated for production today. This revolutionary approach to seagoing travel enabled an amphibious seaplane (the 'Ekranoplane') to rise up out of the water at speed and literally skim over the wave tops, cushioned all the while by the lift generated by its stubby wings against the surface of the water. Unlike a conventional hydrofoil, an Ekranoplane doesn't rely on foils or wings carving through the water – it is still a pure aircraft, albeit relying on an unusual aerodynamic effect to achieve its wave-skimming flight. It doesn't bear much relevance to the flying discs in itself (though some of the Russian craft equally look as if they belong in *Star Wars*), but the concept does go to highlight the depth of Bartini's brilliance as an aerodynamicist and therefore lends weight to his earlier 1930s work in the field of airflow around certain wing forms – precisely the sort of work that would have had a positive impact on the development of a flying disc.

The same is true of the work in aerodynamics pursued by Alexander Lippisch. Some of Lippisch's work was detailed in *Last Talons of the Eagle*, specifically how he designed a powerful coal-powered ramjet fighter with a delta wing 'lifting body' profile. This design approach has carried through several NASA experimental vehicles, reaching its apogee in the modern space shuttle. But Lippisch had also been pursuing the development of a pure flying wing project, along similar lines to that of the prominent Horten brothers. As his work in this area developed alongside theirs, the advances in aerodynamics they highlighted were noted in many German research circles, not least those connected with the disc projects, as the work carried out by both the Hortens and Lippisch related directly to their own efforts. Remember, too, that during the 1930s and 1940s aerodynamics was still something of a black and arcane art, with few of the applied physical principles we see in the work of aircraft designers today. Back then, designers relied on testing models in crude wind tunnels or the results of flying prototypes, to inform them of a design's efficacies or shortcomings – and the designers working on the discs would have been saddled with *exactly* these same gaps in knowledge as their colleagues working on more conventional aircraft. After all, at least designers in other areas had a bank of anecdotal knowledge to fall back on – the disc teams were the first in their field and learning as they went along.

But before we roll our story on to deal with the main figures in this intriguing mystery, there remains one without whom the patchwork would be incomplete. His name is Viktor Schauberger.

Schauberger was born in 1885 into a traditional Austrian family of foresters, who for generations had helped manage the ancient woodlands at Holzschlag, near Lake Plockenstein. Viktor was no different in following his father's footsteps into the trade. After the First World War, and by now an experienced forester, he was granted responsibility for a district of 21,000 hectares owned by Prince Adolf-Schaumburg-Lippe, near Steyerling. As he familiarised himself with the territory, often alone for days in this undisturbed wilderness, he began to see nature around him in a different way, especially watercourses. Without going into too much detail here, the essence of the grand theory that he eventually distilled for himself was that water was *alive*; in some way possessed of a life force, or energy. What Schauberger came to recognise, was that a truly natural watercourse, allowing water to flow freely, builds up an energy in that water which, at the right temperature, travels in the opposite direction to the apparent water flow. He remembered something his father had told him regarding the phenomenon: namely, that when a river is exposed to the sun, it turns lazy, it 'folds in on itself'; but at night it wakes, especially under a full moon, and somehow changes its density, becomes more vibrant and buoyant in some way. More *alive*.

After refining this new-found knowledge, he started up a business designing water flumes for local logging companies, exploiting this mysterious energy force in their design and so floating down logs in previously unheard-of quantities *at night*, with no more water in the flumes than had been used before. After an initially rocky start to his business, things started picking up for him as once-sceptical clients began taking up his unique design. He could soon afford to take out patents for his new design of flume, the royalties from which would support him and his family in the years to come, in a strange mirroring of Horbiger's experience. In 1934, as a result of an acquaintance with a local businessman, Schauberger met Adolf Hitler in Berlin. Hitler was apparently keen to hear of the wonderful advances this ex-forester and fellow countryman was making with his new flumes. However, Schauberger was dismayed that the private audience he'd requested with the Führer ended up being gate-crashed by one Direktor Wiluhn of the Kaiser Wilhelm Institute. Undaunted, he spoke without interruption for an hour. Hitler seemed impressed at the end of the meeting, but as they left Wiluhn reportedly rounded on the Austrian and accused him of 'filling the Führer's head with nonsense'.

Nonsense or not, Hitler asked him back for a meeting the very next day unaware that a miserable Schauberger, dispirited at Wiluhn's dismissive patronism, was already travelling back home. Little state interest was then shown until 1938, when the new governor of annexed Austria, Julius Streicher, presented a grant of ten million Reichsmarks to Schauberger out of the blue, with access to the well-furnished lab of Professor Kotschau in Nuremberg. Schauberger wasn't about to quibble at this chance, and after recalling his son Walter from an engineering course at Dresden University they set to work as a team to unravel the secrets of 'living water' in controlled conditions.

Initially the task appeared simple, but in practice positive results were hard to come by. The reason Schauberger always gave for such lacklustre results was that the water used in the lab was 'dead' to begin with, and that, in order to see results, there was no alternative but to use water that retained something of its natural vigour. With no such water on tap, the duo first set to designing and perfecting an enriching device that would restore their water supply 'to life', something the device apparently did well.

But another, more fruitful spin-off emerged from the Nuremberg lab, other than an efficient water flume, and it's this that earns a place here. It seems that in studying the specific properties of colloidal flow in water, Schauberger had actually come up with some new form of power plant. In 1941 he acquired a small electric starter motor from an aircraft engine and mounted it to the scale prototype of a machine he believed might acquire lift through harnessing this newly discovered energy.

The basic idea was that a battery would start the motor which, in turn, would spin turbine blades in a barrel-shaped drum, about 1.5 metres in diameter and weighing over 130 kilogrammes, through the axis of which lay a hollow cone open at its widest end to the underside. In operation, the barrel was filled with 'living water', which the turbine would then circulate at a tremendous rate (faster than with normal water, apparently) around the inside of the barrel (around the outside wall of the cone). This had the effect of creating a hyperbolic, centripetal spiral like some micro-tornado within the water, which, at its top, would pass through a smaller water turbine linked to an impeller at the pointed end of the cone.

To get some idea of this, take an empty plastic 1.5-litre bottle with a slender neck and three-quarters fill it with lukewarm, soapy water. Screw the top on and shake the bottle back and forth (not up and down). You should soon see the same sort of micro-tornado effect in the water, the soapsuds serving to illustrate the motion. OK, so it's a centrifugal cone, not centripetal, but the visual effect is similar. When you see it working, imagine that the cone of turbulence is rising vertically (as opposed to descending) with the impeller so mounted, as to sit at the pinnacle of the spiralling column of water, taking its power directly from the turbulence. As the impeller spun, so it would suck in air from vents around the top of the barrel before expelling it through a diffuser at the broad end of the cone to the ground. This continual cyclonic blast of air generated lift: like a Dyson vacuum cleaner in reverse, it would *blow* instead of *suck*. A feed from the small turbine would then take power back to the main motor effectively to create a closed system, one that was extremely energy-efficient and ran cleanly, if not providing the Holy Grail of alternative technologists today: 'free energy'.

As Schauberger himself put it:

The destructive and dissolving form of movement is centrifugal in nature – it forces the moving medium from the centre outwards towards the periphery in straight lines ... The medium is first weakened then it dissolves and breaks up. Nature uses this action to disintegrate complexes which have lost their vivacity or have died. From the broken-down fragments, new coordinated forms, new identities can be created as a result of this concentrating form of movement. The centripetal, hyperbolic spiral movement is symptomatic of falling temperature, contraction, concentration. The centrifugal movement, on the other hand, is synonymous with rising temperature, heat, extension, expansion, explosion. In Nature, there is a continuous switch from one movement to the other.

The first test-flight of the machine was reportedly amazingly successful (it apparently shot through the roof of the laboratory and had to be recovered some distance away), but, for reasons that remain unclear, Schauberger's efforts again went unrewarded and unrecognised. By 1943 and now a man of fifty-eight, the worsening war situation required him to submit to a call-up draft, but after reporting to his first posting (commander of a parachute company stationed in northern Italy) it wasn't long before Himmler himself issued orders recalling him to the SS-sponsored technical college at Vienna-Rosenhügel. Once there (and presumably at a loss as to explain why), he was ordered to Mauthausen concentration camp, where he met an assigned contact in the form of one Standartenführer Zeireis and was duly informed of his situation. He had two choices: either recruit some of the (Czech) prisoners to help him build new, piloted versions of his flying device back at the college, or be executed in the camp. The latter option might sound drastic, but we must remember the growing urgency of the German war machine to find solutions to the increasing Allied threat. Also, with Himmler's desire to see his SS in the ascendancy, promoting such long shots as Schauberger's work wasn't unreasonable, even if it took coercion to do it.

No guesses for which option Schauberger took. But soon after this episode, he and his new team had to be moved: their college was flattened in an air raid, so they ended up at Leonstein, near Linz, close to where he was born. It was here that he developed his ideas further, to the point where a full-sized, though unmanned flying disc prototype that used his new engine *apparently* flew under radio control. Unfortunately, this author believes that even within a history as murky and as confusing as that of the discs, there is room for a certain amount of mistaken identity. Schauberger's work was certainly intriguing, and discs were almost certainly flying in 1945, but the two shouldn't be taken together. At least not yet.

At the end of the war, the American forces got to Leonstein ahead of the Russians and found Schauberger and his team of ex-prisoners. After letting the members of his team leave after a thorough interrogation, the Americans held Schauberger in protective custody for six months; it would seem that they knew exactly what he had been up to and wanted to prevent other nations, as well as renegade Nazis, from continuing to use his services. After American agents removed all material they deemed interesting, they left behind odd scraps for the Russians who were scheduled to take over the sector from them. Frustrated at what they had apparently missed out on, the Russians dynamited Schauberger's apartment block, after scouring it for papers and the like.

With the war in Japan by now over too, Schauberger was released and gradually tried to re-enter the water flume business. He had been ordered not to work on his flying machines but always kept a weather eye on his technology and was apparently intrigued at the first post-war reports of UFOs and how they might be incorporating some form of technology similar to his.

This seemed to be the case, as it turned out, for in 1957 he and

Walter were reputedly approached by two Americans who were insistent that they should accompany them to the USA, so that their technology could be verified in greater depth. They agreed, and the following summer they arrived at a remote military base, near Red River in Texas, under the strictest secrecy. Their incoming mail was apparently censored and communication with the outside world forbidden, but preliminary research was begun none the less. By September, with their contracts set to expire, the project was extended. But the Schaubergers now refused to cooperate and wanted out: against the wishes of the unknown project director, who would allow Viktor to leave only if he learned English (work to that date had been undertaken with German-speaking technicians and/or translators, so the director felt that if English were spoken it might be possible to continue a correspondence from afar). Walter, too, was forced to sign a binding contract preceding his 'release' which forbade him from communicating any of his work to anyone but a mysterious middleman in Munich, called 'Mr RD'. Although both men felt in real fear of their lives at this point, the threatened withdrawal of their visas heralding only the *start* of potential US harassment, they both duly signed and left the country in something of a disorganised hurry, returning home to Linz after a nineteen-hour flight. Viktor died only five days later, on 25 September 1958, apparently a victim of shock at what had happened. Walter asserts that on his deathbed, his father kept repeating: 'They took everything from me, everything. I don't even own myself.'

After Viktor's death, Walter eventually established a school of biotechnology at Bad Ischl in Austria, which thrives to this day in adapting natural discoveries such as those identified by his father and putting them to applications for industry, apparently unconflicting with the agreements signed at Red River. If there had been such a conflict, perhaps Walter, too, might already be dead. Such is the awesome secret behind the disc project that even the lives of such great innovators as these could be considered forfeit.

❖   ❖   ❖

The work of such characters as Schauberger and Lippisch remains a vital and intriguing primer for the subject of the flying disc. After all, here were maverick designers and inventors working outside the mainstream of accepted thought and practice who were still able to see beyond the restrictions laboured under by others with less insight. With the possible exceptions of Tesla and Bartini, the Nazi party was to view these and other equally gifted figures as invaluable resources that might produce work of inestimable value to the state. That less enlightened governments might have treated them as cranks didn't enter into the equation, for in Germany the established order of things was changing; ushering in new demands that would have to be overcome if the thousand-year Reich were to survive.

With the rise of the Nazi party in Germany, the orthodox establishment that constituted the bulk of the state educational system, from kindergartens through to the universities, was under pressure to change and adapt itself to the new circumstances facing the country. This was hardly unexpected from such an influential government, but, for those working in Germany's various research establishments, life in both the private and government sector was to become even more closely scrutinised for political ends, as the doctrine of 'Aryan physics' was ushered in. The great strides that had been made in German industry, thanks to its thriving scientific community, were to become increasingly rare events as time went on, as scientists struggled to 'prove' their theoretical or practical work along purely 'Aryan' lines. The subsequent brain drain this caused was later felt most acutely in hi-tech projects such as the V-2 rocket programme, under Wernher von Braun's guidance. Although the V-2 eventually entered service, the project was heavily dependent on skilled *guest* workers brought in from across the newly expanded Reich – there simply weren't enough home-grown scientists to meet all the diverse demands on their skills.

Apply this single facet of life under the Nazis to virtually all

German industry and you unearth one of the main contributory reasons for its eventual collapse. Hitler and his war cabinet had played down the significance of promoting science education at all levels, with the result that, while huge amounts of money were poured into projects such as the V-2 and various research institutes, the *quality* of the science and engineering pursued might be considered somewhat dubious. In Britain and the United States, the educational establishment had continued uninterrupted since the First World War, with the result that, year on year, graduate scientists were making great strides in the fields of physics, chemistry, electronics and so on. But in Germany the situation was somewhat different. Where once scientists from across Europe and America exchanged ideas and published papers on their work in a great melting pot of ideas at the hub of Europe, now Germany began to gradually exclude itself from what its leaders saw as an impenetrable community of Jewish physicians.

The rot could be said to have set in properly from 1933, when the NSDAP assumed totalitarian control of the country. Up to that point, Germany boasted several great universities, such as Heidelberg and Göttingen, and a fine record in breaking new scientific ground. But as the Nazis took power and ever greater numbers of students and lecturers became indoctrinated in the somewhat warped beliefs of the regime, the quality and objectivity of the science produced dropped in turn. Students were all but coerced into joining either the Hitler Youth or the German Girls' League, although few girls attended university anyhow, as Nazi policies preferred young women to settle for home and family life – bringing up the new Aryan generation. With these new demands on their time, such impressionable young minds were gradually moulded to accept the 'Aryan' physical model of the world and universe: there was simply no time or opportunity for undertaking research or self-discovery for themselves. 'Jewish physics' (the model freely adopted by the world's academics) were universally derided within Germany as being somehow 'phoney' and below contempt – why else would Albert Einstein never return to live in Germany following his emigration in 1915, if not to avoid the ongoing persecution and general mood of oppression he felt in his home country?

But this chapter in the story is concerned with more than the erosion of academic standards in pre-war Nazi Germany. Important and relevant though this is, it was but one symptom of a new Völkisch culture that was shaping a new generation of engineers and scientists whose ideas and beliefs, though once seen as outlandish, were now more mainstream, more politically acceptable. We've already seen how someone like Horbiger could achieve influence with his bizarre ideas, yet he, and others like him, were merely fortunate to be living in a system with a warped view of the world and of its place within it. One hopes that they would not be given such patronage elsewhere.

Put simply, Nazism offered a dogmatic (though somewhat perfectionist) German industrial and scientific culture, a new outlet through which it could occasionally shock outside observers, following a long tradition of pursuing the outwardly trivial – and what could be more trivial than developing a system based on arcane Aryan lore? Before the birth of Nazism, the First World War saw the renowned firm of Krupp Steel build the world's biggest mortar for the Kaiser – the Paris rail gun – yet it fired only nine shots into the suburbs of Paris before it needed a new barrel. All along, Krupp knew this was likely yet still convinced the army to provide the finance, *just to prove such a big gun could be built* and hang the expense. This same attitude, magnified a thousand times over, was to inform and guide the Nazis. Wrapped up in their new mood and attitude towards science, was a growing belief on the part of the elite as well as the man on the street that it was within Germany's gift to create and build a new series of wonder-weapons that owed little to established scientific or strategic thinking. This was the so-called 'master race' after all; a confident nation that used blitzkrieg to subdue most of Western Europe in a matter of months. With that in-built feeling of superiority came a desire to extract the biggest 'bang for their buck' from every avenue. As we shall now see, this somewhat characteristic weakness was to influence future weapons development with greater impact than building one rail gun could ever bring to bear.

Last Talons of the Eagle described how the Versailles Treaty of 1919 had effectively scuppered Germany's chances of developing new military hardware, with the result that the aero industry, in common with much of industry in other sectors, was almost brought to its knees. A secretive though very gradual movement towards building new aircraft and other vehicles with a dual military capability was nevertheless instigated from almost the day the treaty was signed. As manufacturers recovered through exports of civilian aircraft, the various generals and industrialists behind these covert plans began pursuing new technologies (such as jet turbines) not covered by the treaty which, if developed, might give them a head start when the time came to announce a new air force.

The leading player behind the rebirth of the Luftwaffe was Hermann Göring, who, despite his portrayal as a pompous bombast, was no fool – a colourful if somewhat eccentric character perhaps, but no fool. He recognised in the 1930s the problems that the Nazi party was storing up for itself by not recognising the importance of research and development to the creation from scratch of 'his' air force; let alone the other armed services (who at least had been allowed to re-equip on a small scale under Versailles). The Luftwaffe *was* an entirely new air force and therefore needed world-class equipment as quickly as possible, if it were to pose a credible military threat. The only way to achieve this was to encourage local manufacturers to innovate and come up with new, superior aircraft and equipment. Under Göring's guidance, the controlling board at the RLM (German Air Ministry) recognised the importance of providing good working conditions, salaries and rations over and above rival occupations.

As a result, the emerging aero industry laid down production plans on the basis of the innovations emerging from the new research institutions that Göring's money and patronage had established. Before the war, this approach had a major spin-off for the economy as a whole, as industry could generate foreign currency through exports of these advanced products. For example, it might be a surprise to learn that during the 1930s, once Germany's industrial rebirth had begun, its main trading partner in areas such as engineering was the Soviet Union. Here was a country desperately backward in its industrial infrastructure, and Germany needed as much foreign exchange as it could get, so it exported not only finished goods, but also the means to make them: machine tools, raw materials, support staff and so on. On 1 September 1939, on the eve of its invasion of Poland, Germany even handed over a brand-new battleship to this supposed ally in the east.

The Luftwaffe's nine new research and development centres were all lavishly equipped with a 'cost-no-object' approach, and each specialised in one of the following: flight-testing new aircraft designs; new weapons; air medicine (from 1942); aircraft aerodynamics; the aerodynamic properties of bombs and torpedoes; gliders; developing engines; electronics research into radios and radar; and finally, a technical academy which taught ballistics and other high-level subjects not covered by any other site. These sites represented a huge investment, but even then this wasn't the whole story as the RLM had institutes of its own, under the auspices of the Technisches Amt – its technical office. This office was intended to take the pure research emerging from the other sites and 'productionise' it; in other words, to develop the research to the point where end products might enter service. We already know that the Luftwaffe had adopted a policy of compartmentalisation, by fragmenting its research and development efforts, so there is every chance that the various technical breakthroughs required for the disc project in the fields of radio, radar, aerodynamics, exotic materials and propulsion systems would have been achieved. Each team would operate autonomously, unaware of achievements being reached by similar teams elsewhere and equally unsure of the 'bigger picture' to which their work was ultimately contributing. A figure with oversight, such as someone from the Luftwaffe itself, would have coordinated these efforts to ensure they culminated at the same time.

By creating such 'centres of excellence', or 'technical campuses' such as you might find today, the RLM and the Luftwaffe actively promoted innovation from such exalted staff, so you might safely assume that a Luftwaffe-sponsored flying disc project would be a perfect project for them, representing the necessary 'quantum leap' in technology they appeared to be looking for. After all, elements of the RLM reasoned, why spend millions of Reichsmarks developing a new, though essentially conventional aircraft engine when, for more or less the same budget, you could come up with something as radical as a jet turbine? Though the arguments were certainly persuasive, unfortunately the essentially conservative civil servants controlling the budgets were often scared off by the unknown and opted to plough funds into the safe, conventional and essentially 'boring' projects. The pioneering jet engine programme, for example, got as far as it did only through the individual efforts of certain manufacturers such as Ernst Heinkel, who doggedly – and secretly – continued to work on it from a purely commercial view. If decisions over its future were based on feasibility and the chances for operational use – the same criteria used by the men in the ministry's procurement and evaluation departments – then such programmes as these or the rockets would never have been sanctioned in the first place, let alone pursued, and the outcome and duration of the war might have been very different. That Germany remained substantially ahead of the Allies in the fields of aerodynamics, helicopters, jet propulsion (even after the surrounding procrastination), hydraulics, radio, radar etc. is testament merely to the head start they enjoyed, thanks in part to the persistence of certain manufacturers and not to any superior organisation or enlightened staff.

An example is that of the famous Me 262 jet fighter. Not only could it have entered service *at least a year* before it actually did (if it had received a higher manufacturing priority) but after Hitler had seen it at an airshow it was further delayed. After asking Herr Messerschmitt whether the 262 carried a bomb, the designer replied that *it could*, not that *it did*. Hitler then stubbornly chose to see the plane as a fighter-bomber, so the plane's role was altered to incorporate the fitment of bomb racks. Nowhere in the Nazi military was there a mechanism for contradicting the Führer – even when his judgement proved incorrect. This only got worse for the Luftwaffe, as Göring became increasingly sidelined and made irrelevant by a system reacting against his personal idiosyncrasies and ambitions.

As far as the disc project is concerned, while the Luftwaffe would seem the most obvious service under which the discs could have been developed, there is little chance that a project as radical as this would have ever been selected for development, let alone pursued with the degree of utter secrecy which appears to have been the case, if only because no manufacturer was at the heart of the project to drive it. Worse, all three services suffered from the same administration indisciplines and petty fiefdoms, coupled with indecisive and latterly, confused leadership. So it's easy to imagine that when presented with something as radical as this, they would either have snuffed it at birth or developed it at a breakneck pace which, in the latter case, means we would know about it. That's not to say that admin problems *definitely* prevented the project from proceeding – just that they would have made its progress somewhat tortuous.

Yet one might still comment that surely the discs were on a par with building a liquid-fuelled rocket; the design principles of which would one day carry a man to the moon. So why didn't the Luftwaffe, or any other service, take it on? One reason might lie in the fact that each branch of the armed services often sponsored its own research project, to the exclusion of others, regardless of whether spin-offs might be a positive boon. The obvious examples involve the Luftwaffe sponsoring the V-1 flying bomb, with the army backing the V-2 rocket. The V-2 was the result of a near ten-year development that began at the Kummersdorf proving ground back in the 1930s, when a young Wernher von Braun and his colleagues were first recruited.

But the V-2 was something of a millstone around the army's neck and never fulfilled its potential. It was too advanced for its time; as any pioneer in a new field will later tell you, it's usually only when technology matures through successive generations that success and acceptability are assured – not necessarily for the inventor, as we shall see later in the case of the discs. Consider for a moment that in one massed Allied bomber raid, more high explosives were dropped on German soil than the entire V-2 project ever delivered to England and you begin to realise its futility.

Such follies as the misguided V-2 were seen as a demonstration of the superiority of German engineering and, by extension, the Nazi state. The Allied press (as well as the German propagandists) all believed throughout the war, and for a few years afterwards, that the V-1 and V-2 were state-of-the-art technologies, that somehow nothing else on earth could compare with their advanced engineering, guidance systems and the like. Yet this was simply not true. Yes, the V-1 made for an effective 'robot-bomb', but it was powered by an engine almost as simple as a waterwheel and carried a relatively small load of high explosive, extremely slowly, for only a few hundred kilometres. The bomb's simple gyro-compass offered no guarantee of its landing anywhere near the target zone, but it *was* designed to be mass-produced, so such simplicity was a built-in design feature in such a cheap one-shot weapon. By contrast, the highly expensive V-2 rocket took years to perfect, and even by the end of the war, when the USA started test-firing some captured examples using German technicians such as von Braun, things didn't always run as smoothly as you might expect of a 'state-of-the-art' weapon. Quite simply, the army had over-engineered the V-2 and had lost sight of the originally simple objectives: namely, to deliver economically a one-tonne warhead on to a city like London with no prior warning. What Germany *needed* was an effective weapon; what it *got* was a white elephant twenty years ahead of its time, when a faster, cheaper V-1, with a heavier warhead, might have been more effective. But not as effective as putting the Me 262 into early production might have been – or for the disc designers to have received more support.

The Kriegsmarine (German navy) had research and development programmes of its own, but these, too, were beset with problems and shackled by a leadership generally less receptive to new technologies even than those colleagues in the army or Luftwaffe. Like the British Royal Navy, the Kriegsmarine was considered the more stuffy, 'senior' service, so you might be shocked to learn that here, too, mystical beliefs had crept in. Throughout the war senior admirals at naval HQ in Berlin routinely suspended pendulums over sea charts in attempts at 'dousing' for the positions of Allied convoys so as to direct their U-boats to intercept missions! When a conference was called in 1943 to discuss new technical developments in submarine propulsion, it was reported that many of the scientific delegates 'left in disgust'. Apparently, many of the technical advisers representing the Kriegsmarine were completely ignorant of even the most basic principles behind the new technologies, and the scientists had to go back to basics in their lectures. Most likely this would not have happened in either Britain or the USA, as the lines of communication between laboratory and HQ were too open for such clashes to occur as a result of ill-informed senior staff.

Unfortunately for Germany, such compartmentalisation was a recurring issue that stifled much scientific effort and potential in the years leading up to and throughout the war. By contrast, in the USA all research assumed to have military applications was sanctioned and organised into bespoke divisions by the Office of Scientific Research and Development (OSRD). It was their job to ensure that all scientists and engineers working on projects within each division (from developing specialist radar to better tank suspension) could talk to each other and have access to each other's work as required. In addition, scientific and engineering teams were allowed to visit the battle-front occasionally and witness the fruits of their work in action; such exposure to real-life problems ensuring the vital 'GI-proof' nature of their work. Of course, there were still problems, but at least those that appeared could be nipped in the bud and resolved before too much time had elapsed. But Germany had no comparable structure to their scientific effort. Yes, Germany managed to develop both the V-1 and V-2, but neither project came without tremendous problems, and one might argue that neither was developed to its full potential by the war's end. For example, the V-1 had its inaccurate guidance system, while the V-2 suffered from a multitude of problems, ranging from faulty gyroscopes (that caused midair explosions) to the fact that something so complex, with so many disparate parts, as the rocket motors was a recipe for trouble in itself. Having both types built by slave and 'guest' workers, who were able to sabotage production in any number of ways, was another cause for concern. In almost every area of weaponry and technology, German industry was failing the country. When the Soviet army started fielding the superb T-34 tank, the best the Germans could offer was a bigger variant of its Tiger model – but saddled with a bigger gun and heavier armour, it then needed a larger and less troublesome engine. As a result, Tigers were soon either bogging down under their own weight or being stranded with engine breakdowns in the middle of nowhere: what use would their 'improvements' be then? This pattern was happening throughout industry and made worse by an evaluation process that allowed such gross errors through.

If a manufacturer responded to a ministry tender – say a

requirement for a new tank design – the army staff officers charged with evaluating the design often worked in isolation of the field conditions the equipment would ultimately face. A proving ground is no substitute for the real thing. Not only that, but these officers often had no technical background, so they couldn't make considered judgements on points of interest or concern. And if representatives from a rival manufacturer were present, one can only begin to imagine the backstabbing and political shenanigans which must have gone on to influence where contracts were awarded.

The scientific culture was also one of segregation. Scientists were kept apart from those who would use their work in the field and generally would meet them only when undertaking demonstrations during official visits. To the military establishment, these laboratories and institutes were treated like some demented uncle that no one likes to speak of and who one visits in sufferance. And with such isolation came 'bad science': for example, the practice of using concentration-camp inmates as live dummies for altitude pressure tests in a decompression chamber. As the pressure varied, their resulting torment was filmed and used by the Luftwaffe as instruction for aircrews in high-altitude work.

Under such oppressive, yet still unusual conditions, therefore, we shouldn't be surprised that so much faith was put into the 'wonder-weapons'. The Allies could rely on steadily increased production of aircraft, tanks and shipping to sustain their war effort, but what of Germany? With its limited resources, both in raw materials and manufacturing capacity, at first it sought salvation in quality as opposed to quantity – only to find, too late, that it had backed the wrong horse. When one learns that Germany continued making consumer goods until well into the war, as a sop to its national morale, while in Britain civilian production of goods such as radios and cars had more or less ground to a halt in favour of war production, is it any wonder that the German war machine eventually collapsed? So much for Goebbels' famous phrase of instigating 'total war' – this was introduced only when German high command realised that not enough equipment was being built with which the war could be fought. Impressive results *were* being achieved in manufacturing, but by then the war was already as good as lost.

In the end, then, the failure of German military research across all three services boils down to three main points. Firstly, there was a failure to ensure that planned research and development met anticipated future requirements. Secondly, the protracted selection process was continually subjected to individual, corporate and military self-interest which would invariably distort the honest outcome, and, finally, there were insufficient communications between the civilian engineers, scientists and the military. Yes, German industry came up with the goods on a number of occasions – but it could be argued that because so much was being done, in so many areas, it was inevitable that, against the odds, the right project would win through against the competition.

But before we go away with the idea that something such as the flying disc project could *never* have been maintained under such chaotic circumstances, let's not forget that the SS were more than capable of enveloping projects within their ranks and ensuring that deadlines were met, as they had so convincingly demonstrated in taking over both the V-1 and V-2. Regardless of the fact that it was too late to make either project a convincing war-winner, and that Himmler was merely seen to be extending his tentacles of influence, the SS was more than capable of sheltering the entire flying disc project under its wing from day one. It had the resources; it had the security; it had the motive (ultimately to usurp the Nazi hierarchy and create an autonomous region of its own away from the Fatherland); and it had the will. Observers often ignore the SS when debating the existence of the flying discs. Either they go through the various arguments, as we have just done, but fall short of considering the SS outright or they simply fail to see why the SS would *want* to become involved and overlook Himmler's long-term goal in the process. Observers rightly dismiss the Kriegsmarine, the Wehrmacht and the Luftwaffe as being too incompetent to handle something as secret and critical as the disc programme, but then overlook the fourth service – the SS. The SS was the only body capable of managing such a feat and, as such, were probably involved right from the entire project's inception.

chapter four

'There is no failure except in no longer trying.'
Elbert Hubbard, *The Notebook*.

Up to now, our story has focused on a tapestry of myth, interwoven by secret groups, talk of Antarcticans and the gradual shift in German society towards a largely fabricated Völkisch past. At first glance this has little to do with the discs, but it *does* underpin the flying disc story and helps us understand something of the political and military imperatives for developing such a craft, i.e. the accelerated demands of war. We've also looked at the work of a few noted individuals in a search for clues as to the overall foundation of this new technology and at the role the SS would appear to have played as its sponsor. But it's time now for us to take a look at the discs themselves in greater depth, as well as those pivotal figures most closely associated with these original 'flying saucers'. Or perhaps this should read 'in as much depth as possible', for nearly all of what you are about to read remains conjecture and rumour. *No* hard and indisputable evidence has *ever* emerged regarding the German disc projects. After sixty years, if any detailed files are in a secure vault somewhere, they are still classified and are likely to remain so for the foreseeable future.

But if all we have to go on is rumour, then we should begin with perhaps the most well-known 'false start' of all the stories – and something we know was actually built. In 1980, a German aviation magazine published photographs of the first full-sized aircraft designed by an obscure pre-war model-aircraft engineer by the name of Arthur Sack. Built in early 1944, his Luftwaffe-sponsored 'AS6 V1' ('V1' in this instance meaning 'first prototype', not the flying bomb) employed a circular wing of around 4.8 metres in diameter, which was of conventional construction and bisected by a flattened central fuselage. With the exception of a prominent cockpit canopy, a front-mounted engine salvaged from a crashed Me 108 and a conventional tail section from an Me 109 fighter, the wing had a pronounced lenticular profile on both its upper and lower sides and was almost perfectly circular in plan. But things didn't look good when its first test-flight at the Brandis airfield had to be abandoned after the rudder control proved ineffective. For the second run, five different takeoffs were attempted and abandoned before the pilot realised that, when taxiing, the control surfaces were next to useless. They were positioned within the low-pressure zone that extended under the whole wing and could therefore never work. Somewhat optimistically, however, Sack and his team believed that this could be overcome by using a more powerful engine; but with war restrictions prohibiting the acquisition of anything better, they settled for tweaks to the basic airframe in an attempt to improve control and lift. By mid-April they were ready to try again, but, after several long taxiing runs, the aircraft resolutely refused to lift into the air and the effort was abandoned.

Although Sack tried to solve the problems on a limited scale until the end of the war, his flying disc project was to prove the most fruitless of those undertaken in Germany. By coincidence, the AS6 was almost a carbon copy of an American design that had first appeared in 1942 and was built by the Chance-Vought company. Officially named the V-173, but more commonly known by its nickname 'the flying pancake', it was intended for use on aircraft carriers and possessed the STOL (Short TakeOff and Landing) abilities needed for such an application (though Vertical TakeOff and Landing – VTOL – is more desirable). As well as having a low stall speed of only 40 knots (ideal for approaches to a carrier's landing deck), it also boasted a reasonable top speed, though it never entered service with the US navy and was little developed as a result of aerodynamic shortcomings, which came to light only during flight testing, but at least it got airborne.

What both Sack and Chance-Vought had failed to appreciate was that by adopting a circular wing they both had a foot on the ladder to success. The only problem was that they were looking at the circular wing as just that – a *conventional* wing – and were expecting it to behave as such. Both failed to realise that while the *shape* might have been correct, it was what you did with it that would make the difference between success and failure. Surprisingly, both designs were worked on long after they appeared dead in the water, in the belief that they might one day produce successful prototypes. At least with Sack's work, there is a good chance that his results were being passed on to others already working on more viable flying disc aircraft and that they would have taken lessons from his failure. As to who they were and where they might have been found, we need look no further than Flugkapitän Rudolf Schriever.

In 1940 this serving amateur aircraft designer and Luftwaffe officer was assigned to Heinkel's Eger factory as a test pilot. As time passed, he predicted with obvious foresight that if the war should ever take a turn for the worse there would be a need for agile, VTOL-capable fighter aircraft to work around the envisaged lack of accessible and viable airfields. This is exactly the thinking that would later go into the Hawker Harrier jump jet: after all, why settle for an exposed airfield that's costly to defend and keep operational, when you can take off from and land on forest clearings or roads? Two years before Arthur Sack's doomed AS6, in 1942 Schriever was to take his ideas through to a working scale model of something he nicknamed 'the flying top'.

No photographs or 'official' details are available, as it's not thought a patent was ever openly applied for, but imagine a tail-less helicopter fitted with a dozen or so wide blades (which are so broad they almost overlap) and enclose these within a shroud that's partially open on both sides, but which still allows for these hub-mounted blades to be adjustable for pitch. Supported in the upright position by four extendable legs, its shape apparently resembled a child's spinning top in profile – hence the name. A small gas-turbine motor was mounted where you'd normally expect the fuselage or 'body' of the helicopter to be, together with the remote-control radio system and fuel tank, and all are contained *within* the wide-diameter spinning hub. From rest, the engine's thrust would be directed on to the underside of the rotor blades, through possibly three or four diffusing nozzles, causing the hub on which the blades are mounted to spin at extremely high speed. The blades, meanwhile, adopt an oblique angle, intended to 'draw' air in from above the device, expelling it downwards through the lower shroud to generate lift. As it climbed, the blades would level out, as the underside shroud progressively closed up. Jet thrust would now be expelled through an exhaust pipe or diffuser mounted in the fuselage to give forward motion. The upper vent would still be open to accept incoming air, but this, too, would close off as the amount of air taken in at faster speeds compensated.

This 1.8-metre-high device apparently flew under remote control while tethered in a hangar, exciting observers from the RLM (against form, the Air Ministry were still its sponsors at this early stage), who then authorised the development of the envisaged (and manned) full-scale version.

In incorporating a cockpit, the basic structure of the new craft (now named 'Flugelrad' or 'Flying Wheel') was to be somewhat different from its smaller forerunner, though it kept its basic mode of operation and incorporated several lessons already understood, though never embraced by others such as Sack, who persisted in trying to use circular wings as *wings*. Little lift or control is feasible with such a configuration: hence its predictable failure. Yet even Lippisch tried to make it work with his 'Kreisflügel' experiments. But in researching the work of German helicopter pioneers such as Professor Focke and in building his 'top', Schriever had learned that for himself.

When you throw a frisbee, it flies straight and true. It's stable in flight, with little wobble or motion until it slows, and yet it's a disc shape, so why does it work so well? The answer lies in the fact that it's spinning all the while and is therefore able to use gyroscopic forces to stabilise itself, in the same way as a real spinning top or a gyroscope does. When its speed of rotation slows down, you see the characteristic 'wobble' as its gyroscopic forces diminish and the frisbee becomes unstable – just as Sack's AS6 would have been. Schriever could see that his concept offered a winning combination, as it sited the engine, pilot, flight controls and fuel tanks centrally – as in the fixed hub of a bicycle wheel. As the wheel – with rotor blades for its spokes – spun about the pilot in the hub, it would create the in-flight stability required, so all you had to do was make the thing go up and down and back and forth.

By the time that Schriever began planning the Flugelrad in early 1943, the engine-maker BMW was well into developing its promising new 109–003 turbojet. Seeing it as suitable, Schriever duly assembled a small team and travelled with them to a BMW plant in the suburbs of Prague, Czechoslovakia. The team comprised an engineer skilled in aerodynamic and helicopter theory, Klaus Habermohl, an Italian aerodynamicist and expert in heat-resistant alloys, Giuseppe Belluzzo, and a mysterious engineer by the name of Dr Ing. W. O. Schumann (thought by some to work for the SS). BMW rented out part of their premises to Schriever; by moving in, he hoped for factory support and maintenance for his chosen engines. It's at this point that it seems likely the SS took over the project from the RLM. The most likely scenario would be that Schriever approached the RLM for more funding but got turned down, so he then approached the SS who, seeing the potential in his work, orchestrated the move to Prague and assigned him a new budget. As originally planned, the Flugelrad Mark I would have had a larger gas turbine than that fitted to the 'top', but the new deal with BMW moved the design straight on to the Mark II version. Some reports mention that the actual engines used were in fact the same Walter pulse-jets as used in the V-1 flying bombs, but this assertion can be dismissed on the three known drawbacks associated with the type: namely, its lack of real power, no throttle control (it really was all or nothing) and the unavoidable and terrible vibration problems it generated in operation: probably sufficient to shatter the Flugelrad's blades in flight.

Once he was settled in Prague, Schriever and his team commenced the actual construction in one of the workshops at the plant. The Mark II was around 6 metres in diameter and 2 metres high and closely resembled a frisbee or discus, with a prominent, domed cupola mounted in the inner, central, non-spinning part of the hub, in which would sit the solitary pilot. The outer, free-spinning hub supported sixteen wide rotor blades, whose edges were extremely close together when horizontal and levelled out; these could be altered in pitch as before, to allow air to pass through from one side of the disc to the other. Around the outermost edge of the blade tips ran a protective 'shielding ring' which held the blades in place and prevented undue oscillation. Four telescopically sprung and non-retractable wheels supported the craft and kept BMW's bulky turbojet (directly beneath the pilot) from fouling the ground. No shrouding was considered for the rotor blades at this stage, however, for the Mark II was purely a 'proof-of-concept' device, intended only to prove that Schriever's theories would work on a large scale. The method of propulsion, however, was still based on his 'top' and involved treating the large rotor assembly essentially as a windmill.

Think of a child's windmill, of the kind you might buy in a seaside kiosk. When you blow directly on to the face of the toy, little happens, but when you turn it on its side and then blow, the blades flash round. It was this same principle that Schriever's design exploited. By attaching a clever variably ducted diffuser to the exhaust nozzle of the turbojet, the pilot could angle the jet thrust into the blades of the Flugelrad, which, if angled at the right pitch, would then spin sufficiently quickly to draw air through as before and generate lift in the process. As the pitch of the blades changed, this lift energy would be modulated, as in a regular helicopter. The thrust could also be augmented by siphoning off some of the jet thrust. In order to alter direction, this extra thrust would simply be redirected laterally from left to right.

In keeping with the secrecy surrounding such a project as this, the SS had to ensure that any test pilots assigned to fly this radical-looking aircraft could be entrusted to keep the secret. Luckily, a Luftwaffe unit had test pilots willing enough to volunteer. KG-200 was *the* special squadron. Among many other top-secret roles, it used to ferry spies in and out of enemy territory, test-fly captured Allied planes and approve new aircraft types before their certification. So with sufficient pilots on hand, by late summer 1943 the Flugelrad Mark II was ready to take to the air for the first time. Once again, there are no known photographs of the craft, nor contemporary flight records. What little we know has come from German newspaper reports from the 1950s and from the odd eyewitness, as well as circumstantial evidence, but there is enough to assert that this full-scale craft didn't perform as well as hoped, perhaps through being underpowered. Apparently, it could rise only a metre off the ground and hovered gingerly over a distance of some 300 metres before its pilot brought the show to an abrupt and bumpy end. There's not even circumstantial evidence to corroborate claims that this design continued being tested with equally poor results – I prefer to believe that Schriever pursued design improvements, rather than persist with something known to be compromised. After all, there simply wasn't the time for such indulgences, so it's likely that a second working prototype – the Flugelrad Mark III – followed quickly on from the disappointing Mark II.

This time round, the craft's diameter was increased to a little over 7 metres; the cupola was widened to provide room for a second crewman (to act as flight engineer, overseeing the turbojet), and a new tail fin/rudder was fitted, which, it was hoped, would provide more stability. Apparently painted in a lurid shade of yellow, this bizarre craft first flew a little over a year later, but even at this stage in the development of BMW's engine, problems were still legion. While the latest units offered substantially more power than before, they were so unreliable as to render the effort hardly worthwhile; a factor that was already precluding their serious consideration for more conventional aircraft applications. An engine that needed servicing every ten hours or so hardly fitted in with Schriever's tight schedule. Another seemingly insurmountable problem was that insufficient lift was being generated. Even though adequate (though unreliable) power was now available, Schriever was running up against this unforeseen aerodynamic shortcoming in his design. Some commentators have also reported that KG-200 officers at one stage threatened to withdraw their support for the tests, on account of the number of their colleagues being killed. But I dispute this point of view, as it presupposes that more than one or two examples of each mark were built and were badly damaged, if not written off, after each crash. The team probably had accidents, but I believe that casualties were low if not non-existent and that discs were simply rebuilt after each (minor) mishap, such as undercarriage failure. As luck would have it, while these disturbing developments were becoming clear, an opportunity arose for Schriever and his team to help out on another project. Leaving the BMW engineers to work on the problems, they travelled the few hundred kilometres north-east, to Breslau in East Prussia (now the Polish town of Wroclaw).

The reason for their unscheduled secondment to Breslau was to work on *another* flying disc programme that had been transferred from Peenemünde and was struggling to meet its objectives. It would seem that the SS was supporting this team, too, at least since its departure from Peenemünde – putting Schriever to work on it would therefore have been entirely possible. The main driving force behind this project, the designer/engineer Dr Richard Miethe, had originally been part of the V-2 design team, but in time had began work on another flying disc project. We don't know if he had been drafted into an existing project team or whether this had sprung from his own initiative, but his name is as synonymous with this story as anyone else's, and Miethe *does* appear to be one of its leading lights, along with Schriever, Habermohl and the others. Little is known about him, other than he was a great friend of none other than von Braun's, so it would appear that the disc programme was his first recognised achievement of any note.

Chosen by Germany as the site for the world's first dedicated rocket research centre and test range, Peenemünde was an isolated site, separated from the mainland by the river Peene and open along three sides to the Baltic Sea. Apart from a nearby bird colony, on the otherwise uninhabited Usedom island, the site was completely deserted. The government had bought the land almost as soon as its suitability had been identified and, in 1936, the Organisation Todt construction corps began work in almost complete secrecy. The site would eventually require thousands of forced labourers but, initially at least, work involved merely setting up camp: building a mini-town for the workers and their families to live in, as well as the first laboratories, workshops, test stands and so on. Just like the efforts later put in by the Americans in building a secret town for the construction of the atom bomb, Peenemünde appeared on no map, yet by 1937 scientists had already begun to move in.

When asked what they associate with the name Peenemünde, most people who have an interest will immediately name either the V-1 or V-2 projects. Both weapons were developed there, and after the site was bombed by the British in August 1943, during Operation Hydra, they were both moved to scattered facilities in the hinterland, out of sight of the Allies. But other things were going on here that most people have never heard or thought of. That Miethe's flying disc programme began its life at Peenemünde is something this author believes with little doubt. After all, here were ideal circumstances in which such a project could develop. Take a large group of highly paid and fevered boffins, all striving to deliver Hitler's Wunder Waffen. Add unlimited resources, as well as the obvious benefits of complete secrecy and isolation, considered so essential by the authorities, and it seems only natural that the discs were going to be worked on here, as in other sites with similar regimes.

The British bombing in 1943 caused most damage to the barrack quarters; the labs were mostly unscathed. Work on his disc could have continued here, but the SS probably chose to relocate Miethe following the raid, which might explain how he ended up at Breslau to pursue his concept alone; no other team members are mentioned as being with him. With his experiences of working at Peenemünde, however, he would have been adequately qualified to begin work without a team, hoping his credentials would help him recruit one once there – something that appears to have happened. There is every chance that his sponsors were the SS; they would have been aware of his talent as an engineer from their position of oversight on the V-2, and Himmler would most certainly have wanted to take Miethe under his wing, once he'd showed signs of progress. Remember that the SS were also backing Schriever, so while the two teams may not have even heard of each other, their SS masters could see sense in eventually bringing them together.

History is rather confused on the issue of what Miethe had chosen to call his craft. 'Kügelblitz' ('ball lightning') has been bandied about at times, along with names such as the 'Vril' (the society had apparently devised the 'mysterious' engine used by Miethe) and the 'Diskus'. The author's guess is that the craft was actually called the 'Haunebu', an occult term linked with the Germanic 'tree of karma' and the ariosophical belief in the polar origins of the Aryan race. Some commentators would assert that the Haunebu and Vril I craft were one and the same – if not very similar – but there is no anecdotal evidence to support the existence of the Vril I, whereas Miethe's disc almost certainly did exist. If a name needs to be attributed to it, then from the mythology surrounding this subject Haunebu appears the most likely.

Whatever its name, the craft was of a totally different configuration from Schriever's Flugelrad. Whereas the Flugelrad had large blades rotating around a fixed central cockpit, through which jet thrust could be vectored, Miethe's Haunebu had no blades and took the form of a smoothed and solid disc, of around 9 metres in diameter. It had a bubble-shaped cockpit in the centre, on either side of which were two sets of propellors; each set probably powered at this early stage by a conventional aero-piston engine. This Haunebu – the Mark I – was intended only as an evaluation tool – a stepping stone to using full jet power that would appear in the Mark II. The Haunebu's main point of interest was that it was one of the very first aircraft to employ a little-known phenomenon at that time with which to generate lift – 'the Coanda effect'.

Its Romanian discoverer, Henri Coanda, first noted the effect when flying a primitive rocket-powered aircraft he had built in 1910 (an amazing achievement in its own right). In flight, Coanda could see that the flames and exhaust smoke from the front-mounted engine tended to hug the fuselage as it streamed out, rather than dissipate in the air as he expected. It took another twenty years of study by him and others to realise that this was a hitherto completely unknown aerodynamic effect, and it was duly named after him by his peers. The effect works for liquids as well as gases (in both cases, the denser the better), and you can experience this yourself every time you open a carton of fruit juice. Pour too slowly and the juice dribbles down the outside of the carton and on to the ground, but pour at a more acute angle and the juice flows out faster – into the glass, avoiding the kitchen floor.

This is the Coanda effect in action, and what Miethe did was to exploit it with the thrust energy from the two jet engines he'd built into the Haunebu Mark II, with the help of engineers recruited for him by the SS at Breslau. As on the Mark I, around the front edge of the disc was a series of shrouded intake slots through which air was sucked by a compressor driven off the turbojets. This huge volume of air would then be ducted through to the jets, in order for the combustion process to take place. The resulting thrust energy would be ejected through two variable nozzles, mounted behind streamlined cowlings, one engine out to the nozzle on the upper fuselage, the other to a nozzle mounted on the underside (if only one engine was fitted, it would go to both). As in the Flugelrad, the pilot could direct these nozzles – in this case aiming the thrust at the smoothed disc fuselage (the outer skin of which was made from a heat-resistant alloy). The Coanda effect would ensure that, rather than dissipate ineffectually, each thrust stream would stay a cohesive and intact energy body as it flowed to the trailing edge of the disc, where the streams would then combine to add still greater impetus to forward motion. The basic shape and profile of the disc was aerodynamically more efficient than the Flugelrad's somewhat compromised design and was far superior to Sack's, because the disc wasn't used to emulate a conventional wing by generating lift. A STOL capability was also achieved by angling the lower nozzle to the ground, like the later Harrier jump jet, and allowing its brute power to roll the craft forward and into the air. At a suitable altitude, the pilot would engage the second jet or nozzle to provide thrust to the rear, and a smooth transition to level flight could be achieved, with the lower nozzle swivelling up to match its companion in providing rearward thrust. Any directional change would be easy to accomplish, as by moving the joystick the pilot would move the exhaust nozzles to effect the heading – a nozzle could presumably even swivel through 180 degrees to slow the craft in any heading.

What problems Miethe may have experienced no one knows – perhaps, like Schriever, he was having reliability problems with the turbojets he was using, or perhaps, like the smoothed-disc approach used by Arthur Sack, he was finding the handling of a non-rotating (and non-gyroscopic) disc too unstable. In any event, he had built two working prototypes of the Haunebu, and it was these that he demonstrated to Schriever and his team upon their meeting. Whatever its drawbacks, the Haunebu's use of the Coanda effect was evidently far superior to the Flugelrad's compromised system, and once Schriever had arrived I have no doubt that it was quickly decided to pool those ideas which, together, had the best chance of cracking this unique approach to flight – just as the SS had probably always planned. From the moment that Miethe joined Schriever's small circle, both the Flugelrad and original Haunebus were destined to stay in their own developmental cul-de-sacs.

So perhaps with mixed feelings at leaving the two Haunebus in Breslau, at the end of summer 1944 Miethe travelled to Prague with the returning Schriever to develop a new craft which, while also called Haunebu, was to combine his knowledge of the Coanda effect with Schriever's gyroscopic rotating blades. Miethe was also to look at the newly rejigged Flugelrad Mark IV. In Schriever's absence, it had been built up according to instructions he'd left prior to his trip. After hearing of its past problems, Miethe persuaded Schriever to re-sculpt the leading edge of the blade's collar to give it more of a wing-like profile and to remove the heavy (and useless) tail section in an effort to generate more lift. A short hop of, say, 120 metres took place that winter (perhaps at Prague's Khbely airfield), but the design had made no real leap forward and was cancelled by the SS for good. Soon after these flights had taken place, both the Mark IV and the earlier Flugelrad prototypes were completely destroyed by Waffen SS soldiers to prevent them falling into the hands of the advancing Soviet troops (as had, by now, befallen the two Haunebus). This destruction was described by Schriever himself in 1952, and while it must have been an immense setback to the team, they had at least amassed many blueprints tracing their progress. SS personnel had also dutifully filmed at least one of these short flights, recording it for posterity. Since then, the footage has languished in a German vault somewhere. If it could be found, it would be the only visual record that would show the craft in flight. The noted ufologist Bill Rose has apparently been shown stills from the film and pronounced them 'genuine', though with what criteria he reached such a deduction remains unclear.

But the team was already moving ahead with the Haunebu Mark III and had little time to dwell on the failure of the earlier concepts. Evidence suggests that, with the Soviets approaching Prague, the team was relocated once again, this time to an underground facility in the Harz Mountains (probably to an SS-run site such as the Mittelwerke at Nordhausen, where assembly of the V-2 was scheduled to begin). Within this secure and secret site, development could restart in earnest, but key figures such as Habermohl and Miethe were still occasionally required to travel back to Prague to liaise with the BMW engineers over their ever-improving engines. The distance between the two sites isn't that great, so this was a feasible logistical exercise and appears to have had a bearing on the eventual fate of the team members at the end of the war.

The Mark III Haunebu took a further step forward in its design at this time, as it lost both nozzle fairings and integrated the two jet units further into the body of the disc, which grew slightly fatter in its cross-section as a result. The Coanda effect was retained, but now jet thrust would be expelled via screened vents at the near rim of both levels of the disc fuselage (air intake for the jets following a similar route at the front). A shrouded rotor blade was also now fitted within the body of the disc to provide gyroscopic stabilisation, as in the Flugelrad. Miethe had realised that he would have to improve the basic aerodynamic package. By dispensing with the nozzles and making it more 'slippery', the craft would have a lower wind-resistance and be capable of higher speeds. From the winter of 1944 this became as much a focus of development at the underground site as integrating the rotor.

At this point we should look at a new alloy material emerging from German labs at the time and which I suspect Miethe wanted for the Haunebu's fuselage. Luftschwamm ('aerosponge'), or sinterised aluminium/magnesium alloy, had one specific property above all others, which lent itself perfectly for use on the Haunebu – it was *porous*. Its development had indirectly occurred as a result of investigations in the 1930s into an aerodynamic effect known as the 'boundary layer', which threatened to impose a maximum top speed on aircraft unless it was overcome. In a nutshell, the boundary layer is a minutely thin layer of air which sits on the leading edge of a wing as it moves forward. This layer acts as a 'lubricating buffer' between the aircraft and the air around it, and allows for that mass of air to be easily pushed aside as the aircraft moves forward. An aerodynamically efficient design will always channel this displaced mass of air efficiently to the rear, reducing heat from friction and giving increased speeds into the bargain. Conversely, an inefficient design will have a slow top speed through its inability to cleave the air effectively and requires more power from its engines to match the speed of a more efficient aircraft, increasing fuel consumption in the process. Common to both aircraft, however, is the problem of how best to deal with the 'transition point' ('TP'). As speed increases, the boundary layer thickens, and, as it flows to the rear of the aircraft and/or the wing, it mixes with incoming, turbulent air from the wake and forms an eddying effect into the slipstream, which can create lots of drag. So the aim for the designer of a high-speed aircraft (and the Haunebu was nothing if not a high-speed craft) is to minimise the effect of the boundary layer and TP, if not remove them altogether.

During the 1930s, designers in both Britain and Germany, looking at the problem, first tried moving the boundary layer away from the wings, in order to shift the TP. To do this they each adopted an approach that used jets of compressed air from tiny holes in the leading edge of an aircraft's wing to disrupt and move the layer, but this approach was inefficient and didn't fully achieve the desired effect. A British design team then switched to *sucking* the boundary layer through the same small holes in the leading edge and dispelling it harmlessly through vents at the rear; the TP was moved far enough back not to cause problems (the ensuing patent didn't go unnoticed in Germany). As time progressed and the designers found their countries once again at war, the development on both sides continued at an accelerated pace. While the British work culminated in a rather compromised material called Porosint (an alloy of phosphor and bronze), which was intended for use in an aircraft's leading edge wing construction, the Germans had produced their own version: Luftschwamm. Another exotic alloy material developed in Germany was called Impervium, and this became available for commercial use from 1935. Capable of withstanding incredibly high temperatures, which caused it to change its colouring in the process, it might be that this alloy also found a role in the development of Luftschwamm – providing additional thermal insulation for the pilot, engines etc.

Luftschwamm seems to have originally been formulated for use within the V-2 project, but given that the SS were now in control of both the V-2 and the Haunebu it's not inconceivable that Miethe was informed of the material's properties. A certain V-2 scientist by the name of Dr Waldemar Schierhorn was a noted authority on aluminium alloys, having contributed in part to the development of the missile's internal construction, and he would seem a likely source of such information, given Miethe's friendliness with his boss, von Braun. In any event, Miethe would have seen Luftschwamm as a solution to the boundary layer problem overshadowing the Haunebu Mark III, for if the disc's fuselage could be made from this amazing material, the internal rotor from the flugelrad could draw in air from the boundary layer, directing it to the jet engines, the thrust from which could then be channelled through a Luftschwamm diffuser at the rear. As it exited the Luftschwamm, the Coanda effect would come into play and help maintain the integrity of the channelled airflow, ensuring it didn't decay and cause unaerodynamic drag.

Work by the British team on Porosint had led them to conclude that the material suffered from too many problems (one being that it would soak up rainwater like a sponge and double, if not triple, its weight), which outweighed its obvious benefits. German researchers might well overcome some of these drawbacks with Luftschwamm, but other issues, such as the intense heat build-up at the leading edge of the disc as it speared through the air (remember that the protective boundary layer was being sucked away), would appear to have been insurmountable and would probably have forced Miethe to compromise on his plans. The analytical science of materials and technology simply didn't exist to perfect Luftschwamm, though in the various craft that would follow in the years to come the solution it promised would appear to be the accepted norm.

With these setbacks, Miethe and Schriever were forced to recast the Haunebu's constitution for a fourth time, and in doing so the profile of the Haunebu Mark IV took on the familiar shape we think of when visualising the 'classic UFO': namely, an inverted saucer laid on the rim of another. This lenticular shape retained the good aerodynamics of the Mark III but also gave extra space for the twelve or more jet engines, plus their fuel tanks, that would now be powering this beast. Schriever's original rotor idea was also no longer required, as this new system of channelling thrust would negate the need for extra stabilisation. Miethe was still desperate to use the Coanda effect, however (after all, it was the most elegant solution to channelling propulsion thrust), as much as he wanted to eradicate the boundary layer problem. This he was able to do by radially mounting the engines equidistantly around the edge of the fifteen-metre diameter of the disc, their grilled air intakes facing the hub. When starting up, the engines would have taken their necessary air in at these intakes. The resulting thrust energy would then have been directed through three variable nozzles at the very rim of the disc (three nozzles per engine), using the Coanda effect to carry that thrust down to the underside of the disc to create lift. As the pilot transited from a climb to horizontal flight, his joystick movement would redirect a number of these nozzles as required to alter direction or provide thrust. Because thrust was emerging from points all around the disc, balance was retained without the rotors. It was an effective compromise, but it seems improbable that this craft actually got built, for the war was drawing to a close and something of this size would have placed too great a strain on dwindling resources. Added to that, the BMW engines planned for were still not delivering anything like the desired reliability or power output, and with at least twelve of them the craft's fuel consumption would have been horrendous. With fuel stocks as parlous as they were in Germany at the time, this would have been too much. Furthermore, BMW hadn't yet entered full production with the units, so to procure them for this one project would have been a hard job even for the SS. If we assume that the team were at least aware of the pressures on them from the SS, they would undoubtedly have been forced to look to an easier solution – a quick fix.

So in the final few months of the war, I believe Miethe and Schriever ended up designing a smaller version that incorporated, say, four Junkers Jumo jets. These units were already proven in

the Me 262 jet fighter-bomber and, given they were being manufactured in the same underground factory, it would have been easy
for the team to use their SS connections to 'borrow' a few. This
was to be the compromised Haunebu Mark V, and out of necessity
its development was swift. Its profile was nothing like that
proposed for the Mark IV, but then this craft was merely a 'proof-
of-concept' vehicle; the team realised that all they had to do was to
get it airborne and nothing more. The Mark IV would stay in the
shadows and wait for sunnier days. Mounting the four engines in
the same manner as in the larger craft resulted in a much smaller,
lighter machine all round, and this enabled the performance gains
promised in the aborted Mark IV to be realised, over and above all
previous models built. Swift progress was made, and on 14
February 1945 the first test-flight of this apparently awkward
looking machine was undertaken in the grey skies above the
factory, with either a KG-200 pilot or Schriever himself at the
controls.

This first came to light in the testimony of witness George Klein,
who in 1954 gave an interview to a Swiss newspaper in which he
claimed to have seen the flight take place from the extensive
underground site of Kahla in the Thuringia region, a site developed
under SS supervision. Among the few details he alluded to was
the astonishing performance of sea-level to 40,000 feet in under
three minutes, plus a top speed exceeding the sound barrier – not
bad for a first flight! Some researchers have looked into Klein's
testimony in greater depth and have reported that weather
conditions on the day 'were totally unsuitable', being misty, snowy
and very bleak, and that the flight couldn't have taken place as a
result. This may well have been the case, but I would argue that it
was precisely *because* the weather was so bad that the flight took
place at all. Bad weather would have meant no aircraft, Allied or
Luftwaffe, would have been in the skies overhead to interfere,
removing the possibility of any outside witnesses seeing the craft
in flight. Therefore, I would tend to agree with the rumours

suggesting that Klein – if he was telling the truth – was connected in some way to the project: he would have to have been, to be granted access to the test. Whether his report is *entirely* accurate, however, is open to debate. I, for one, doubt that it is.

Again, what happened afterwards no one knows for certain, and there have been many rumours to account for the short time to the end of the war. One of the favourites put forward would have us believe that the SS had set up a disc production line somewhere in the Harz Mountains (at a site such as Nordhausen) from where, after the Third Reich had collapsed and as part of a last redoubt, they would operate aerial armadas of discs – either 'death ray'-equipped Flugelrads or Haunebus, depending on who's telling the story. But with even the comparatively advanced Haunebu Mark V still so compromised, the SS would not have countenanced such a move, preferring more proven weapon systems instead. The idea of these craft using such exotic weaponry is also laughable. Yes, there might have been the odd unusual weapon in development, but to suggest it was operational is plain wrong. Then combine the fact that these discs used advanced materials and engines in their make-up, together with the weak-ened position of the Reich at the time, and it's inconceivable that even the SS could have laid on a production line for something like this, whether in Germany or Czechoslovakia. Given the likely proximity of the Soviet advance, it would not have been sensible for the SS to do so either. One-off prototypes – even short production runs – might once have been feasible, but to conceive of mass production on a scale comparable with, say, the Volksjäger jet-fighter programme is a misguided folly, and in any event, by the time of the Haunebu's first flight, the Russians were practically knocking on the door. There was precious little time to organise this 'Alpine redoubt', and when the Allied armies eventually moved through Bavaria, they found no evidence of a planned defensive stronghold, other than a few ammunition dumps and fuel barrels. The redoubt had existed only in the frenzied imaginations of some

SS men and Goebbels' propaganda ministry.

So what could really have happened to the single Mark V after its sole test flight? Some believe wholeheartedly in the idea that a U-boat lay ready and waiting to whisk the dismantled disc and its technicians to Neu Schwabenland, from where the war could continue, but this seems a little hard to believe. While U-boats may have been on hand, thanks to misleading orders and paperwork from Dönitz's office, even a dismantled Mark V would have taken up too much room and restricted the number of passengers. It seems obvious that the SS technical staff overseeing the team would have opted to blow it up and rely on blueprints from then on. After all, with the successful flight of the Mark V they knew the principle worked, which in turn gave them grounds for believing that the full-sized Mark IV might also. Leaving behind a prototype as secret as the Mark V, which had already served its purpose, was deemed too much of a risk.

But nevertheless, as hinted at in Chapter Two, I'm fairly sure that plans and blueprints for all the disc designs, together with machine tools for creating jet engines (as well as Schauberger's engine), found their way down to the isolated Base 211 one way or another. It's a good bet that long-range U-boats had been visiting the site on an ad hoc basis throughout the war, and with conventional shipping from a friendly South American country (or even Japan) supplying the base with its industrial raw materials and rations, supplies could have come through undetected. With the manufacturing capacity that may have been assembled there, further disc development and even attempts at a limited production run might very well have been feasible; unlikely, but feasible.

But whatever was planned wasn't to involve the design team, as at this point the SS would appear to have deemed them surplus to requirements and moved them back to Prague and the BMW plant, away from the underground facility and their work. This would have served two purposes. Firstly, to allow the project to be crated up without their knowledge, and, secondly, to throw a false trail for those investigating the mystery after the war: civilians and military officials alike. The SS had no thoughts of surrender and, by covering their tracks in this way, could continue the struggle elsewhere. What the team actually did once in Prague, no one knows, but it can't have been much, as Schriever's old Flugelrad prototypes had long since been destroyed. Perhaps they polished their alibis and stories and waited for the inevitable collapse and the freedom it promised . . .

This wasn't long in coming, as on 9 May 1945, in the teeth of the Allied advance, the BMW plant finally stopped working and was overrun by Czech patriots and DPs ('displaced persons' – refugees) out for revenge, which caused the remaining German technicians there to flee for their lives. This would appear to have included the team members, who began moving westwards to-wards a friendlier reception than that facing them to the east and Stalin's army. The one exception would appear to be Habermohl, who somehow got separated from the others and ended up a *guest* of the Soviet Union for an unknown number of years. Given that his specialisation was in jet engines, one can only presume that that's the field he was used in, as the Soviets might not have known of either the discs or the fact that he had been involved in their development.

His colleagues, however, fared somewhat better in their flight and were received by the Western Allies, as hoped. According to his own account, Schriever was offered post-war work by the Americans as well as by groups thought to be renegade Nazis in Argentina (believed to be connected with Base 211). In the end he settled for an apparently lowly position unconnected with his previous occupation – delivering copies of the US forces' news-paper *Stars & Stripes* to American bases throughout Germany. On the face of it, this would appear a peculiar career path for him to take, but it was known at the time that SS networks, such as 'The Spider' and 'Odessa', were using men in such positions as fronts for moving out of the country numbers of personnel wanted for war crimes. It's quite possible, therefore, that Schriever had taken the job to play his part in the continuing secret war. Of course, it might have been the only job open to him, but in that case why did he turn down the other offers? He died in the late 1950s in his new home town of Bremerhaven, without leaving much in the way of a written testimony about his time during the war and we have only a few interviews with newspapers to corroborate his story. Nonetheless, there remains a waft of smoke about the fire which refuses to go away. His claims of working in the Projekt Saucer team have an irresistible air about them, as do his claims that UFOs photographed in the 1950s bear resemblance to his (and Miethe's) original designs. He also claimed that blueprints were stolen from his laboratory, which effectively scuppered his chances of returning to the project, although this claim doesn't really add up and, I believe, is something of a convenient smokescreen to account for his unexpected occupation as delivery driver and, perhaps, to misdirect enquiries.

As for Belluzzo, little is known of his post-war life; he remains a man of mystery. And Miethe? After the war he moved to the USA as a result of being picked up on the Operation Paperclip lists at the apparent recommendation of his old friend Wernher von Braun, something recently confirmed by the former Assistant Secretary of the USAF, Alexander Flax, in a TV documentary on the subject. While working primarily for the USAF on various projects (which are still classified but which one can make easy guesses at), Miethe was also seconded during the 1950s to work for the A. V. Roe aircraft company in Canada. He apparently spent time there on the failed AvroCar project, although subsequent research and disclosures under the American Freedom of Information Act has revealed that his likely involvement was more with a project known as 'Silver Bug' and that the AvroCar was indeed what many observers had always took it to be – a convenient (though expensive) red herring intended solely to put people off the scent. We shall be reviewing these projects in greater depth later on.

So that's the story. Some or all of it may be true, but until the official files are opened no one in a position to know the truth is either denying or confirming it. And yet . . . It does sound plausible. When researching *Last Talons of the Eagle*, I came across a number of bizarre projects that sounded equally unfeasible but which turned out to be very real indeed. All that's missing in this case is the photographic and written evidence to prove it once and for all.

But reading testimonies and contemporary reports is not enough if one is to build up a complete picture of the story. Perhaps an overview of the German war effort in terms of its capacity for secrecy and some of the technologies it was known to have developed might lend further weight to the claims covered here, and this is dealt with in the next chapter.

chapter five

'There is no need of spurs when the horse is running away.'
Publilius Syrus, *Moral Sayings*.

As we've seen in the previous chapter, there certainly appears to have been a flying disc programme *of some kind* in Germany during the war. While the technology might not have been as advanced as some unreliable observers have suggested, none the less a programme intended to develop aircraft of this configuration was in evidence, using engines and materials to hand. But in order to develop and run a project of this scope in wartime, with this degree of absolute secrecy, certain factors need to be present for it to have a chance of success, and that's something that now needs to be examined in greater detail. After all, with the passage of time and the continued silence of the authorities conspiring to leave the project in the shadows, perhaps we should shed a little light on an adjacent spot and look for glimpses of the *real* prize in so doing.

In the immediate aftermath of the Operation Hydra raid on Peenemünde in August 1943, the most visible projects being undertaken there – the V-1 and V-2 – were moved off-site to scattered locations throughout the expanded Reich. Miethe's two Haunebus were also likely moved at this point. Some elements from these projects ended up at existing research facilities, owned either by private business, the army or the Luftwaffe, while others were housed in purpose-built underground sites, constructed or adapted expressly for them under SS supervision. The SS, too, had long since had its own research centres in operation since Himmler had realised that, for it to achieve its long-term goal of predominance in the country, it would have to develop something of an omnipresence – and the twin fields of science and technology were no different. Operation Hydra gave Himmler an excuse for taking these projects under his organisation's wing. He blamed spies in the army and Luftwaffe for giving away Peenemüde's secrets, and he vowed to Hitler that under the SS such lapses in security would never happen again. Developing its own concealed manufacturing sites was seen as simply the next step in Himmler's plan for SS supremacy and – who knows? Perhaps the German military industrial base as a whole might have benefited from this approach had Himmler been given greater scope by Hitler. But, crucially, the other leading lights of the Nazi government mistrusted his motives in wishing to undertake such a responsibility (perhaps already fearing the position of the SS), so the wider underground factory plan – which would have required many hundreds of thousands of workers and millions of Reichsmarks to complete – was scaled back to cover just the rockets. The discs would also have been part of this plan, of course, and this author believes them to have been hidden in with the administration of the more visible projects.

SS Gruppenführer Hans Kammler began planning three elements to the dispersal of the V-2 project, a responsibility that had been awarded to this bright young SS officer and model Nazi. Firstly, he set up a new V-2 training range at an SS camp at Blitzna, in Poland. Secondly, a development works nicknamed 'the Cement Project' was established in an underground cavern in the cliffs above Traunsee, Austria. However, Speer ordered this to be scaled back in July 1944 on orders from Hitler to concentrate less on long-term projects and switch more to arms manufacture. From that point on, the Traunsee site switched to the production of tank components.

With Niedersachswerfen near Nordhausen in the Harz Mountains as the manufacturing plant and third element, Kammler's plan seemed complete. Originally, the extensive underground workings at the site were owned by the WIFO company, which extracted minerals there, but under a sweeping 'Führer order' the company was all but evicted by the SS which, thanks to Kammler, had a wide remit to develop the site in preparation for receiving the various Wunder Waffen. Examples of the rumoured V-4 'radiation bomb' were thought to be already stored here, but with the cancellation of this programme the V-2 was scheduled for Nordhausen in its place.

With new galleries blasted into the Kohnstein mountain by 60,000 slave labourers employed by Organisation Todt, the site was to become the largest underground factory ever built, consisting of two parallel tunnels each 2,600 metres long and wide enough for a double railway track to be laid down. If you can imagine these two in plan as the outer rails of a ladder, then between them ran forty-six 'rungs' – connecting tunnels, each two hundred metres long – in twenty-seven of which the V-2 rockets were to be assembled, with jet engines being produced in the remaining tunnels. The overall floor space was just over 125,000 square metres, and the available space was 750,000 cubic metres – more than the entire underground space available in all of Britain for manufacturing and storage at the time. Twelve ventilation shafts circulated air and kept the temperature at a constant 17°C throughout, while helping to eradicate moisture in the air – a constant hindrance to working with electronics and machine tools under ground. It was a huge undertaking. But what engineers such as Kammler were building up great knowledge of were the principles behind successful tunnelling and underground construction in general – at a rate unseen hitherto. Moreover, it is likely that such knowledge filtered back to the few civil engineers on Base 211 throughout the war, as they created their new base under the ice.

Conditions for the OT workers, who lived and worked under ground, were as grim as you might expect, but after an apparently shocked Albert Speer visited in December 1943, representing his new Ministry for Armament and War Production, a nearby camp ('Dora') was built to house them. Here, they could at last see daylight and breathe fresh air; their rations were also improved, in an attempt at increasing their efficiency. Their only reason for finding themselves in such dreadful conditions was that they were Jews, Gypsies or Slavs from the occupied eastern territories in Russia. Over 20,000 were said to have died in building the facility, from starvation, exhaustion and the brutality of the SS guards.

As the first tunnels opened up, the army weapons office transferred the development contracts away from Peenemünde to the newly renamed Nordhausen Central Works – or Mittelwerke as they've since become more commonly known. They were called 'central' as their location is more or less in the middle of Germany. Other underground factories were intended in the east and south, at Riga and Vienna respectively, but the deteriorating progress of the war cut short these plans and efforts were solely concentrated on completing the core plant of Nordhausen, with other smaller plants following close by. For example, the discs are believed to have been moved to Kahla; a site that lay within Nordhausen's sphere of influence and which served as the location of the test-flight witnessed by Georg Klein.

After pushing the labourers hard to prepare the site, the Mittelwerke opened for business on schedule in January 1944. By the time it closed in April 1945, its 16,000 production workers had made over 6,000 V-2 rockets. Though the jet engine side of the site was planned from day one, it was never actually completed, in common with further extensions intended to house a Junkers aircraft factory, a liquid-oxygen plant and a synthetic-oil refinery. Another separate installation was planned nearby at Woffleben, which was intended to make the Henschel Hs 293 guided missile and V-1s, but this, too, was never completed. Other secret installations discovered only after the war include the Hermann Göring Institute at Volkenrode; a complex in the mountains ringing Lake Garda in Italy; a site near Taunus, twenty-nine kilometres to the north of Frankfurt am Main; and another at Verdun, France. A significant find was also reportedly discovered by the Russians at a Czech town called Podmokly, in which several V-2 fuselages were found, together with a stockpile of uranium and a number of cyclotrons (uranium-enriching machines) apparently used in the V-4 programme. With the twin demonstrations of the awesome power of the atom bomb soon to be unleashed on Japan, Russian scientists were then forced to re-evaluate the importance of what they had discovered. The machines were crated up and shipped eastwards, ending up at the Black Sea resort of Soukhoumi, from where it was reported that Russia commenced its first atomic experiments using these very machines and the stockpiles of uranium.

But aside from concealing facilities within mountains, there were also other huge installations already committed to: various bomb-proof U-boat pens scattered across France and Germany, the 'Atlantic wall' coastline defences and sundry V-2 launching bunkers. All were proceeded with on the grounds that they were essential for national security, whereas it was felt that the rest of industry could be adequately defended by anti-aircraft guns and fighter aircraft.

Kammler himself appears to have had a colourful war as a result of his headlong drive for recognition and glory. Before 1939 he had been just another civil engineer employed within the Luftwaffe but, if the stories are true, with the outbreak of war he recognised that if his career was to advance with any real speed, he would have to join an altogether more dynamic institution. The SS duly beckoned, and almost from the word go it seems that Kammler was involved in running top-secret technology projects at an SS research centre based at a Skoda factory in Pilsen, Czechoslovakia. Himmler was so impressed at his administrative prowess (no mean feat this: impressing Himmler with his *admin*) that he placed a triple ring of security around Kammler's group, by which it was hoped secrecy would be maintained. This in itself should tell us that already Kammler was no ordinary engineer. Thereafter, with his group now renamed 'Kammlerstab' ('Kammler staff'), funding arrived via the Skoda board of directors and looked for all the world like just another financial transaction – conveniently hidden away in the company records. After the integration of Skoda into the Hermann Göring Werke, a quasi-military industrial combine, the group's covert existence was all the more secured. As the Kammlerstab's director, Kammler would have been able to foster development of both Miethe's and Schriever's disc projects with ease – even when Peenemünde was still running.

He first came to Hitler's attention when a sketch of his ideas for the layout of a concentration camp was shown to the Führer by Himmler. So impressed were they both that it's said that Kammler's sketch was to act as the template for all the camps to follow. Soon promoted to SS-Brigadeführer, with responsibilities for SS construction projects, in December 1941 he laid down a five-year plan that would result in new barracks and concentration camps across the Reich, from the fjords of Norway to the oilfields of Baku, on the Caspian Sea. But Kammler's most visible achievement was handling the V-2 dispersal. It passed off *relatively* smoothly, and as a reward he was appointed to Speer's own new Jägerstab – the new industrial ministry, intended to increase production of fighter aircraft and other arms. Still in the SS, Kammler was charged with production planning, and in the teeth of ever-dwindling raw materials and labour resources this was a role he settled into comfortably. As the war moved into 1945, he had used his influence and skill at playing the political game, to the point where he now had virtually full responsibility for both the V-1 and V-2 programmes, the Volksjäger fighter project as well as all jet aircraft (and engine) production and much more besides. His marked skill in extracting results, from seemingly impossible situations, had earned him recognition from all quarters. Once he had both Himmler's and Hitler's ear, it seems inevitable that Kammler should have gone as far as he did. To Hitler, Kammler appeared trustworthy and, with so much else going wrong, Hitler felt he had no choice but to show faith in that trust.

With his direct control over several sites, including the Mittelwerke, together with his general influence in the SS, it is Kammler who seems the most likely SS figure behind the disc project, right from its inception, when Schriever first went looking for funds. The Flugelrad was so radical that only Kammler, with his own experience of unknown, secret projects at Skoda, could be relied on to manage the project. On his later arrival at Peenemünde and the necessary review of operations he would have undertaken at that point, Kammler would have learned of Miethe's plans and would no doubt have also backed him, seeing his work as complimentary to Schriever's. Later on, when both projects were running out of steam, Kammler would not have thought twice about splicing them together, in the hope that the teams would make progress once combined – which they appeared to do.

For Kammler, moving the combined team from Prague and into the Kahla complex would have been an easy administrative task, compared with moving the V-2. Blasted out of the Grösseutersdorf mountain, this site wasn't as large as Nordhausen but had good rail and road links straight into the mountain and was big enough to swallow up a project such as the discs with ease.

But perhaps the biggest mystery surrounding Kammler is his disappearance in the closing days of the war. Some conflicting reports from members of his personal staff suggest that he shot himself in a Bavarian forest, but this is hard to believe of him. A man as driven as Kammler would surely have thought of death as the easy way out. Remember, he had joined the SS to further his career, so while he might not have *completely* believed in its notions of brotherhood, he was content as long as he got something out of it. Seeing the end of the war as inevitable – regardless of what he might report to Himmler or Hitler – this pragmatic figure would have viewed the disc project as an ideal new focus to go for, and it's therefore highly probable that he would have organised its dispersal to Base 211; just as he did so successfully with the V-2 from Peenemünde. This author finds it hard to believe stories of his suicide. Someone so obsessed with the minutiae of life and his career would have viewed engineering his disappearance simply as a means to an end – that of starting over again, somewhere else, with a new life of challenges.

The question under discussion, though, is whether or not a capacity for secrecy existed in Germany which might have shielded knowledge of the discs right up to the present day. Well, considering that Peenemünde's activities weren't discovered until 1943 after years of operation, and that the Mittelwerke, Kahla and many of the other sites remained hidden until after the war, it does seem to point to a positive conclusion. The Third Reich was spread over most of Europe, so for Allied reconnaissance aircraft to cover every metre of it on a regular basis would simply have been beyond their resources. Occasionally, they would strike lucky with a piece of intelligence from a local resistance movement on the ground, or a fluke overpass by an aircraft, but these were rare events, and it should not be surprising that so much was achieved in secret.

And with research and development in all areas of aerospace going on throughout the war, thanks to Göring's enlightened protectionism of the Luftwaffe, such effort would surely have borne fruit.

From the point of view of private firms such as BMW, unless the company was effective at hoodwinking the authorities (who were continually inspecting labs and production lines), then any new innovation emerging from its labs would have been picked up and further refined where necessary by a body within the Technisches Amt before being passed on to the disc teams for inclusion, as well as more conventional, rival aircraft manufacturers. Industry in general certainly wasn't in a position to refuse such interference and would have treated the spread of industrial knowledge by the state as a mixed blessing.

So if we then safely assume that the industrial and technical capacity was there, what of the operational side to the story? What of the men who, most likely, would have been assigned to fly the disc prototypes? The KG 200 (Kampf Gruppe) squadron have already been mentioned as the most likely team. When you consider that even its one-time commanding officer, Colonel Werner Baumbach, fails to mention the unit in his memoirs, you begin to realise just how elite and secret it was. And how ideally suited to the job.

KG 200 originally sprang from an irregular and clandestine squadron attached to the Abwehr (military intelligence) and the Luftwaffe's secret 5th Air Branch, whose job was to photo-reconnoitre parts of Europe, North Africa and Russia – a risky task its pilots undertook in both civil and military aircraft. As the war ground on, the Abwehr's reputation began to suffer through its rumoured involvement in plots to remove Hitler. Perhaps disillusioned at this distraction from its original purpose, one of its pilots – Captain Edmund Gartenfeld – formed a new breakaway unit of his own in summer 1942. By February 1944 his 2nd Test Formation had grown to number four squadrons, at which time it was officially recognised and renamed KG 200. After moving to Gatow airfield near Berlin, KG 200 then came Baumbach's control and divided its previous (and some new) responsibilities into two Gruppen (groups). The first group was further divided into four 'flights'. I/KG 200 delivered and retrieved agents from enemy territory; II/KG 200 undertook special operations near combat zones using a pair of American B-17 Flying Fortress heavy bombers that had been cobbled together from aircraft lost on daylight raids; III/KG 200 was concerned with transport and training and was based on the Baltic island of Ruegen and later Flensburg; lastly, IV/KG 200 handled technical matters. The second Gruppe handled all the various operational miscellanea that didn't square neatly with the duties of the first: i.e. providing Pathfinder aircraft for bombing sorties, radar-jamming aircraft and the bizarre Mistel composite aircraft. This last idea involved mounting a fighter, such as an Me 109, on a frame atop a stripped-out bomber deemed too old for further service, which was then packed with an eight-tonne warhead of high explosive. A group of these ungainly contraptions would then be flown to a large infrastructure target, such as a bridge or power-station, where the pilots would release the bombers, which would then descend to the target in a gentle arcing 'death dive'. These two Gruppes were the only ones developed by KG 200 during the war, but another pair were planned; the third would have used Fw-190 fighters in an anti-shipping role equipped with torpedoes, whereas more infamously the fourth would have had operational responsibility for the planned 'suicide planes' on which the Reich's future fortunes were once pinned. The aircraft planned for this role were merely V-1 flying bombs adapted to carry a pilot who would guide it to a target. When adverts for volunteers appeared in 1944, the KG 200 officers and the plan's supporters elsewhere were overwhelmed by the number of applicants willing to lay down their lives. In the end the scheme was dropped for fear of an adverse effect on the nation's morale.

But even though this outlandish idea didn't get off the ground, KG 200 were involved in plenty of others and would have been ideally suited to helping out on the disc project. One other scheme worthy of inclusion is the development of an ingenious system for dropping secret agents into enemy territory from fighter aircraft which, ordinarily, were unable to carry passengers. Later on in the war, many German fighters were fitted with external bomb racks, so this plan involved mounting a barrel-shaped plywood container to them, called a PAG (Personen-Abwurf-Gerät or personnel drop device). Up to three agents would lay on canvas biers inside the PAG, with their kit packed within the conical foam nosecone that was designed to absorb much of the impact on landing. Once over the target area, the pilot would release the PAG, which would then drift silently earthwards, suspended from three parachutes which triggered on release. The procedure was apparently safe and was used many times.

To recap, we have explored the possibilities of resupplying Base 211 with raw materials and essential supplies via shipping from both South America and Germany, as well as by submarine (although no submarine of the day could carry more supplies than a conventional freighter). We know that German shipping was active in the South Atlantic throughout the war, and friendly South American countries such as Argentina and Paraguay would have allowed such voyages to take place. We've pieced together a highly plausible timeline that links together all the known figures in the story, and we've seen that as a result of sticking to achievable goals and claims those goals might have been feasible. In this chapter we've looked at the possibilities for secret development from all sides – both in terms of testing and manufacturing – and these lessons could equally be transferred on a smaller scale to Neu Schwabenland. Because there's no evidence or sightings that conclusively prove the existence of these craft, doesn't mean they didn't exist.

Schriever's main breakthrough with the Flugelrad was in recognising the importance of using a rotating element in a circular aircraft to achieve gyroscopic stability. This vital step was indeed radical, yet it was merely his reinterpretation of then-emerging helicopter technology, and we should recognise that he wasn't alone in his attempts at forging something new with it. Friedrich von Döblhoff, an Austrian baron, in 1942 began building the first prototype of a small, one-man helicopter he'd designed. While in this early stage it lacked the ability for independent forward flight and relied on tows to get airborne, its unique propulsion system was raising a few eyebrows. A small petrol engine fitted with an Argus supercharger was mounted to the main spindle above the fuselage, at the top of which rotor blades were fitted. This supercharger sucked in air through a vent before compressing it and mixing it with pre-heated petrol from the fuel tank. This volatile mixture was then channelled up into the rotor head itself and thence into each of the three hollow rotor blades, along which centrifugal force drew it. At the tip of each blade was a small ramjet combustion chamber, which worked along the principles of the noted engineer Dr Ing. Pabst. Under the localised high G-forces generated in each ramjet and the speed of outside air entering the chambers, the mixture was ignited and its thrust channelled through a small nozzle to the rear, thus spinning the rotors without the torque problems experienced in driving them directly from an engine in the fuselage. In short – a jet-propelled helicopter! Although five prototypes were built in all, with semi-enclosed bodywork and more powerful engines, after the successful short hops of the first machine, serious production was never considered. At the end of the war, the remaining machines fell into American hands and were lost amid the booty found by the GIs as they advanced into a shattered Germany, and it's unclear what happened to them thereafter.

Whilst Döblhoff's design had merits, the thrust capacity of the Pabst ramjets and the power of the petrol engine weren't as high as required, and the rotor assembly also lacked a variable pitch control, which curtailed its effectiveness. But this was a strange omission, given that at least two manufacturers were by then already producing helicopters for consideration by the Luftwaffe and Kriegsmarine, leading us to conclude that Döblhoff merely wanted to prove his concept before getting into the complex engineering behind an articulated rotor.

During the last months of the war, the established aircraft company of Focke-Wulf also looked into the principles embodied in the Döblhoff, with its Triebflügel design. Had it progressed beyond a few scale models, this advanced, streamlined interceptor would have sat vertically on the ground, on a landing wheel assembly incorporated in its tail section. Three variable-pitch rotor blades were mounted on a revolving collar, set flush with the fuselage's outer skin, which spun around its middle halfway up the fuselage. At the end of each of these blades would have been mounted a Pabst ramjet, larger than that found on Döblhoff's craft.

In case you're wondering, the essence of a ramjet involves a narrowing cone-shaped air intake (with few moving parts, if any), which, at high speeds, mixes the inrush of air with either a solid or liquid fuel – to get up to the operating speed *these* units required, they each incorporated a customised Walter rocket within their housings. Before takeoff, the pilot would angle the blades to a point at which they created no lift (neutral pitch), with the rockets firing straight down. With the Walters lit (of a design similar to that fitted in the Me 163 Kome), the aircraft would shoot skywards and, having built up sufficient speed, the pilot would then bring these blades simultaneously to a higher angle of incidence into the airflow. As the angle changed, the thrust and bite of the blades into the air would set the collar spinning, creating a single, giant propeller – similar to the principles embodied by the Döblhoff. Just like a helicopter, these blades would generate lift and continue spinning, courtesy of the ramjets now operating at their tips, fuel for the launch rocket already depleted. On reaching the operational height of around 30,000 feet, the pilot would then level out and alter the angle of the blades to bring the rotational speed of the blades and their ramjets into line with the desired forward speed of the aircraft. With the collar spinning at around 220 rpm, the blades would experience Mach 0.9 at their tips – quite enough for efficient ramjet operations. Construction of the first prototype was weeks away from commencing at the end of the war, and a lot of testing, both on models of the airframe and the engines, had already been completed.

It would therefore seem that, with the ramjet now 'proven', the technology was being assimilated by groups elsewhere. If this seems somewhat sweeping, remember that by 1945 the SS effectively controlled the bulk of, if not *all*, new aerospace developments and had their finger on the pulse. Figures such as Kammler were well placed to monitor developments such as Döblhoff's and Focke-Wulf's. In addition, Kammler oversaw the developments emerging from the SS and Luftwaffe research labs, the very sites that would have produced the breakthroughs in radar etc. Göring's influence had considerably weakened by this point in the war, leaving the Luftwaffe something of a spent force, so there was little protection for the many thousands of employees at the labs. For them to continue in their posts, the patronage of the SS was almost a necessity – especially if their work depended on essential, and scarce, supplies.

The prevailing theme of 'achievable development', then, might also be attributable to *another* project, similar to and developed in parallel with the discs – one that casual observers have long misidentified as being part of the disc project: that of the Foo Fighters. Unlike the flying discs, however, this project does at least seem to have had its share of witnesses.

With the incessant waves of American and British bombers flying over the Reich day in, day out, many solutions were being suggested to combat them. Something had to be done to protect both civilians and industry. From introducing new flak pieces (anti-aircraft guns) with greater range, to developing one-man armour-plated gliders intended to be flown directly into the fuselages of enemy bombers, ideas were plentiful.

From summer 1944 onwards, key figures such as Albert Speer knew full well that if the industrial infrastructure continued to suffer at the hands of Allied bombers, the war would be over sooner rather than later, and at this point in the proceedings that outcome appeared inevitable. The surrender of the Reich was still not an option seriously considered, so Speer and the SS had to ensure that industry continued producing submarines, tanks and aircraft unabated. Adequate fighter aircraft cover was considered the most pressing need, as if they could attack the British and American bombers, then industry could carry on. But with so many expensive aircraft lost, both in terms of skilled pilots as well as the financial cost, cheaper and more effective means of wrestling air superiority back from the Allies were being sought constantly. One approach lay in developing a whole range of 'conventional' ground-to-air missile systems, which were well on the way to reaching operational status just before the war ended. There's no doubt that given a few more months these would have been devastatingly effective, thanks to their relatively sophisticated infrared tracking sensors that would have locked on to the hot engine casings and exhausts on Allied bombers (adapted from a system built by AEG and fitted to some night fighters, codenamed Spanner).

But Germany didn't have a few more months. It needed something *fast* if it was to put up a credible resistance. Luckily there were engineers working on the problem, with the foresight necessary to recognise that a possible solution *did* exist; its constituent parts were scattered around the various technical institutions already mentioned. Perhaps under Kammler's guidance, these unheralded engineers began working to combine some of those technologies into something that might offer a useful defence. It is the first fruits of their efforts which the Allied (and German) pilots began seeing in the winter of 1944: the Foo Fighters.

The name comes from the French for 'fire' ('feu'), and the phenomenon was given the 'Fighters' tag by witnesses trying to make some sense out of what they had seen. The German pilots who had seen the same thing started referring to them as

'Feuerballs' in turn, though in common with their opponents they had no idea of what they were seeing.

Put simply, what these pilots reportedly encountered were spherical balls of energy; each pulsating with a vivid orange-red iridescence and seemingly under intelligent control. Their only purpose seemed to be in pacing aircraft, and, no matter what manoeuvres pilots undertook to shake them off, the Foo Fighters were still there, keeping a regular distance. Sometimes witnesses reported seeing more than one at a time; clusters of these glowing balls of light drifting through Allied bomber formations were reported on more than one occasion.

The first sighting would appear to have occurred on either the night of 22 or 23 November 1944. RAF pilot, Lieutenant Edward Schlüter was flying a Bristol Beaufighter night fighter on a regular mission over the Rhine some thirty-two kilometres from Strasbourg when he and his crew noticed ten red-glowing spheres apparently pacing them. At this point the plane's radar set packed up and, given that a night fighter relies totally on such equipment, Schlüter made for home, he and his crew mystified at what they'd seen. Four days later, one Lieutenant Giblin was flying his Beaufighter to the south of Mannheim when a single, though much larger, orange ball of light appeared to be pacing his aircraft from several hundred metres above, apparently without any interference to his radar. Its presence wasn't registering in the radar sets at the nearest ground station, but this may simply have been due to the inability of early radar systems such as these to differentiate between aerial bodies flying in such close formation. If the Foo Fighter was shadowing more closely than it had Schlüter's aircraft, this may explain the size difference. But whatever the truth of the phenomenon, it was unable to differentiate between the air forces. The sightings continued into December in the same pattern, with Foo Fighters pacing both Allied and German aircraft alike – German pilots thought the phenomenon an Allied secret weapon, while the Allies thought the opposite. But once reports started filtering back from the skies over Japan, so the Allied military staff gradually came around to recognising the phenomenon as a new weapon of the enemy's.

The Luftwaffe was effectively a beaten force by November 1944. With the exception of the misguided Operation Bodenplatte, which took place on 1 January 1945 using the last elements of a cohesive force to attack Allied airfields, the Luftwaffe was putting up very little resistance. Yet how could it, when fuel stocks had dwindled to the point when orders were issued forbidding aircraft to taxi out to the runways under their own power, and instead be towed by oxen, in a measure to save fuel? Production of fighter aircraft had scaled new heights all the while, but unbelievably there was no fuel for anything but 'essential' combat missions – and even these had to be authorised at the very top. As a result, the Allied night fighters were reportedly having to settle for attacking sleeper trains and overnight road convoys, rather than Luftwaffe opponents, and this was having the effect of boring the crews in the process. This apparent state of affairs has led some post-war researchers into the Foo Fighters to suggest that RAF crews were fantasising the whole thing in order to inject a little fun into their routine, and that once the story entered the public domain it all got a little out of hand and became too difficult for them to own up.

Personally, this author disputes these claims, given the professionalism of the crews themselves. Yes, mischevious hijinks and one-upmanship might have coloured one or two reports, but there is never any smoke without fire, and when senior officers on both sides start reporting the same phenomenon, there must be a kernel of truth in there somewhere. The first the public got to hear about the story was a small article in the *South Wales Argus* that had been picked up from the Reuters news agency and published on 13 December 1944. Note that this in turn might have been lifted from the *American Legion* magazine, published earlier that month, which carried the personal opinions of several American pilot officers on what they thought lay behind the phenomenon.

> The Germans have produced a 'secret' weapon in keeping
> with the Xmas season. The new device, which is apparently
> an air defence weapon, resembles the glass balls which adorn
> Christmas trees. They have been hanging in the air over
> German territory, sometimes singly, sometimes in clusters.
> They are coloured silver and are apparently transparent.

The story caused quite a stir and got picked up again, by no less a journal than the *New York Herald & Tribune*, on 2 January 1945. A large-scale sighting followed this on 12 January, when several bomber squadrons reported Foo Fighter sightings to HQ at Dijon. A high-level investigation was then ordered, only to be shelved when it was realised that the Foo Fighters appeared to show no aggressive traits, so were clearly not a threat.

But if the Foo Fighters weren't downing aircraft, what might their purpose have been and what link might they have had to the flying disc programme? For a few answers to this question we should look to the one primary source of information on the subject – the work of the Italian author Renato Vesco, whose 1968 book, *Intercettateli Senza Sparare (Intercept – Don't Shoot)* took a long look at the subject. Although several researchers have since poured scorn on some of his more dubious claims, Vesco none the less presents an intriguing case.

In seeking to understand what might have gone into the Foo Fighter design, he pulls together several strands of research known to have been pursued at the various SS and Luftwaffe scientific institutes. These include producing a localised electromagnetic disrupter, for interrupting the ignition systems of conventional aircraft engines; a device for scrambling an aircraft's radio communications; and an infrared tracking device that could latch on to an aircraft engine's exhaust, like the system for the new anti-aircraft missiles. The device would attempt to maintain a constant reading, so whatever craft it was fitted to would appear to be pacing its target, once acquired. Known as 'Paplitz', this system was manufactured by the Elektro Akoustik Institute of Namslau, and when fitted to a conventional aircraft and tested in March 1945 it was sensitive enough to keep both the 'hunter and hunted' at a distance of only 12 metres apart – something similar to the Foo Fighter.

To this day no one knows what the first Foo Fighter actually looked like – no authentic blueprints or photographs have ever surfaced, and, because so many of the sightings were at night, it's impossible to gauge accurately their size and shape. However, it's a fair bet that the main body of the device would have been a sphere of around two metres in diameter, around the circumference of which would perhaps have revolved six variable-pitch rotor blades, as in the Triebflügel. At the tips of three of them would have been fitted a smaller Pabst ramjet similar in size to those on the Döblhoff; these craft were relatively small so required less power to do their job and so didn't require an engine on each blade.

The lower section of the device might have been slightly elongated (giving the overall outline of a laden ice-cream cone), which would have lent the design a lower centre of gravity and prevent it from gyrating wildly. Some have suggested that such a design might also have been fitted with a set of air brakes around the base of the 'cone', which would have greatly added to its aerobatic abilities and make it easier to pace aircraft taking evasive manoeuvres.

By mounting the bulky electronic avionics pack in the upper half of the sphere, it would be protected from the heat and vibration of the engine and spinning bearings as the blades outside whizzed around. There would also have been room here to mount the receiver for the infrared tracking system which, by facing forward, would not have been blinded by the flash from the jets. There might also have been a small warhead, triggered by the infrared system, but since no recorded loss of an aircraft was ever attributed to a Foo Fighter no one knows if this was simply down to the fact that the sightings were of unfinished prototypes. Likewise, there is speculation regarding its use of a simple 'quick retreat' mechanism. Some Allied gunners in the bombers were known to shoot at the Foo Fighters and reported seeing them move away at extreme speed. Vesco surmises that this was due to the outer panels of the device being dual skinned with metal sheets charged with different electrical polarities either side of an insulating layer. As a bullet passed through, it would cause these two sheets to touch, thus closing a simple circuit. This would be linked to an emergency throttle setting on the craft, which would override the infrared system and cause it to scoot off at high speed to avoid taking further hits. In any case, these components are purely speculatory as we just don't *know* what went into these devices – we can only make a best guess.

The Foo Fighter would most likely have been launched from the back of a truck, railway flat car or some other improvised ground station, its operators waiting until an aircraft could be either seen, heard or observed on radar before launching it, in order to conserve fuel that might otherwise be wasted in searching for a target. We must also now speculate on the various propulsion systems that might have been fitted to the Foo Fighters. One idea is that at the pointed end of the cone was mounted a small RATO ('Rocket Assisted TakeOff') solid-fuel rocket pack, larger versions of which were often used by Luftwaffe transports and bombers to assist them in their takeoffs. The ground crew would fire this up from their launching platform and stand back as the craft took off with the speed of a firework. Its burn duration wouldn't have lasted long, but enough to achieve two things: firstly, to get the Foo Fighter up to operating altitude and, secondly, to ensure sufficient climbing speed to get the ramjets working – a pump within the body of the device would have been sending fuel out to the ramjets since takeoff and, once lit, they would have started

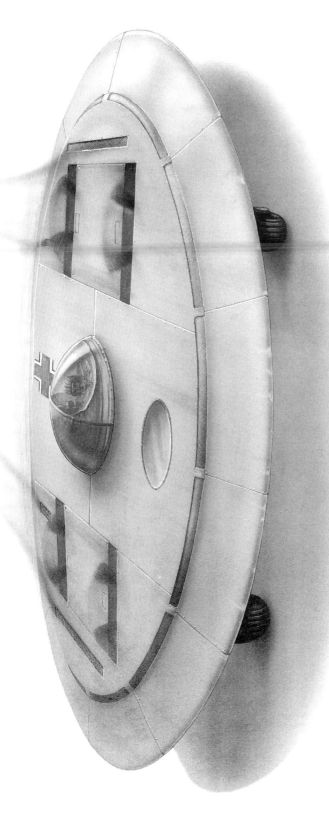

Miethe's Haunebu MKI

Many designs have been offered for Miethe's second Haunebu, but the first (MKI) is almost always ignored. Miethe's initial aim was only to prove the Coanda effect, so for simplicity he would most likely have used conventional piston engines and propellers. Note the inclusion of a lenticular porthole on the front apron, through which the pilot could have sighted the runway during takeoff and landing.

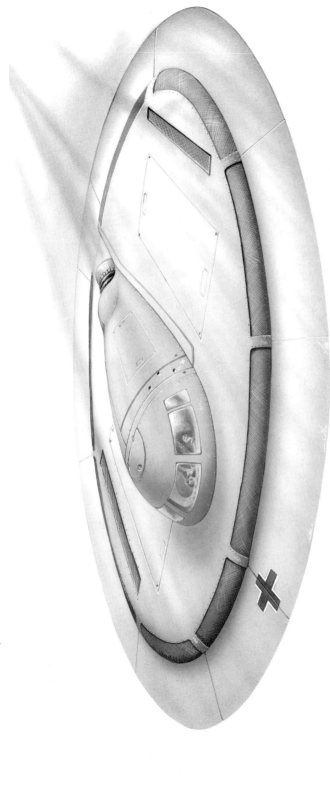

Miethe's Haunebu MKII

With the jet-powered Haunebu MKII model, Miethe was looking to refine the Coanda principles beyond the MKI. Note the cowled jet intake on the upperside, mirroring the upper teardrop cupola and the tapered, manoeuvrable jet exhaust nozzle at the rear – one of a pair, with the second out of sight on the underside. This classic layout draws inspiration from the many sources of information that have appeared since the war.

Schriever's Flugelrad MKII

While this design didn't cover itself in glory and was soon replaced with a more airworthy MKIII, one can see in this view how the diffuser mounted on to the exhaust nozzle of the jet engine might have played over the underside of the rotor blades. Angling the blades down and tilting the nozzle upwards would have started them spinning like a helicopter; the idea being that the pilot would then angle the blades upwards to gain lift.

This was Miethe and Schriever's last-ditch effort at finding a workable disc design and, with the Red Army practically at the door, one or two test flights were supposedly made. A witness later claimed that it had attained at least 40,000 feet and had broken the sound barrier; a record not officially claimed until 1947 when Chuck Yeager achieved the feat. The story goes that, following the flight(s), the MKV was blown up and its blueprints smuggled out of the Reich, bound for pastures new.

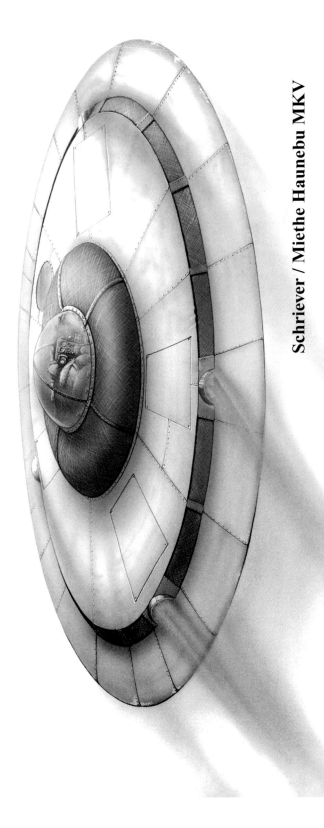

Schriever / Miethe Haunebu MKV

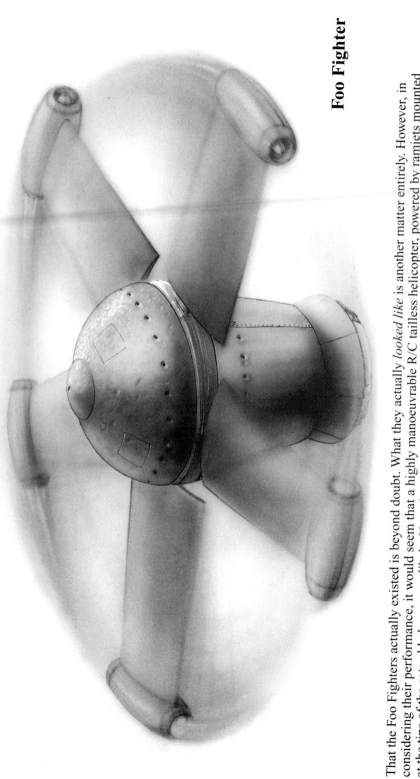

Foo Fighter

That the Foo Fighters actually existed is beyond doubt. What they actually *looked like* is another matter entirely. However, in considering their performance, it would seem that a highly manoeuvrable R/C tailless helicopter, powered by ramjets mounted at the tips of the rotor blades, seems likely. Note the recovery parachute at the base, the I/R sensor in the nosecone and the bleed holes just below it, from which fuel would burn to create the distinctive visual effect.

In this accurate rendering, one can see the main drawback of the Omega – *it wasn't a disc*. Instead of playing a part in the TG's programme, its purpose had been to evaluate German lessons regarding Coanda; from the engine vents at the side of the fuselage/wing, this does seem to be the case. With work completed, its 'inefficient' design was forgotten, but some elements were later used in the AvroCar.

AVRO Omega

Project Y – Silver Bug

Revealed only in 1995, the already forty-year-old Silver Bug project represented a level of technology one notch below that of the TG's Alpha discs and was planned as the ultimate 'red herring'; to be unveiled should investigations get too close to the TG. For a decoy, its performance was astounding, combining a top speed (thought to be in excess of Mach 3.5) with some of the agility of the Alphas.

Contemporary Alpha Disc

Strip away thoughts of aliens behind the discs and this is what a contemporary TG Alpha might look like, with a typical unmarked Huey helicopter alongside for scale. Capable of a wide variety of roles including personnel insertion/retrieval, this probably represents the smallest size of manned disc now being manufactured. Note the tread guides for the pilot(s) running up the side of the disc's fuselage, high gain aerial and various warning lights around the perimeter.

spinning and taken over from the RATO when it expired. The small RATO unit might then have been released, to drift earthwards by parachute for recovery later, as existing full-sized models already did. The Foo Fighter, meanwhile, would have begun homing in on its selected target, thanks to the infrared system locking on to the heat signature of the target aircraft.

Another option would suggest that the device was fitted with its own on-board petrol engine or gas turbine, which would have spun the rotors while on the ground to a sufficient speed to get the ramjets working. They would then have taken over the RATO's job of getting the craft airborne. Another alternative to this is that the actual launching station incorporated a motor and drive shaft, which in turn would start spinning the device's rotors – once they were up to speed, the ramjets would fire and lift it clear. Or maybe the answer lay in a combination of all three – we simply don't know.

No matter what propelled the Foo Fighter skywards, it's a good bet that, in operation, the craft acted autonomously. A controller at the ground station might have been able to monitor the fuel status and a basic telemetry from the infrared transmitter, but would have been unable to interfere in any way with the operation. For a start, while a televisual guidance system had already been developed for experimental versions of Henschel's Hs 293 air–ground missile, its picture quality was terrible and reception unreliable. Likewise radar: no system then known was capable of being miniaturised to fit inside something so small – especially if the infrared system had to be housed too – so an operator would be powerless to respond once a target aircraft started evasive manoeuvres. As fuel levels dropped to a critical level, the Foo Fighter would back off from its quarry in preparation for its return home (assuming it had not been shot at). The margin remaining was intended to return it as close to the ground station as possible; hopefully in one piece, thanks to a parachute packed in the base (above the RATO pack, if fitted), which would open out freely and in the process cut the supply of whatever fuel remained. All this would make the job of recovery that much easier; the operator perhaps locating the device with triangulation on a repeating radio signal.

Much has been written of the Foo Fighters since the war, and conclusions drawn have usually varied between the intervention of benevolent alien spaceships that were observing the conflict, through to simple atmospheric effects such as ball lightning and so on. Other suggestions over the years include Allied pilots being confused by a 'mist' of ignited fuel from the engines of their own aircraft, through to electromagnetic effects as a result of interactions with the radar and radio sets on board the aircraft, causing strange atmospheric anomalies. All these 'explanations' fall down on closer inspection, however, for one reason or another, and the only one that seems to emerge somewhat unscathed is that presented here. After all, there was certainly no technical precedent to overcome in design or construction, and the pressing need for such a weapon, driven by a group such as the SS, would have sidestepped any minor obstacles. In short, this author for one believes the Foo Fighter to be a wholly credible and feasible weapons system, the prototypes of which were certainly brought into testing in November 1944, but the project was never put into production or used in anger, due both to the changing course of the war and the role of the SS.

The development programme could therefore have been in two distinct phases. Firstly, as an unarmed prototype, it was seen merely as a psychological weapon intended to unnerve the Allied pilots and lead them and their superiors into thinking that even more exotic reprisals could be expected from their foe. Secondly, the Germans doubtless intended to send up waves of Foo Fighters, once perfected, night after night, day after day. Underground installations such as Nordhausen and Kahla would make these relatively cheap and expendable 'aerial mines' in huge numbers, and their combined effect would have been to prevent any Allied incursion over German skies – the air superiority so desperately sought. This was something they would have been singularly effective at doing, as it would seem there was no defence against them – the edge Hitler was looking for and so lacking in the V-4 radiation bomb. The Allies hadn't even begun to evaluate the Foo Fighters for countermeasures, so Hitler might very well have bought his country time enough to develop the other main bricks in the Reich's defence wall – the jet fighters and missiles. But against the Haunebu and the Foo Fighter, even the jet fighters were antiques, and this is where Kammler began to make his own play, probably with Himmler's consent. Each project had a bearing on the defence of the Reich, but only these two – the Haunebu and the Foo Fighter – stood a chance of being developed into true war-winning machines; devices that would give Germany that vital edge and be economically feasible as much as strategically. But time was running out for both projects; Kammler, with his unique knowledge, would have known that.

Though the Haunebu Mark V reportedly flew in February 1945, the project was quickly disbanded and crated up for pastures new. The Foo Fighter appears less and less in reports after March 1945, so could it be that this, too, was a project dismantled by Kammler? Certainly by then he and his cohorts would have been satisfied with its capabilities and would have attempted to put it into mass production, if it were not for pressing problems else-where. The Russian army was massing to the east and, when its momentum shifted up a gear, would prove virtually irresistible. Likewise in the west, the Allies had found a new urgency after the close shave they had suffered in the Ardennes offensive, in the autumn of 1944. The resultant Battle of the Bulge, was Hitler's attempt at winning Germany a little more time and breathing space, but in the end delayed the onward advance from the west by only a month or so – still not long enough for Wunder Waffen to make full production and displace established projects such as the V-2. All the while, Germany's industrial base was being blasted and was less and less capable of saving the country.

The war was finished, and with it went any chance of either of these amazing weapons entering service in the colours of the Third Reich. But there's evidence to suggest they were destined to see service elsewhere.

chapter six

'To whom you tell your secrets, to him you resign your liberty.'
Spanish proverb.

With the end of the war, Germany experienced the inevitable power vacuum. As the British and American armies advanced from the west and the Russians from the east, the country was held in a vice-like grip. The Allies scrutinised its interim government and war-weary population for signs of a Nazi resurgence and dissected its industry for signs of the fabled Wunder Waffen.

If remnants of both the Foo Fighter and Haunebu programmes had already been spirited away to Base 211, then what else might have been left behind for the scientists of the victorious countries to pick over? History is familiar with the many projects already mentioned, such as the jet fighters and missiles, and there was certainly a great deal of such material on hand; both blueprints and actual machines were to be studied for years afterwards. But these were small beer compared with the Haunebu craft and the Foo Fighters. It's not known if Soviet pilots had reported seeing the Foos, so we can't say whether the Russian secret service (the

NKVD) had a mission to unravel the mystery, but there's certainly every chance that Britain's MI6 (hereafter referred to as the SIS – Secret Intelligence Service) and America's OSS (Office of Strategic Services, the CIA not yet having been formed) would have been more than interested. After all, while the phenomenon might have been dismissible in public, behind closed doors there would have been much consternation at what this unknown apparition might represent. If it really was a new type of aerial technology, the officials had only to look at the way in which it ran rings around their all-too-conventional aircraft to know this was something that couldn't be ignored.

But if examples of these craft were themselves no longer around, the next best thing would have been the technicians and designers who built them and the pilots and ground crew who repaired and flew them. In short, all the people who had been left behind when the last U-boat sailed for Antarctica. There was no chance of the Allies, on all sides, letting these and the many thousands of other scientists involved in other areas slip through their fingers. With little sign of Germany being forced to pay war reparations, as in 1918, governments viewed the potential economic dividend in scooping up all this advanced engineering and technology as their best chance of obtaining some measure of compensation on the part of the vanquished.

But the SIS hadn't always been so willing to look at scientists as an intelligence and economic resource. This was famously demonstrated in the case of *The Norway Report*, in which various German scientific advances were highlighted: for example, glider prototypes of the Me 163 Komet then being tested at Peenemünde, two new torpedo designs, a new radar system and a new proximity fuse for anti-aircraft shells. The report was sent to the SIS in the months before the war broke out by an anonymous Norwegian benefactor, concerned at the leaps in German technological achievements. But the SIS haughtily dismissed it out of hand, with the cavalier attitude of 'Well, if we can't make it, neither can they'. This blinkered attitude was to be completely reversed in the years of struggle ahead, of course, as British scientists perfected ever more sophisticated, if not vital, innovations; especially when America entered the fray in 1941. Even from the earliest days of the lend-lease programme, British scientists and industrialists visiting America were able to witness at first hand the benefits of true mass-production techniques and were able to similarly re-equip their factories as a result. Progress was slow, but as better aircraft, ships and tanks began appearing, the SIS could see the growing importance of economic intelligence. With the end of the war in sight by 1944, this new focus was beginning to show itself.

But there was another simple yet urgent reason why the Allies would want to pick up German innovations and scientists. Allied submarines and tanks might have been improving throughout the war, but compared with the best German equipment they still lagged far behind. German type-XXI U-boats, with their innovatory Snorchel engine breathing system, could cover many hundreds if not thousands of kilometres submerged, making them true *submarines* as opposed to submersibles. German tanks had better armour and harder-hitting guns that fired ammunition superior to the vast majority of Allied types. The Allies might have had a lead in the development of the atom bomb, but only because the Germans had chosen not to pursue their own simplified, though no less terrifying version – the V-4 r-bomb. Instead, in the tradition of the Krupp rail gun, they had opted to put their efforts into more exotic weaponry – rocketry and flying bombs. Although such weapons had mixed success, until the very day of their first use, Allied scientists were convincing themselves and everyone else that such advances were not possible. A more pragmatic Churchill was scared enough of the *potential* in these new weapons that he ordered Peenemünde be flattened in 1943, but it was already too late to stop the projects, as we've seen; the first operational flight of the V-1 was less than a year away. It was the strategic lead promised in such high technology, as it was perceived to be, that was shaping the post-war initiative of the SIS, OSS et al – and which was to spark off a mad scramble for technological military ascendancy that would continue to the present day.

Governments now realised that, in the post-war world, those countries that had marched together in a united cause would find themselves once again economic rivals. The military ties would remain, but in the demilitarisation and reshaping of industry that was to follow, it was going to be every man or country for itself. The SIS – along with the intelligence agencies of the other victors – would have to fight new economic battles if *reparation* was to be won. Unfortunately, at first Britain's efforts at capturing such intelligence appeared almost farcical. Amazingly, the RAF arrogantly decided there was little of interest to be gained from examining the Luftwaffe's facilities and failed to nominate personnel to go to Germany and search, which left the Royal Navy and the army to rely on their own assault teams for the job, known as T-Sections. After reports of unruly behaviour on the part of a Royal Marine T-Section (which earned it the nickname 'the Bodily Assault Team'), the Admiralty, together with the Chiefs of Staff in Whitehall, ordered them to work alongside more organised and disciplined American units, such as the ALSOS team, then involved in tracking down the secrets of Germany's atomic projects. But this embarrassing episode merely highlighted how amateurish the British effort had been all along, and by how much the initiative and momentum had been lost through the undisciplined and boorish behaviour of those on the ground. By contrast, the Americans had put together a long shopping list of technology and scientists – and was not afraid of putting the necessary resources and organisation in place to achieve these goals. On the face of it, the SIS had failed, once again, to predict accurately Britain's post-war needs – or so the damning official records would have us believe.

Consider these two anecdotes as apparent evidence of this failure. When the Soviets invaded the SS-controlled V-2 test site at Blitzna, Churchill cabled Stalin to ask if it might be possible for a joint Anglo-American team to visit the site and see the missiles for themselves. Stalin agreed, but, after a journey made deliberately tortuous by the Russians, the team was told on arrival that the Germans still held the site – whereas in reality the Russians had held it for the past fortnight and were busy removing the missiles through the back door. By the time the team gained access, what remained was of minor importance or interest but, as a gesture of goodwill none the less, their hosts filled a few crates with 'V-2 components' to examine back in Britain. When opened, these revealed little other than spare parts for aero engines – which didn't go down too well, as one might imagine.

Another gem perhaps reveals more of the French attitude to this post-war spirit of looking after one's own interests. Through necessity, the Germans had invented an artificial substitute for rubber, called Buna which, throughout the war, was made in a French factory. When British investigators reached the plant, keen to learn the production secrets behind Buna, they were told by the management that nothing could be divulged on account of the non-disclosure agreements they had signed with departing German personnel! In short, the secrets of this important material were intended to remain with the German scientists and the French manufacturer. History does not recall whether or not Britain ever learned Buna's mysteries, but these two incidents shed light on what was going wrong with Britain's policy at this time. The country was being too 'polite'; too willing to play by the rules of warfare and international diplomacy, while other countries were pouring resources and manpower into securing their own reparations from the vanquished.

Alongside ALSOS, American efforts had matured under pro-active (some might say risk-taking) leadership. With the resources at America's disposal, herculean efforts were being undertaken in order to secure the country's likely post-war economic and strategic superiority. The new enemy was now perceived to be Russia and, as the only other acknowledged world superpower, it was essential to America that no stone was left unturned in its quest for the best scientists and their work.

Even before the war in Europe had ended, the Americans had a daily train running to the Channel ports (the 'Toot Sweet Express'), on which was carried as much booty as could be mustered: tanks, aircraft, V-1s and V-2s . . . The list was endless, yet hardly any of the material was destined for Britain, as once the train arrived at the coast, its cargo was loaded straight into US aircraft carriers and freighters bound for home. It wasn't only familiar material which was being crated up, as the OSS were finding a whole host of exotic projects, which were practically unknown even to the British and others. For instance, Professor Lippisch, the designer of the Me 163, had been working on a new delta-winged ramjet-powered fighter project which, thanks to Germany's continuing oil shortage, was ultimately intended to run on coal granules. A full-sized, though half-finished, glider proto-type was captured at the war's end, and the Americans not only persuaded its designers and engineers to complete their work, but then proceeded to crate up the entire glider and haul it slowly back to the Channel, and a waiting aircraft carrier, on the back of a tank transporter. An immense security effort was put in place to explain this strange-looking wooden packing crate as it travelled through the French countryside, yet the team reached their objective and the DM-1, as it was known, flew for the first time in the USA. American aircraft carriers and freighters were shuttling back and forth across the Atlantic with important material like this for weeks, if not months, before Britain got a look in.

After America's first tentative foray into acquiring military and economic intelligence, it quickly came to be seen as the most desirable side to whom the German scientists from all disciplines could surrender. With its apparently unlimited resources, America must have seemed to Germans wishing to continue their work to be the goose that lays the golden egg. It might appear odd that such figures would want to continue working, but in the main these were civilians, whose work had dominated the past five years or more of their lives. Their projects had become almost vocational, so when it looked unlikely that a defeated Germany could offer them continued employment, approaching one of the victorious powers with that aim would seem an obvious move. America remained the favoured choice, and hundreds took that option. Perhaps the most famous has to be Wernher von Braun, who surrendered to the Americans, along with most of his team after they had been relocated by the SS to the small Alpine town of Oberammergau, a place famous for its once-a-decade Passion Play.

This was quite a prize, and the V-2 rockets which the Americans also 'found' at Nordhausen were seen as the best chance America would get to steal a march on Russia. With such large numbers of scientists joining them, the Americans had to organise something fast in order to accommodate them, so the OSS devised Operation Overcast; a large clandestine administrative effort geared to processing the applications for resettlement, based on the value of the work on offer.

When a breach of security led to this being compromised, a replacement was set up, named Operation Paperclip, after the paperclips attached to each man's file, which denoted whether or not he would be sailing to the USA. Werner Osenberg, one-time commander of the Gestapo's scientific section and now in the employ of Allen Dulles, head of the OSS, drew up an initial list of over six hundred men who would make the trip; some had been attached to von Braun's rocket programme, which now looked set to continue. Others, from various 'medical research facilities', would resume some of their interrupted concentration-camp experiments. At a few US army camps, this involved psycho-chemical experiments conducted on unwitting GIs, into drug-induced states for extending military operations. The pharmaceutical cocktails administered were intended to suppress the need for sleep, as well as emotions such as fear and fright – all useful in prolonging the effectiveness of soldiers out in the field (experiments in exactly this area are still being undertaken today in the British and American armies). Security for these six hundred 'Paperclip Boys' was noticeably relaxed, with the local population and press suitably reassured that the toughest screening and interrogation had weeded out all the true Nazis. However, this wasn't strictly true.

Rudolf Hermann, an expert in aerodynamics who had conceived of building an orbiting Nazi weapons platform in space, was stationed at Wright Field air-force base and gained a certain notoriety after insisting that he wear a Nazi-style brown shirt and give daily speeches at roll call, on the vital importance of staying loyal to Hitler. Von Braun's brother – apparently in America on no stronger pretext than *that* – was caught trying to sell an ingot of platinum to an El Paso jeweller . . . On his apprehension by the authorities, he was unable to explain how he'd acquired it, but with no reason to rock the boat the case was dropped – as on many other occasions when the motives of certain Germans appeared less than honest.

De-Nazification proceedings were continuing apace, nonetheless, as part of the Germans' resettlement packages, and those who stayed on eventually won American citizenship. As for Operation Paperclip, it was eventually wound down in 1973 – the Germans had helped put a man on the moon, but with the Apollo project now winding down, America no longer had any need for its first generation of imported rocket pioneers. Incidentally, Dr Miethe himself was certainly brought to America as part of Paperclip – a fact confirmed in a TV interview by Alexander Flax, former Assistant Secretary of the USAF. But this author does not believe he went to the USA with the promise of building new discs, but as a result of trading on his past experience and friendship with von Braun. In 1945–6, America was concentrating solely on building up its newly acquired rocket technology and didn't want to dilute its focus with such frivolities as flying discs.

Yet while British observers on the ground could see what was going on, nobody seemed ready to take responsibility and grab some of these ever-dwindling resources for themselves. When W. S. Farren, director of the Farnborough Aircraft Research Establishment, eventually arrived in France in July 1945, it was only after enduring a month's worth of bureaucratic red tape. Farren and his team went to a Messerschmitt plant, only to find it swarming with American soldiers and technicians; a sight repeated in practically every location visited. In his report, he wrote: 'The British representation at these targets appears unsystematic, hurried or in many cases non-existent.'

Other observers ruefully echoed this sentiment, but still things didn't change. Various excuses were offered, such as insufficient manpower, but this is lamentable and pathetic when one considers that Britain, together with her Commonwealth partners, had several hundred thousand troops on the Continent in a position to help. But this stubborn and pig-headed message of 'Well, so what? We've won the war' was a refrain echoed in British industry, whenever concerned onlookers challenged it to send representatives to Germany. Rolls-Royce had been making just over 100 jet engines a month up to the end of the war, yet throughout Germany the comparable figure had long been over 2,000 a month. This production expertise was there for the taking but, as happened time and again, timid and blinkered British management and government policy combined to let the country down. Britain may have won the war, but it was in imminent danger of losing the peace.

But Britain wasn't alone in adopting a muddled approach to achieving reparation. Russia's intelligence service, too, had a negligible presence, and this lack of trained scientific professionals in the front line to evaluate the booty led to countless treasures being simply blown up or 'lost', due to ignorance on the part of the troops. But things were to turn around dramatically under Operation Osvakim. The subsequent humiliation of Allied observers at Blitzna was the first indication that the Russians were taking things more seriously. Their momentum reached a peak in 1946, when over three thousand technicians and their families were moved deep into Russia; divided into two groups, they were to work on a series of advanced aircraft projects. The first group continued its previous development of the DFS 346: a rocket-plane project aimed at breaking the sound barrier; rumours that they succeeded before Chuck Yeager's famous flight in 1947 still persist today. The second group was to continue developing the Junkers Ju 287 forward-swept-wing jet bomber. This revolutionary design was far ahead of its time, but its aerodynamic shortcomings eventually led to its receiving more conventional wings – though by that time its momentum had been lost and it never entered production. In addition to these two complete projects, the Russians found numerous jet engines and machine tools, V-2 rockets and a few other complete aircraft designs. As well as Blitzna, they also 'inherited' Nordhausen from the Americans – but only after von Braun had helped his new masters to 'steal' a hundred V-2 missiles, which later surfaced in Arizona.

With one exception, it seems unlikely that the Russians would have been the recipients of any part of either the disc of Foo Fighter projects. Although the Russians had been despised publicly for four years, most German civilians accepted the realities of the situation on the ground and just got on with their lives; hence the cooperation with the aircraft projects. Fervent Nazis, though, such as the men of the SS, would never have elected to help the Russians, given the venomous feelings towards Russia generated in them since before the war years. The Nazi propaganda machine had long portrayed the Russians as nothing but subhuman Slavs, although this mood took popular hold only after Hitler had launched his invasion of Russia, Operation Barbarossa. The trade between the countries until then had been too valuable to be spoiled through a dip in relations: even though evidence has since emerged that if Hitler hadn't launched an attack first, Stalin would soon have countered, taking advantage of the perceived weakness of the Wehrmacht in already fighting a war on two fronts. With organisations such as Odessa and the Spider, set up by ex-SS men to look after the interests both of comrades and the now-defunct Reich, there is every chance that not everything was being passed on to the Russian 'enemy' as willingly as perhaps it was to America, France and Great Britain, the Foo Fighter and Disc projects being the most obvious examples (although France seems never to have been involved with the discs). The 'exception' mentioned earlier was the capture by the Russians of Klaus Habermohl.

We're in the dark as to exactly what the Russians knew of his past work, but it would be a good bet to assume that, in exchange for favourable conditions under the new regime, he might have begun trading secrets and knowledge. But with neither blueprints of the discs to hand, nor his familiar engineering team, progress towards reconstructing a disc would have been painfully slow, and far more likely is that he applied his talents to developing conventional jet engines. Along with Miethe over in America, as well as other ex-team members, he would also have been acutely aware of Odessa's long reach in protecting such secrets – and the discs etc. were of course still worthy of continued secrecy.

While Britain wasn't as proficient at acquiring secrets as America, at least it wasn't as bad as the Soviets. In spite of its past bungling and ineptitude, Britain *did* succeed in enticing a few key engineers to cross the Channel, one of whom was Professor Walter, designer of a revolutionary diesel-electric U-boat and the rocket system in the Me 163 Komet. He and members of his U-boat team were housed by the Admiralty in Barrow-in-Furness, with the intention of lending their combined expertise to building a new generation of British submarines. Even here, things didn't go well. Their sojourn was cut short when local residents, whose homes were forever cold due to coal rationing, complained to the authorities after seeing smoke billowing from the chimneys of the large house in which they were staying (they were eventually repatriated). Not that such local animosity wasn't the only problem faced by guest workers. Firstly, Britain's high rates of income tax were levied on their salaries, making these free civilians question why they should be working in Britain at all. Secondly, they were issued with only short-term contracts – hardly an inducement to leave Germany in the first place. It seems a typical British reaction, to want to look a gift horse in the mouth.

The RAF, in time, also realised to its cost how much initiative and time its stuffy arrogance had lost them and sought to rectify matters with Operation Surgeon. This was intended to cut out and remove what remained of the Luftwaffe's research establishment, centred on Volkenrode, and move it to Farnborough. But this was too little, too late, and although some scientists and engineers made the move, they were still up against the twin issues of local hostility and oppressive taxation. This was all music to the ears of Britain's domestic intelligence agency, MI5, who had been vocal in their opposition to the idea of German nationals living and working in the UK, fearing some sort of build-up of fifth columnists and agitators.

But to paint the intelligence efforts of SIS, MI5 and the government of the day in such an unflattering light is perhaps unfair. *Perhaps* the very reason why Britain appeared uninterested in the V-1, V-2 and jet fighter programmes is because it had simply (and somewhat miraculously) acquired something of far greater value, *something that would make everything else pale into insignificance* ... knowledge of the discs. Not through one of the disc scientists actually surrendering to the British, but more likely an ex-project technician looking to cut a deal for his freedom, in trading blueprints of either the discs or Foo Fighters, or both. When Kammlerstab officers were preparing for their exodus, it's quite possible that duplicate copies of these plans might have been spirited away by just such an opportunistic staff member. Since no working models had been built of the various discs, one can only conclude that Britain received the data as blueprints, perhaps on microfilm. Whatever was received, after being examined, I have no doubt that its significance was realised at the highest level and that, from that moment on, certain wheels were set in motion.

Luckily for Britain, while MI5 was and remains concerned with matters closer to home, the SIS has always enjoyed a somewhat wider, geopolitical remit, in the pursuit of which it has built close ties with the military. Thus we see a likely situation in which the public is told of limited dealings with German nationals, so as not to enrage opinion (the chimney episode being a perfect reason for this), while the *real* business went on unabated elsewhere, within military circles. Sure, the SIS had mishandled the collection of intelligence in the immediate post-war weeks and months, perhaps to the merriment of MI5, but once we assume it was gifted the blueprints, things would certainly have changed.

They would have had to, for this was something the importance of which cannot be overstated – a completely unknown aerospace technology with the promise to revolutionise air and space travel for ever. Something this big would have transcended the personalities involved. Funding and authorisation sufficient to develop something of such real worth would have materialised from somewhere, while MI5 was left handling the scrapings of the German scientific war machine at home; something it clearly had no desire to do wholeheartedly. I must once again stress that there is little concrete evidence in the public domain to support this theory, only circumstantial events. But it would certainly be an interesting exercise were we ever to unearth a little of the true story, to shed a chink of light on to whatever was exactly going on.

At the time, Britain could still boast something of its past glories and empire, with India and Pakistan still just about under its control, along with the Antipodes and dominions in Africa such as Rhodesia. There was also Canada, which, with its vast and largely uninhabited forests, prairies and mountain ranges, was to prove an ideal location for the projects. Britain, being a relatively crowded island, wasn't a suitable location for something like this, but

Canada, on the other hand, was near perfect.

This wasn't the first classified dealings with the Canadian authorities either, as in 1943 a top-secret Anglo-Canadian uranium reprocessing centre was opened at Chalk River, near Petawawa, Ontario. Along with another plant at Clinton, British Columbia, and a uranium mine beside the Great Bear Lake, in the Mackenzie district of the North-West Territories, this gave both Britain and Canada strategic resources to match, if not exceed, those of the USA and laid the foundations for cooperation on a much greater scale later on. But such close ties weren't to be without complications. Throughout the war, it appears that the British government had been anxious to avoid diplomatic tensions with America on other certain issues, perhaps to protect lend-lease.

To the north-west of Canada sits the American state of Alaska, which, after the USA had recognised its strategic suitability, now became a focus for military development, providing a buffer against any future Soviet operations across the Bering Strait. In order to move men and material in sufficient numbers there in the event of war, America applied to build a road running through western Canada, linking the state to mainland America, called the Alaska Highway. At intervals along the road (itself opened in 1942) were to be a series of new military and civilian airfields, from Edmonton to Fairbanks, the development of an oilfield at Norman Wells and the laying of a pipeline to convey this oil to Whitehorse. American authorities were responsible for the road and pipeline, with the Canadians responsible for the oil wells and airfields.

At first, the project was welcomed. It would open up western Canada to greater development, perhaps a generation earlier than otherwise, and if America followed up on its pledge to foot half the total bill, all to the good. The British High Commission in Ottawa and London were initially in favour. But by mid-1943 things were moving ahead in areas unforeseen by the British government, and our man in Ottawa, Malcolm MacDonald, was asked to investigate. His report made for difficult reading. In short, the

Canadians were putting so many resources into the war effort that they were finding difficulty in meeting their obligations on the project. The original plan called for Canadian ownership of all the joint undertakings once finished, but time and again this contractual obligation was ignored as construction decisions were taken solely by the Americans. For example, after rethinking the siting of some of the airfields, the Americans simply began building their own airfields without any consultation with the Canadians, on whose land they were, of course, guests. As a result, another 3,220 kilometres of new spur roads were needed to reach these new locations, in addition to the main (2,575-kilometre-long) highway.

These decisions were taken on purely strategic grounds, with little thought as to the post-war needs of the Canadian people, and all this riled Britain and the Canadian administration. But there was more, for other pipelines were being laid, in addition to the one already agreed. The site of Norman Wells was then showing great promise as an oilfield, and it appeared obvious to concerned observers on the ground that these new American pipelines were simply an elaborate preparation for an influx of (American) oil firms, once the war was over. Perhaps more worrying was the fact that the Americans were studiously photographing the territory. To what end, no one could say at the time but, looking back with hindsight, this might have been in preparation for a possible Soviet overland assault, as much as using the construction effort, as a convenient excuse to spy on its largest neighbour. Local people were also told by the Americans that they saw themselves as 'an army of occupation', which didn't go down at all well. Canada had appointed General Foster in May 1943 to handle relations with the Americans on the project, but it was thought by some that he handled the situation with kid gloves, rather than an iron will, and as a result the Americans were taking advantage.

Simply, the Anglo-Canadians were being cut out of their own party: and it wasn't the first time. When one learns that American aid early in the war was conditional on Britain handing over details of its radar systems, among other advances, as well as giving the US unlimited use of many military bases, the depth of British frustration becomes apparent. Being unable to share in the post-war fruits of the A-bomb project was the final straw. The apparent reason for America's reluctance to share the weapon was that Britain had elected a new Labour administration, which was seen – or appeared to be at least – making overtures towards the USSR. Therefore, given that the USSR was the new enemy, they were reluctant to hand over so vital a technology. But the atom bomb might never have been *possible* without the contribution of British scientists and physicists to its development, and this simple fact would have annoyed the authorities most. One can also suppose that there was little mutual respect between the OSS and SIS, each increasingly mistrustful of the other, following the debacle over the T-Sections. To the Americans, the SIS wasn't exactly seen as watertight and, worse, was thought capable of passing untold secrets abroad. They might have been right, when one considers the later activities of Kim Philby, among others – though the US had problems of its own, to be sure. But I don't believe that something of the nature of the discs would have found its way to Moscow or Washington; for a start, the compartmented nature of the project would have restricted access to the full picture to only one or two implicitly trustworthy figures, and it was in the interests of both London and Ottawa that this status quo remain.

Such complications over the highway would have presented the British and Canadian authorities with a few sensitive obstacles to negotiate, once the decision was taken to develop new discs from the prized blueprints and position the pieces in this hugely important game of chess for their advantage. The SIS knew, as much as anyone else in this game, about the underlying tensions between America and Canada/Britain, but it was decided to proceed because, in addition to the atomic projects at Chalk River etc., the war had seen previous joint developments in aeronautic engineering between Britain and Canada begin to succeed. In

December 1944, a summit in London of the Canadian and British authorities agreed that it would be in their shared interests to conduct joint research into aeronautical matters. What they agreed to discuss remains classified, but the following extract from the minutes of the summit make interesting reading:

> It was concluded that for experimental work in Canada in the immediate future, the emphasis would be placed on the kind that is done in-flight. It was not considered advisable at this stage to discuss the programmes of work in detail, but it might be relevant to mention that Canada has *large areas and comparatively uninhabited country* where experiments on radio navigation, on *remotely controlled high-speed aircraft* and on the various forms of guided missiles can be done much more safely than in the UK [author's italics].

The minutes also go on to record that the best approach for such an undertaking would be through the creation of a 'Special Experimental Establishment', with its own labs, workshops and airfield, presumably far from prying eyes. Thus, a new body was established – the Aeronautical Research Council (ARC) – which would bring in Australian designers and scientists too. Its remit was simple: to look at conventional aircraft and their problems at a security level below 'confidential' – in other words, at a publicly accountable civilian level. For more highly classified military matters, this author believes that another body was either already in place or now proposed, to coordinate such material. This latter body would have had no need to call in the German ex-disc team members for their expertise. Firstly, to do so would have raised suspicion as to *why*; secondly, the engineers recruited to this project were skilled enough to interpret the blueprints without further assistance. At least initially.

In a Commonwealth memo of August 1945, it was noted that, when it came to defence matters, while Canada had no existing research and development budget to speak of, if the UK could pay its own way, then it was happy to help out on projects of joint importance. Long-range flight tests and cold-weather trials were then mentioned, together with a final note suggesting that this list might be added to 'after consideration of existing facilities'. One wonders if this consideration included an all-new facility being planned for Bedford, grandly named the National Aeronautical Establishment. Intended to lighten some of Farnborough's load, this new facility was built on a site hitherto occupied by the ancient village of Thurleigh (before it was demolished) and was apparently laid out along lines modelled on an Italian research and development site at Guidonia. With six supersonic wind tunnels as well as a whole host of other test cells and laboratories, Bedford seemed an ideal location, but why was its construction apparently delayed for a time during the early 1950s? In his book, Vesco seems to believe that it was because necessary technicians and resources were having to be recalled from Canada, and, to a degree, I would tend to concur.

Another 'existing facility' considered by Canadian engineers was the large air base at Arnprior, near Ottawa. Built in 1942, it was suggested by the ARC in 1944 as a suitable site for a 'Canadian Farnborough'. However, this site lay too close to the American border for comfort and, following the tension over the highway, a completely new site was chosen 'somewhere' in the southern wooded mountains of British Columbia, in the remote south-west. Even with the Alaska Highway and the city of Calgary, the area today remains a wild and largely uninhabited wilderness and fifty years ago would have made ideal cover for developing a secret base. Just as well the Americans had been photographing the area – their past diligence would now help them identify its location.

The preparations were made in secret, in conjunction with the then Canadian Department of Mines and the Technical Survey's mapping branch; together they would have been best placed to identify suitable sites. It appears that four were selected, in an area of over 1,945 square kilometres; within such a huge area, a base could be hidden with ease. The Alaskan Highway already had innumerable spur roads leading off it, courtesy of the Americans, but there would still have been scope to clear another track off one of these spurs in secret; perhaps guarding the entrance with foliage or fencing. In any case, this would then have led directly to the base, after a suitably long distance. After all, the authorities wouldn't have wanted to run the risk of having stray motorists witnessing strange aircraft overflying the road, so a concealed rough track of about thirty kilometres or so, which led into an adjacent, parallel and therefore hidden valley, would have been sufficient deterrence to ward off casual visitors – especially if guards patrolled its length.

In construction, the runway would have been laid with concrete mixed on site from aggregates brought in either by this road – at night – or perhaps by a secret railway track laid especially for the purpose, although the road sounds more plausible. The runway wouldn't have needed to be full size – perhaps only four hundred metres or so – as the disc craft to be built and tested here had at least STOL capabilities, if not VTOL. As to the buildings, I am in agreement with Vesco on what approach might have been taken. In looking at several German facilities, the civil engineers would have seen that an effective approach to disguise would have been to plan only single, maybe two-storey buildings, in a campus layout, within a dense evergreen forest to break up the outlines of the buildings, which would themselves be disguised. Taking the base under ground would have added another tier to the costs, which an impoverished Britain and equally poor Canada (compared with the USA) would have been unable to provide. The former option was the only viable one (after all, this wasn't a nuclear bunker), and within the low-rise format, hangars, workshops, offices and accommodation blocks could all be hidden from view – even from American spy planes 'en route to Russia'.

With the end of intensive military production, arms

manufacturers in 1945 had to seek new ways of reaping the peace dividend, and aircraft manufacturers were no exception. One such, (later named) Hawker Siddeley, could see an opportunity for developing prefabricated housing out of aluminium panels, using similar mass-production techniques which they'd hitherto used for making warplanes. The material they developed – Airoh – proved very successful and was used in tens of thousands of prefab homes across the UK to house the returning servicemen and their families as well as the many thousands who'd been bombed out of their homes. Other aero manufacturers, such as Bristol, started producing Airoh under licence and, before long, a new industry had evolved. The construction team in Canada, as well as the one in Australia looking to build the new weapons test range in Woomera, saw in this material a solution to their problems and, with the help of the SIS, arranged for ample supplies to be covertly shipped out to them.

For the base in British Columbia, it would have been an ideal material from which to make an insulated sandwich with foam as the filler, as protection against the savage winters experienced there. The long winters and enforced isolation would also have made other requirements necessary: space heaters for the build-ings, sufficient rations of all kinds in the likely event of being snowed in, uninterruptible services such as fuel oil, electricity, sewerage and freshwater and so on.

The peace dividend would have also provided the governments and the SIS with an opportunity to recruit staff for their new project. With orders for military aircraft set to fall off dramatically in 1946, many manufacturers were already laying off design staff in 1945, thus throwing a glut of designers and engineers on to the job market – an employer's dream. Together with the Americans running Operation Paperclip, this meant that the SIS could afford to be choosy in whom they selected to travel to Canada. Single men with few family commitments or ties would have been ideal, though, once stationed there, sufficient entertainment would have had to be offered to keep them focused. The site would have been staffed primarily by civilians and all sides would hopefully have recognised that only with a properly motivated workforce could results be expected, so the surroundings would need to be comfortable, with good leisure facilities, but no schools. This wouldn't have been a place for families, so perhaps married personnel were either not employed here, or were housed in married quarters in the nearest town. But given that no one is saying where such a base actually was – or is – I can't even suggest the name of a likely town.

As far as the logistics of building such a base go, the task would have been fairly straightforward, as long as security wasn't compromised – and during all my research I've not heard a thing about it.

Britain was facing a brave new future in post-war Europe. It knew that its industries were going to suffer an inevitable decline as war production ran down, so it slowly began to look for a peace dividend; stumbling in its first misguided forays for reparations. America settled for rocket scientists and captured V-2 technology, among other headline-grabbing projects. France started to rebuild its industrial base, renewing ties with Germany on a more cordial footing. Germany itself needed to lick its wounds and get used to democracy again. Britain was being steadily sidelined. Its amateurish efforts at acquiring scientists were undermined by a lack of top-level support, and efforts at getting the Americans to share their 'Paperclip Boys' were weak. It lacked a sufficiently large industrial base and strong economy to fall back on, as in other countries, and, worse, it now had a relationship with America in which it was to be denied the atom bomb, faced crippling lend-lease repayments and had to stay afloat financially as thousands of servicemen returned home to an uncertain future.

But it *had* embarked on a serious technical exchange and development programme with both Canada and Australia and was looking to face the future alone as part of the Commonwealth.

This, then, was the strategy. After the SIS's bungling T-Sections somehow acquired duplicate blueprints for both the Foo Fighter and Haunebu projects, the plan was to rely on ties with the colonies as alternatives to the two super-powers. Commonwealth countries were now working together to a common objective: namely, military freedom from a sulking, introverted America now embarking on a Cold War with Russia and increasingly unwilling to share its toys. That Canada now had umpteen American bases on its soil, together with various military agreements on joint exercises and so on, put that country in a similar position to Britain's, thus strengthening their unity of purpose. I suspect that both the Canadians and the British either knew or suspected that the other main powers were studying their technology but, as long as they believed they had the lead, little would stop them in their development of perhaps the most important air-transportation technology to appear since the Wright brothers first flew.

chapter seven

'A lie has no leg, but a rumour has wings.'
With apologies to Thomas Fuller MD, *Gnomologia*.

As we've seen in past chapters, the myth of Base 211 as the last Nazi stronghold is a hard one to suppress. In the sixty-odd years since the end of the Second World War, such stories have become something of the fabric from which all good conspiracy theories are woven. Tales of Adolf Hitler escaping in a U-boat, together with certain of his cronies, to Antarctica, there to be cloned and/or orchestrate the creation of the Fourth Reich, all make for a riveting read and are doubtless set to continue for years to come. But as with so much of the material in this book, the very existence of Base 211 has never been confirmed, which makes the task of chronicling its likely history all the more difficult.

While we're grappling with such enigmatic fantasies, it would perhaps be timely to define our understanding of this whole subject. Such stories *are* ridiculous to contemplate and to take seriously by any objective measure; especially when other fantastical elements are added. Cloning new 'Hitlers', through preserved samples of the Führer's blood and hair, in the manner of the dinosaurs in *Jurassic Park*, might *just* about be possible in the immediate years ahead, but in 1945? No chance. Other stories involve Hitler being cryogenically frozen, after succumbing to illness in the 1950s in South America, his body stored thereafter until he could be revived – but does his non-appearance mean that a cure for whatever killed him has not been found?

In discounting some of this more extreme material, we're left with a mixture of actual events, interwoven with what we might safely assume to be the real, 'secret history' that should prove more palatable to more wary and sceptical readers. First of all, though, I should confirm my earlier suggestion that Base 211 did indeed exist. In writing this book, my judgment could have gone either way, but in the end the weight of circumstantial evidence, as in the story of the discs themselves, presented me with no option but to go with it. As we shall see, Germany was more than capable of establishing a base in Antarctica. To help it achieve this, the courage of the U-boat service was vital.

During the war, the mainstay of the Kriegsmarine's U-boat fleet was the venerable Type VII boat, of which just under seven hundred were built. This versatile craft had a range of up to 16,095 kilometres when surfaced, with a normal patrol range of around 11,265 kilometres. In the early stages of the U-boat war, when boats were able to leave their ports in northern Germany and reach the Atlantic through the English Channel, the journey to their operating 'box', or zone, would be around 3,220 kilometres. Factor in a return trip and the submarines had between 4,830 and 9,670 kilometres in which to operate. However, with the Allies increasing their sonar sweeps of the English Channel, together with the extensive mining of British waters, U-boats soon had no choice but to take the long way round to their hunting grounds, via the tip of Scotland and down the west coast of Ireland. This enforced detour cut short the operational effectiveness of the boats, and something had to be done quickly if their advantage was to be held.

The first response was to move the patrol areas to more inviting Caribbean and South Atlantic waters, where, unmolested, both wolf packs and lone hunters could attack the unprotected and vulnerable Allied shipping operating in these waters. But this increase in the patrol distance placed new demands on the Type VII boats, which lacked the range for such work even when operations from French ports began. New, larger U-boats with longer ranges were on the drawing board but, until they appeared, a stopgap was found in the shape of the new Type XIV 'tanker U-boats', or the 'Milch Cows' as their German crews came to know them. Around six of these special, though essentially unarmed, U-boats were constructed, with the profile of their upper deck and conning tower simulating a regular small freighter at a distance, so as not to raise alarm on the part of Allied shipping. To start with, the ploy worked.

One Milch Cow could supply up to ten U-boats, not just with diesel oil from its maximum load of 432 tonnes, but with freshwater, spare parts, vegetables and meat from walk-in refrigerators and even bread from an on-board bakery. But such versatility was to prove a double-edged sword to GrössAdmiral Dönitz and U-boat command, because in extending the operating range of the Type VII boats by so much, there was less pressure to bring the newer designs into service. Before the arrival of the Milch Cows, if a return trip to the Caribbean took a Type VII U-boat two months, it would leave only a month for operational duties in any three-month tour. Dönitz had ordered that ten boats be operational in that area at any one time, so thirty boats were required to work on an overlapping rota if the area were to be covered as ordered. But once the Milch Cows entered service, having only one of them on station in the Caribbean, allowed ten boats to stay operational for up to a full *four* months, not one, thus extending the rota and reducing the number of U-boats required. As a stroke of strategic brilliance, it was hard to fault. This also ensured that U-boats could use any of the Milch Cows in the Atlantic as an outlying 'home base', en route to and from the Antarctic. If refuelling at Base 211 itself was possible, then this would have allowed the boats to make only one stop per leg of the Europe–211–Europe voyage. Remember, too, that if one Milch Cow could keep ten regular Type VII boats working, imagine what might be achieved if only one was assigned to, say, two or three U-boats exclusively. It would allow for more daring and audacious patrols to the South Atlantic, without even visiting Base 211.

Unfortunately, though, there was one problem that hindered the development of the Milch Cows. Built with a large cross-section that gave an unusually large displacement, they were slow and sluggish and, with no offensive weaponry other than anti-aircraft cannon in the conning tower (their torpedo tubes were replaced by fuel tanks), they were susceptible to air attack by those Allied patrol aircraft lucky enough to spot them. These two factors combined were to see all the Milch Cows lost by the end of 1944. But, by then, early examples of the larger, newer U-boats had begun to enter service, with ranges far in excess of the old Type VII. For example, the new type IXD2 could reach Japanese waters non-stop with its 58,000-kilometre range. With new boats as advanced as this, it would then have been quite possible to reach Base 211 unaided and unseen for the first time.

But the gradual war of attrition was taking its toll, and, as 1945 dawned on a battered U-boat service, its senior officers could reflect on the gradual slide in its fortunes. Its ranks had been gradually depleted of submariners with long-standing experience, as more and more boats were lost to advances in Allied detection equipment. More new boats than ever before were still being commissioned, but fewer were actually being launched, thanks to the bombing of shipyards, the ever-present supply problems and the recurring lack of fuel stocks – all of which were making adventurous forays to far-flung waters increasingly unfeasible. A group of boats had been operating in the Indian Ocean for a while, using Penang in Malaysia as a base, but with the tide in the war now against Germany, all had been recalled to defend the home country. Yet of the twelve boats recalled, only three made it to Europe; the others were either sunk or unable to leave for lack of fuel.

Against this background, while there may not have been the large numbers of U-boats operating in southern waters as some have suggested, there are records to confirm that operations were indeed carried out – and sufficient reason to suggest that *unofficial* operations – i.e. unrecorded and clandestine missions – probably went on as well, just as in any other navy before and since. Whether or not these involved shuttling back and forth to Base 211 we don't know for sure, but the facts suggest that German surface shipping and the odd U-boat *were* involved in unusual activities in the wartime South Atlantic – witness the *Pinguin* as proof of that. An unusual article appeared in the French newspaper *France Soir* in autumn 1946 (and reported in Mattern's and Friedrich's book *UFOs – Secret Nazi Weapon?*), suggesting that such operations were continuing until after the war had ended and perhaps linked to Base 211. It seems that an Icelandic whaling ship, the *Juliana*, had been confronted by a German U-boat in the waters around the Falkland Islands that September, the crew of which boarded the *Juliana* by dinghy in order to buy fresh food, which they paid for in US dollars.

But if the truth regarding Base 211 is something we may never know, then perhaps we should take a look at some of the most mysterious of all U-boat missions *actually* carried out in Atlantic waters, revolving around the U-530, U-234 and the U-977, for clues as to what might really have been going on.

Launched in November 1944, U-977 wasn't ready for its first sea trials under its captain, Heinz Schaeffer, until April 1945. According to Schaeffer's autobiography, before embarking he'd had to order a change of the sub's batteries and an upgrade to the armour plating on the outside of the conning tower, but a shortage of materials led to both requests being rejected. He was then ordered to Kiel, along with his scratch crew, to take on supplies for an as-yet unspecified voyage. With this done, he was ordered to sail for Norway, where he was to meet up with two other boats (one of which was a new Type XXI) and form a convoy out into the North Sea. On the way from Kiel, he put into a Danish port and took on even more stores, before reaching Christiansund South on 26 April. He didn't leave the port until the night of 2 May after receiving orders to 'cause trouble' in the English Solent and hearing that Dönitz was planning to relocate to Norway, the German navy's Berlin headquarters by then almost overrun. However, the main periscope had collapsed soon after leaving Christiansund, which meant that submerged attacks would be impossible. But they had to stay under water for fear of being spotted from the air, so took to running submerged during the day, the engines using the new 'snorchel'* system, and surfacing at night, once safely out of aircraft patrol range – though this wouldn't be for many weeks.

They had been submerged and out of contact for eight days, so the message received from U-boat command on 10 May ordering their surrender came as a shock. Schaeffer agreed to let sixteen of the men ashore (those with families) and make their way back to Germany, but fearing the capture of the boat and the end of his and the remaining crew's apparent plans to go to Argentina and start new lives for themselves, he opted to put them ashore on an isolated part of the Norwegian coastline, where the boat could stay undetected. After that, Schaeffer undertook a remarkable sixty-six-day submerged voyage around John O'Groats and

---

* A valved pipe that lay alongside the outer casing of the U-boat when not in use but, in use, rose vertically, much like a periscope. The U-boat captain would then maintain a steady depth, sufficient for the snorchel's tip to break water, allowing the diesel engines to run under water, taking in air from outside. Usually boats would rely on batteries for underwater running and use their diesels while surfaced, both for recharging their batteries and for propulsion, but snorchel allowed almost permanently submerged running.

Ireland before crossing the Bay of Biscay to Gibraltar, prior to heading west across the Atlantic. In his account, he tells of the hardships that he and his crew endured in that time – how they had accumulated so much fly-infested refuse that they had taken to firing it out of the torpedo tubes, while mould was covering surfaces throughout the boat and growing on their own skin for lack of ventilation. Occasionally, the diesels would blow back their exhaust fumes into the boat, too, coating everything and everyone in black dust. But once safe, they would surface at night and taste fresh air once again. They even stopped to bathe in the clear waters at one of the smaller of the Cape Verde isles and were accompanied by schools of dolphins.

Finally, Schaeffer heard over the radio that another U-boat (U-530), equally unwilling to surrender, had put into the River Plate in Argentina, whereupon the boat and her crew had been handed over to the USA – contrary to what Schaeffer and his men had believed would happen. After all, to that point Argentinian officials had been almost cordial towards German nationals. However, with his oil level running low, Schaeffer had no choice but to put in at an Argentinian port, and he entered Mar del Plata on 17 August 1945 after a three-month odyssey under the worst of all conditions.

Almost immediately, an intensive interrogation began, centring on what might have been Schaeffer's *real* reason for delaying his surrender. An American investigative team that had been questioning U-530's crew immediately refocused their efforts on U-977 and, according to Schaeffer's account, asked only three questions of him:

1. Where had U-977 been when the Brazilian steamer *Babia* had been sunk? (Schaeffer was suspected of attacking her after the ceasefire had been called.)
2. Why had it taken him so long to surrender?
3. Had U-977 been carrying anyone or anything of political importance during its voyage – Adolf Hitler or Martin Bormann, for example?

To these three points, Schaeffer repeatedly denied any involvement with the first, gave the same answer to the second as already outlined here, but for the third question he flatly *refused* to offer any insight. The Americans had been taking a similar line of enquiry with Commander Otto Wehrmutt, of U-530; frustrated by the combined silence of both commanders on this matter, they eventually extradited both men back to a secure camp in Washington DC after freeing the junior members of the crew. The line of questioning was undoubtedly prompted by the non-appearance in Germany of the bodies of the two most prominent Nazis – Hitler and Bormann – together with a growing distrust of the Russian line of enquiry into Hitler's alleged suicide. The OSS wanted answers to these and more nagging questions, and the two senior U-boat commanders appeared to be in a position to give them answers. That their responses were never made public is either because their indoctrination and loyalty worked only too well to create a smokescreen. Or perhaps, when eventually extracted by some *other* means, the truth was too devastating to acknowledge publicly.

What if, as has been suggested, Hitler, Bormann and Kammler, along with a few loyal retainers, escaped aboard one or more U-boats, leaving carefully planted evidence behind them to cover their tracks and make investigators chase shadows for ever more? In Hitler's case, there are certainly enough red herrings to cause onlookers to re-examine the events surrounding his suicide. These include the conflicting testimonies of some key members of his private staff; insufficient quantities of petrol with which to burn a corpse to the degree apparently witnessed; no actual formal and independent identification of the bodies before they were burned and so on. The more one looks into this area, the more questions and anomalies one finds, so perhaps such a convoluted cover-up as is suggested might not be so unbelievable.

So am I suggesting that such high-ranking figures successfully evaded capture, only to resettle in Neu Berlin? Yes and no. I certainly believe that an escape was orchestrated. What I think might have happened is that both U-530 and U-977 were sent to Base 211 on a final resupply mission; their high-ranking passengers, with the exception of Kammler, aboard one or both boats. Even at this late stage in the war, it would certainly have been possible for them to sail down to the South Atlantic and rendezvous with a surface tanker, before pushing on to Base 211. Once at the pack ice, they would most likely have met Kammler and his small party of engineers (who would have taken an earlier voyage to the base), before transferring over any other key figures and disc-related materiel they had carried. This would then leave only a cruise to Argentinian waters, where their secret passengers could be put ashore into the welcoming arms of fellow countrymen and sympathisers. Now fully unladen, the U-boat(s) could then have made for a local port, where it had been assumed a warmish welcome awaited them – and the means to effect either an escape route home or a new life in South America, where large German communities reside to this day. Either Odessa or the Spider would have been capable of organising such a disappearing act and offering support to both passengers and crews, so perhaps it's no coincidence that both U-boat captains ended up living in Argentina after their release. Since the war, historians have settled for the easiest option, namely that Hitler committed suicide in Berlin, yet what if this were simply untrue? To this author, the most unlikely of scenarios might yet turn out to be the most probable of all.

U-234, the other U-boat mentioned earlier, has an equally intriguing history. Originally built as a mine-laying U-boat, in September 1944 she entered dry dock after her first patrol for conversion into a 'cargo-carrying' U-boat, her mine shafts now used for storage. After a protracted spell in the dockyard, thanks to numerous Allied air raids, she eventually left her home port of Kiel on 25 March 1945 under Captain Johann Fehler. Bound for Tokyo, the sizable cargo included drugs and medicines, optical glass for weapons sights, Panzerfäust bazookas, and even a complete, though dismantled Me 262 jet fighter (copies of which the Japanese were hoping to build under licence). But of most interest to researchers long after the war were fifty-five lead cubes, stored in one of the forward mine tubes and each wrapped in brown paper. Over the years, speculation as to what might have been inside these cubes has been rife: some say components for laser weapons, flying discs or stolen art treasures. In fact, the truth is perhaps more sinister, as it casts doubt on the confident findings of the ALSOS mission, which stated that the German atomic programme was essentially stalled at a primitive stage. This conveniently ignored the V-4 bombs and the fact that the cubes aboard U-234 contained 550 kilogrammes of partially enriched uranium, the starting point from which one could extract pluto-nium – the precursor to a viable nuclear chain-reaction bomb. Two Japanese officers were accompanying this vitally important shipment – Captain Hideo Tomonaga and Imperial Air Force Colonel Genzo Shosi. Among the distinguished German pass-engers were Leutnant Erich Menzel of the Luftwaffe, an expert on the V-1, and Captain Gerhard Falk of the Naval Architecture Division, who was to help the Japanese make copies of the latest and advanced Type XXI U-boats. The mission didn't go well at first, after a collision in Scandinavian waters with U-1301, but after repairs to the conning tower Fehler received personal instructions from Dönitz himself to set sail on 16 April. The end of the war was just over a fortnight away.

With British waters successfully negotiated, the boat received a devastating communique on 6 May reporting Germany's surrender and Japan's reciprocal action in severing all diplomatic relations with its erstwhile Axis partner. Understandably, Fehler took that as an omen not to sail on for Tokyo, and instead he decided to sail back across the Atlantic and surrender to the Americans, a better option than returning to Kiel and meeting the Russians, who by now had captured the home port. Two days later, a further pair of messages were received, the first giving them the option of either continuing with their mission or surrendering to an Allied port, and the second banning the transmission of encrypted radio messages. By this time, Fehler had already settled on his safer course of action and ordered the two Japanese officers to stay in their wardroom, having first confiscated their ritual swords. The nearest port at that time was Halifax, Nova Scotia, but not wishing to attract the attention of the trigger-happy patrol aircraft known to be operating in the area, Fehler turned south for an American, not Canadian, port. During this latter phase of the voyage, little had been heard from the Japanese, and when their door was next opened they were found to have committed suicide with an overdose of sleeping tablets. No sooner had their bodies been cast over the side than the USS *Sutton*, which had been shadowing them, moved in with a boarding party to escort them to Portsmouth, New Hampshire.

On arrival at Portsmouth, the U-boat had to undergo a detailed inspection for booby traps before unloading could start, and the job proper didn't begin until July. The early discovery of the lead cubes caused immense concern, but with hindsight their contents could not have caused a chain reaction by themselves, being enriched to around only 0.7 per cent of uranium-235, compared with around 7 per cent required to sustain a reaction. Germany didn't possess as many cyclotron devices as America, which would have enriched the material still further, but that's to miss the point. It's this author's belief that this stock of uranium-235 came directly from the remnants of Germany's V-4 project, previously at Nordhausen.

Note that the point of the V-4 was not to create an atomic explosion, but merely to use conventional high explosives to spread radioactive material over a wide area and so inflict radiological damage on a civilian population. The material carried in U-234 would have been ideal for this purpose and would have given Japan the chance of hitting Allied troop concentrations and civilians with its own R-bombs thanks, ironically, to an already defeated Germany. Some observers have suggested that the Americans actually enriched the uranium themselves and used it in the warheads for the two atomic bombs dropped on Japan later that year, but their construction had already begun by this point and such suggestions are wide of the mark. However, I would imagine that the discovery of this deadly cargo would have sharpened the mind of President Truman and his Chiefs of Staff and *might* have underlined their decision to use their new weapon. Hundreds of thousands of American lives might be lost if a gradual invasion of the fortified Japanese home islands were undertaken, and if there was *any* chance that the Japanese might already have similar weapons to the R-bomb, then any measure should be used to nip matters in the bud. The A-bomb was thus dropped on Hiroshima on 6 August 1945; Nagasaki followed a few days later, with the implicit threat that Tokyo itself would be next.

From just these three U-boat histories, one can begin to build up a picture of the audacity and the willingness of U-boat crews to go the extra mile in fulfilling their duty. Their attrition rates were so high, with over sixty per cent of all crews dead or missing by the war's end, that a certain kind of fatalism pervaded the ranks. National heroes emerged from the service, with 'ace' commanders feted by the public, press and Nazi elite alike. With such motivated crews, anything might have been possible; long-distance trips to Antarctica and all. To his last days, Dönitz was proud of his cherished U-boat service; maybe with greater reason than he made out. For if there really *was* a base in Antarctica, the commander of the U-boat service would surely have known of it.

But despite their reckless heroism, and whatever schemes others such as the SS might have been planning, 1945 ended with the Allies victorious and work getting under way in several countries to unravel the spoils of war and their secrets. From von Braun's team preparing to test V-2 rockets in the heat of an American desert, to teams still in Germany working for Russia on new jet aircraft, much was happening. The British were no different either;

their new Canadian operation would have been establishing itself – settling in to its task. Once this phase passed and 1946 dawned, I would expect the British and Canadians to have made good progress at following the schematic drawings and blueprints at their disposal; especially in such a focused and closeted atmosphere. After all, in the middle of nowhere there are few distractions to take one's mind off the work and every incentive to finish the job early, so as to escape back to the real world. The year 1946, then, would probably have seen the first test-flights of the Anglo-Canadian Haunebu.

For their part, the SS were loath to see the war end without securing something for the futures of their membership. Odessa and the Spider were but two organisations intent on taking up that role after the war, and Kammler would have been aware of the opportunities open to him in a post-war economy. By possibly taking the projects to Base 211, perhaps Kammler was looking to construct a fleet of bargaining chips with which to earn a more profitable and honourable (in his eyes) settlement for his comrades and, by extension, Germany. The SS were now firmly in control – just as Himmler once planned for. As Hitler's bodyguards, they would have spirited their Führer safely away to South America, where he could remain as their titular figurehead; thoughts of a military resurgent Fourth Reich dimming in the process.

Instead, the SS organisations now in place were planning to carve out a new, economic future; Kammler's relocation a vital element of the plan. Perhaps, in some way, the engineers thought to be beavering away in Base 211 on discs of their own, felt the same as those in Canada. After all, they would have been in an even more isolated location, with little or no contact with the outside world and a long, long way from a homeland that no longer resembled the one they had left, both politically and geographically. But unlike the civilian engineers working in British Columbia, it was adherence to the Nazi dogma which would have ensured their continued efforts. Remember that the SS were said to be in charge and, as a result, little dissent would have been tolerated. The workers (or Antarcticans, depending on your viewpoint) would simply have had to abide by the tenets laid out for them, or be silenced. Those running New Berlin could not afford to have disgruntled ex-members confessing to the authorities who, they rightly assumed, already knew of their presence.

President Truman considered the final defeat of Japan in August 1945 as the last word on the Axis aggressors, until the first reports on Base 211 started reaching him from the interrogators of the U-boat crews. As if this wasn't enough, war clouds were forming in Europe once again, this time with Stalin's Russia which, if not translated into a 'hot' war, would certainly turn into a cold version in time. Therefore, Truman's generals would have wanted to cover all the angles in preparation for America's defence. Unlike Alaska, the vast wastes of Antarctica presented little immediate strategic value to the USA, but with the growing promise both of vast untapped mineral and fuel resources to be found there, together with its possible use as a safe launching platform for long-range nuclear missiles, it had to be taken seriously. America was now determined to stake a larger claim for itself, over and above the odd pockets of territory it already held, just as Hitler had done a decade earlier.

To then learn of the potentially serious threat to the national security of America and its allies posed by a bunch of renegade Nazis in Antarctica would already have made for difficult reading. If this group succeeded in perfecting their own Haunebu craft, it might prove devastating, for America still had no comparable project – not even one on the drawing board. With a longer range and vastly superior manoeuvrability than any conventional aircraft possessed by either the US air force or anyone else, these craft could terrorise cities or military installations with no warning. The decision was taken to kill two birds with one stone: firstly, evaluate and remove the threat, and, secondly, stake the claims to territory. To do so, an invasion force was assembled, which would travel to

Antarctica for the final showdown, under the codename of Operation High Jump (OHJ).

This development occurred to the apparent consternation of the British government, which believed that American expansionism was the real reason behind OHJ. Whether it had any inkling of what was *really* going on I can't say, but certainly in studying the various declassified Foreign Office reports concerning the event, there is no sign of any hidden agenda, other than fears expressed about America's ultimate geopolitical and military intentions. Another pressing concern of more interest to Britain came not from OHJ but from an apparently separate (though simultaneous) mission for the American Geological Society, to survey and map Antarctica, being planned by an American naval commander, Finn Ronne. The British Falkland Islands Dependent Survey operation had several men occupying old huts in the existing American territory in Antarctica, and concerns were raised that they might now be discovered and/or removed by Ronne, who was scheduled to depart around the same time as OHJ. But Ronne's expedition was tiny in comparison and incorporated twenty scientists; in which field they specialised also remains unknown. However, odd press reports link them to a search for deposits of uranium.

The American press were heavily briefed on the reasons for OHJ and were told that it had two purposes: firstly, to search for deposits of uranium (confusion with Ronne?), and, secondly, to test new cold-weather equipment, then under consideration for US forces, along with tests of new guided missiles. The exercise was originally scheduled for the Arctic regions but was apparently moved to Antarctica for fear of scaring the Russians. But, of course, this wasn't strictly true, for it omits the real 'two birds, one stone' philosophy. During the exercise, like Germany a decade before, American aircraft were scheduled to drop their national flag at the apex of each photo-reconnaissance flight, thereby claiming the land for itself – and this included much of the continent's coastline. It would therefore seem that the American

State Department was seeking to win territory through the 'back door' of a military exercise. Neither this, nor the possible assault on Base 211, was even hinted at during the press briefings. Those of the opinion that there was *no* hidden agenda would laugh at such apparent paranoia but, as I have suggested all along, often the truth really *is* stranger than fiction.

The Americans had only one real choice of candidate to head up this expedition – Rear Admiral Richard E. Byrd. This charismatic explorer had enjoyed an unorthodox career for many years before the war and had achieved many records, such as being the first man to fly over the North Pole. He had, you will recall, also advised the original German *Neu Schwabenland* expedition in 1938 with a slideshow illustrating the conditions they might expect in the Antarctic. During the war he had been involved in several secret American operations and deliberately kept out of the limelight to avoid undue attention; OHJ was to be a return from apparent retirement. For a mission as important as this, the US navy had need of his expertise of these waters and appointed him 'polar consultant' alongside the operational commander, Captain Richard H. Cruzen. Once the decision to go was taken, planning took up much of 1946 and, once assembled, the fleet set sail on 2 December from Norfolk, Virginia. We know that it comprised one submarine, two seaplane tenders, an aircraft carrier and nine other icebreakers, oilers and destroyers, together with six Sikorsky helicopters, six flying boats and six other aircraft, as well as at least one full sled-and-dog team from Alaska. It also carried enough supplies to last the force around eighteen months, in case they found themselves icebound. Over four thousand soldiers would also be making the trip, which made it look less like a scientific mission and more like the invasion force it really was.

Once again, from this point on our story divides into both an official account and one that runs counter to the accepted version. For the record, over 1.3 million square kilometres of Antarctic territory were mapped, and the mission was deemed a great success. Byrd flew over the so-called Point of Inaccessibility, over 1,600 kilometres from open sea in any direction, and several times over both the magnetic and geographical South Poles, making extended detours towards the Indian and Pacific Oceans in the process. However, the weather apparently closed in more severely than Byrd thought was safe and, rather than risk being trapped in the ice for the rest of the winter, he advised that the mission be cut short. The group then returned to the USA somewhat earlier than planned.

But as far as our story is concerned, a somewhat *different* picture of OHJ now emerges. From sources as diverse as an almost mythical pamphlet, issued in Germany during the 1970s by a neo-Nazi group entitled Brisant and brought to our attention by the British writer W. A. Harbinson, to other writers on the subject such as Vesco, we hear hints and rumours of a military disaster on the part of the Americans, at the hands of the (by-now) perfected Haunebu discs of Base 211. The legend goes that Byrd's considerable force landed close to Neu Schwabenland, taunting the Antarcticans to show themselves. This then occurred, but the conventional aircraft being used by the Americans were no match for the discs, whose weapons cut through the American planes like a hot knife through butter (apparently a weapon similar to Tesla's 'death ray'). The Americans had no response to this onslaught and, having lost many men and several aircraft that first day, the ragged fleet retreated after only three weeks on the continent, arriving back at port in March. During one candid exchange with a reporter on his return, Byrd reportedly said:

It was necessary for the United States to take defensive actions against enemy air fighters which come from the polar regions ... [and that] in the event of a new war, the US would be attacked by fighters, that are able to fly from pole to pole with incredible speed.

Whether Byrd ever *actually* spoke these exact words remains unknown, although those who tell the stories go on to assert that the admiral was kept under a close shroud of security for the rest of his days (he died in 1957), bound to keep the real truth behind OHJ a secret for ever. How the authorities could rely on the participating servicemen or reporters to keep quiet we are never told; perhaps their own loyalty and various gagging orders did the trick?

After looking at all the stories, then, what of the reality behind Base 211? This author for one finds the more amazing of the stories surrounding the base, such as discs fresh from production lines repelling OHJ, a little too much to accept. I can believe with little hesitation that the Germans had a base of some kind on Antarctica. As I've shown, there's no reason to doubt that, for the Germans, such a base was more than feasible. Indeed, in looking at the possibilities opened up by the U-boats and Antarctica's close proximity to South America, there is every chance this was so. Thanks to the arrival of Kammler, the Antarcticans might even have had access to the same Haunebu blueprints as found by the British and attempted to build their own versions. But realistically there was simply insufficient time and resources for the Antarcticans to build up a *fleet* of the discs, as has been suggested.

One of the more remarkable stories of German manufacturing achievement during the war can be seen in the story of the Volksjäger: a simple jet fighter, designed from scratch and test-flown within three months. Had there been a little more time and reserves of jet fuel to hand, this simple aircraft might have played a large part in stemming Germany's losses elsewhere and, if not wholly reversing the invasion of the country, then certainly giving a breathing space. But such an achievement occurred only with considerable manpower and the help of dozens of companies throughout what was left of the Reich, all pulling together in one final effort. Down in Base 211, such efforts as this were simply unrepeatable. Some reports have suggested that over a *hundred thousand* people might have been located there, but I would refute this notion as being wholly impractical. Out of this huge figure, if you take away those involved in administration (these were fastidious Germans, after all), health, security, plant maintenance and construction, you might be left with say, seventy thousand people involved in Haunebu construction! That's a hundred thousand people, in one spot in the vast permafrost of the Antarctic wilderness, expected to design and build a fleet of the most highly advanced aircraft in the world and relying on ad hoc supply visits from U-boats and shipping! I don't think so.

Now consider the complexity of each one of these craft and you begin to appreciate that successfully re-creating an example from blueprints isn't exactly like following instructions for an Airfix kit – and that's before you consider the efforts required in simply fashioning the aircraft, getting the jet engines plumbed in and working reliably. All these were problems that would have to be overcome in Canada, of course, but at least there the team would have had all the advantages of regular contacts and supplies. Now assume that the first craft flies as expected (unlikely in itself) and consider what would be required to gear up for *production*. I can't see how there would have been sufficient raw materials on hand to do this, let alone the quantities of fuel required. Yes, the odd load might have been shipped down, but again I can't see it happening. Base 211, as some would have it, is a non-starter in this guise.

As originally conceived, it also seems unlikely that Base 211 was ever thought suitable for a last redoubt. As Germany's military situation worsened, it's likely that the base was visited several times as part of SS preparations for an eventual Nazi government-in-exile, scheduled for either Base 211 or somewhere in South America. It was planned to evacuate several prominent Nazi and SS officials to escape capture and war crimes trials at the hands of their enemies, just as many rightfully ended up facing at the Nuremberg proceedings. The famed 'Alpine National Redoubt', centred in southern Germany, was a work of fiction that originated in Goebbels' Propaganda Ministry, but which muddied the waters over Base 211.

It is for these reasons, then, that I offer the following hypothesis, which takes a middle line between all the conflicting myths and stories and offers something of a more believable scenario.

Firstly, a strong case can be made to support the notion that the original 1938 expedition found a suitable location for a base. Successive clandestine missions both by U-boat and surface shipping took equipment and personnel to Antarctica – I would guess that no more than twenty or thirty people. At this stage, Base 211 was simply another secret outpost of the Nazi secret service and would have been used as a communications base, for running covert operations in South America, South Africa and, perhaps, Australia and New Zealand. Other than acting as a radio listening post, it may also have been used as a stopover for U-boat or surface shipping crews passing through. The amount of German shipping in the area during the war certainly makes such a purpose feasible. As for its layout, it seems likely that there might have been some basic, insulated wooden huts on the surface, with more extensive underground workings hewn from the ice, as previously suggested. It's unlikely, though, that a subterranean tunnel had been found. Such a feature would show up on the recent satellite-generated topographical maps of the area; needless to say, such a feature isn't to be seen (unless paranoid thinking leads us to believe such images have been doctored at source).

On his arrival at the base, together with a small number of engineers and skilled forced labourers from Nordhausen, it wouldn't have taken Kammler long to see for himself that the reality on the ground hardly matched its billing on paper and that a great deal of work was needed before they could even think of building a new Haunebu. Raw materials and supplies organised and shipped down from South America by Odessa would have been basic at best – perhaps enough to construct just one, possibly two Haunebu craft, but certainly not the multitude which have been suggested. So let's assume that at least one working Haunebu was constructed sometime in 1946. The newly enlarged staff of, say, eighty to a hundred, all told, would have had to work in very basic and probably freezing conditions in order to get the job done, and we can bet that that in itself had an adverse impact, resulting in fatalities and incapacitations. Supplies from Argentina and elsewhere might have been forthcoming, but the existence for those at Base 211 would have been basic at the very least.

I would therefore suggest that by the time Byrd's Operation High Jump task force landed in January/February 1947, there was still no sign of the waves of Haunebus long rumoured. In the end, resistance with conventional weapons was probably bitter and fanatical and the odd Haunebu might have been used, which might account for the rumours of killed and wounded GIs, but it would have eventually crumbled under the sheer weight of American numbers, leaving Byrd free to return home ahead of time – with the prize of a captured Haunebu or plans at the very least. The Americans wouldn't have cared if the craft was whole or in pieces, as its reconstruction and 'retro-engineering' would now occur, maybe using the unique insights of men such as Miethe to achieve that aim. Once the Base 211 garrison was overpowered, the Americans then had the job of understanding just what it was that they'd found.

Yet in complete contrast, British and Canadian engineers were working on *their* Haunebu version long before the end of the war with Japan: 1946 would have seen them build their first working prototype at the new base in British Columbia, from a purely logistical standpoint probably using British jet engines as opposed to German. Unlike their more isolated rivals in Antarctica, their base wasn't *that* remote – after all, it was within the territory of a collaborating partner and had both air and road access to the outside world which, weather permitting, could easily allow unlimited supplies to reach it. Likewise personnel. Consider the secret town built to house workers at the Chalk River facility, along with the ultra-secret town built in the US desert to house those working on the Manhattan Project (constructing the atomic bomb), and one begins to see that an equally concealed facility might easily have been built to house a few hundred – or even a few thousand – workers, certainly more than enough people required, with a greater degree of comfort than those few in Base 211 would have had. With the first prototypes working well, as 1946 turned to 1947, thoughts of a limited production run were surely being entertained.

In October 1938 the young Orson Welles directed and starred in an infamous radio adaptation of H. G. Wells's classic, *The War of the Worlds*. In describing an invasion of the USA by Martian spacecraft, Welles inadvertently caused a near national panic, with several people committing suicide at the 'news' and a number of Americans grabbing their shotguns in order to defend themselves. Such was the general level of panic, despite the oft-repeated message that the transmission was a work of fiction, that the authorities were genuinely alarmed at the reaction. America, it seemed, was still capable of believing anything at face value, and this was to have inestimable value to the intelligence community in the years to come.

The Second World War came and went, and 1947 was soon dawning on a country filled with new levels of prosperity and optimism for the future. The Russians were still a looming threat on the horizon, but with America flexing its muscles around the world, little serious credence was given to threats from Moscow by the average man in the street. America was, after all, still the only atomic power in the world at the time. The official reports out that winter, blandly describing the activities of OHJ, were one of the first examples of this new appreciation of the power of the mass media to spread disinformation as accepted truth. Truman probably thought that the threat posed by the discs was now finally past – that America held the only evidence of their existence and could develop them at their leisure.

But on 24 June of that year, Kenneth Arnold, a flying instructor based near Seattle, happened to see something most peculiar, as he flew over the Rainier Mountains in Washington State – a group of nine or ten silvery objects flying in tight formation. Though an experienced pilot, Arnold hadn't seen anything like them before in his life, and as they flew by he was able to get a closer look, thanks to the clear conditions. He described their profile as like two saucers joined at their rims to give a strong lenticular silhouette and, when local papers picked up the story, it was this description which then entered the lexicon – 'flying saucers'. Numerous sightings continued during June and, in public at least, the authorities were playing them down, as whatever was behind them didn't appear a threat to national security – a fatuous statement in itself, as this is *precisely* what these objects were doing, by flying in American airspace without permission.

In private, however, the US air force and the Chiefs of Staff were frantic to know what was going on. With more and more sightings reported, the national press were getting wind of the story and soon there would be more questions than answers levelled at them; a straight denial of the existence of the flying saucers wouldn't be good enough. It's at this point that I like to think someone at the highest level remembered Welles's broadcast of nine years earlier and the furore it caused, for even when presented with a fictional 'truth', the American population at large proved itself unable to cope (and who's not to say it wouldn't be the same for many other countries?). It was this experience, then, which was to inform America's policy towards the subject of these UFOs from then on. *Whatever* these sightings turned out to be – whether Martians, Russians or Nazis – the population at large was to be kept ignorant for fear of upsetting public order on an even greater scale than seen hitherto. Instead, people were to be drip-fed nuggets of the truth, wrapped in blatant disinformation and denial. The newly formed CIA was already working on a system of 'compartmentalising' classified secrets – in which even those closely involved on the inside were aware only of pertinent facts on a need-to-know basis. The German recruits to the organisation, such as Reinhard Gehlen, brought their own experiences of counterintelligence and disinformation to bear. From now on, as far as government policy on these 'flying saucers' was concerned, the subject was to be hidden behind an elaborate, official edifice of smoke and mirrors, where nothing would ever be simple and straightforward. This situation continues to this day.

The CIA and others didn't have long to wait before their new approach could be tested for real, for in early July an event was to occur near the New Mexican town of Roswell which was to enter the realms of legend. The desert surrounding the town housed the 509th Army Air Force bomber base – then, the only dedicated A-bomb squadron of the Army Air Force and a highly sensitive, strategic spot. For the first three nights of the month, local radar operators at the base began reporting several strange anomalies on their screens: 'blips' that were moving faster than any known aircraft of the time. Diagnostic tests on the equipment proved inconclusive, yet still these strange events were being seen – and correlated by radar sets in the nearby White Sands air base. Teams from the army's Counter Intelligence Corps (CIC) were dispatched to Roswell to work out what was going on, arriving on 4 July in time for another lightshow that evening, seen equally well by civilians in the town. Then all of a sudden one of the radar operators tracking the craft reported that one of the fast-moving traces had 'winked out' – disappeared. One second it had been moving in excess of 1,000 mph; the next, it had gone.

The CIC team wasted no time in seeking to locate the craft, which it reasonably assumed to have crashed somewhere. The betting was that this was some form of advanced craft from Russia, flown in on a reconnaissance mission to photograph America's most secret installations – and if that was the case they had to get to it with all speed. But they weren't alone in witnessing the crash of the unknown craft – a team of archaeologists researching native Indian artefacts had already contacted the sheriff with a report of seeing something ablaze zoom over their heads and crash off in the distance. The sheriff, George Wilcox, ordered the fire department out to a spot some fifty-nine kilometres to the north-west of the town. They were to arrive sometime in the early hours of 5 July – unaware that the CIC team was also on its way from the air base and would get there first.

Once the CIC had posted a picket of army sentries to seal off the large perimeter of the crash site, no civilians could enter; neither 'Mac' Brazel, on whose ranch the crash site lay and who had reported seeing the wreckage, nor the firemen and sheriff. But as spotlamps were hoisted to illuminate the scene, the few witnesses to have seen the wreckage reported seeing umpteen scraps of a strange aluminium-foil material, which several of those involved in the unfolding story, such as the base's security officer, one Major Jesse Marcel, later claimed to possess before all were confiscated. Along with fragments of an equally strange wooden material that sported some form of hieroglyphic writing, the foil could not be torn, cut or drilled through and resisted all attempts at being folded over on itself. Reports in recent years have also highlighted the possibility that the debris found on Brazel's ranch was simply that – a load of scattered wreckage. The *actual* craft, from which it had come, lay in a rocky gully a few dozen miles away. Witnesses to this second site, who have come forward piecemeal since 1947, report seeing CIC personnel on the scene *before* news of Brazel's ranch had broken, which leads to the conclusion that they knew where to find the craft. What they found was a surprisingly intact craft that sported a deep gash along one side of its flat, delta-like fuselage, a shape quite unlike the lenticular 'saucer' shape one might expect following Arnold's description, but certainly close to Miethe's Coanda-effect Haunebu design. There were also lurid descriptions of seeing up to five 'unusual' bodies at the scene, with enlarged heads, grey suits, large almond-shaped eyes and so on –

the classic, very first description of a 'grey' extra-terrestrial being, an 'EBE'.

It is at this point that I must once again break away from the accepted mythology, which in this case would have us believe that what crashed at Roswell was a spacecraft piloted by EBEs.

If aliens *were* involved, why would they pick on Roswell? Surely there were better places or means of catching the interest of the American government than buzzing a sensitive air base close to a dusty town in the middle of the New Mexico desert? It was hardly the most auspicious site for a rendezvous between the ambassadors of two worlds ... And what might they have been hoping to achieve in visiting this location? From simply letting the powers-that-be know of their existence, to acting out the prelude to full-scale invasion, this writer has heard all the theories – and has been satisfied by none. These include the possibilities that these were 'ET-tourists' – alien visitors on some kind of joyride which ended, unfortunately for them, in a crash. That they were ambassadors of a returning alien race, which occasionally visits the earth – and us – to see how the human race is progressing. That they genetically engineered mankind to differentiate us from the other apes. That they came to warn us of imminent invasion from a more belligerent species, of atomic war, of our moon's disappearance etc. In recent years, the vogue has been for stories involving 'abductions' by alien visitors, the mutilation of cattle by unknown means and assailants and for cults to proclaim that either the world is about to end and/or that salvation awaits those who commit suicide and in return join their celestial brothers.

None of the possibilities involving *aliens* makes much logical and plausible sense and can therefore be dismissed. But we're forgetting something. The Anglo-Canadian base in British Columbia.

When one looks at a map of western North America, the Canadian province in question is very close to the Rainier Mountains, where Kenneth Arnold first saw his flying saucers –

easily within flying range of a small fleet of Anglo-Canadian Haunebu craft. Remember also, that nearly two years would have passed since such a secret base first began looking at the Haunebu blueprints – ample time in which to build, perfect and then manufacture a small series of these craft, and then demonstrate their superiority direct to the same American administration that was seen to be unreasonably withholding the atomic bomb (among other secrets) from its most important ally of the day.

The British SIS would surely have known of the location of the 509th bomb group, so what greater point could be made than overflying the site with their new craft a few weeks later in early July and scaring the Americans into thinking that someone else was behind the incident? Unfortunately, one of the craft unexpectedly crash-landed on to 'Mac' Brazel's ranch on the fourth night of these flights, and with the arrival of the CIC the secret was out. Britain and Canada were now recognised as possessing the most advanced aerospace technology anywhere in the world, and this positively enraged the Americans.

But they couldn't admit this publicly, for rightful fear of attracting accusations of having let the competition steal a technological march on them – and with the Russians apparently snapping at the country's heels, this would not have been welcome publicity. So the CIC and the CIA together put their new intelligence policy into action. All evidence of the craft having come from Canada was erased from all but the highest records from day one. The all-too-human crew were removed at the earliest opportunity and in their place were left manikins. Intended to resemble humanoid, though distinctly 'alien' creatures, these would have been fabricated in short order and shipped down with the CIC team. Those apparent witnesses who reported seeing strange humanoid creatures either at the second crash site, or even at the Roswell base itself, were therefore accurate in their observations – but saw only manikins and not real corpses.

From that point on, the legend of having been visited by

extraterrestrial beings gathered momentum like a snowball rolling down a hillside, picking up scraps of other stories and reports as it careered out of control, too big for its original builders either to stop or to change its direction. Which was just what the CIA and CIC were looking for. As long as the public were prepared to embrace the romantic mysticism of visitations from aliens, it meant that the real work could continue with little external scrutiny or interference: namely, building flying discs. America had now inadvertently been gifted a badly damaged though largely intact Anglo-Canadian Haunebu craft to add to whatever had been retrieved from Antarctica.

In time, Britain would gain the nuclear technology it so craved, which leads us to believe that, ultimately, its gamble of flying its discs over the border into the USA was to pay off. With the secret out, there was now no reason for Britain, Canada and the USA not to pool ideas and resources on the disc projects. As the 1950s dawned, this is precisely what would happen. Dr Miethe's past experiences would now be drawn on in the exciting developments to come.

As for Base 211, I would suspect that it was subsequently abandoned following the success of OHJ. Post-war Germany relinquished its official claims on Neu Schwabenland, lacking both the resources and motivation to maintain a base there during the long years of partition. The various SS factions also saw little sense in maintaining a presence there – with the disc project now lost, their future lay in more subtle and opaque economic dealings around the world and blatant military posturing no longer mattered. Whether Kammler escaped the clutches of OHJ and returned either to West Germany or elsewhere, or whether he really *did* die in 1945, remains an open question.

chapter eight

'A weapon is an enemy even to its owner.'

Turkish proverb.

'Geography has made us [America and Canada] neighbours.
History has made us friends. Economics has made us partners.
And necessity has made us allies. Those whom nature hath
joined together, let no man put asunder.'

John F. Kennedy, address to the Canadian Parliament,
Ottawa, 17 May 1961.

Operation High Jump had removed the last Nazi outpost from
Antarctica and had gifted America with the bones of its own disc
project. At first, I expect they believed themselves to be the only
ones with this technology, and perhaps it was this belief, as much
as their denial of the atom bomb to their allies, which prompted
Britain and Canada to show their hand. The first flights over the
Rainier Mountains were planned; the crash at Roswell certainly
was not. But from that point on, once the Americans had found
the crashed saucer crewed not by aliens but by regular air-force

pilots speaking English with British or Canadian accents, it's my guess that all parties would then have begun collaborating, begrudgingly or not, in a top-secret, high-level, tripartite group – hereafter referred to as 'TG' – to perfect the basic design and share the issues of finance and future production and research and development needs – the British point already forcefully made.

But then, what could America do to show its anger at Britain and Canada without causing undue public concern and interest? Threaten these allies? How? Truman's hands were tied by the Soviet threat, and he couldn't afford to risk destabilising the status quo in Western Europe in any way, for fear of a surprise Soviet offensive. It was in this heated atmosphere that the TG was brokered, giving the discs a secure future as a result.

But in the years to come, events elsewhere would lead to further collaboration in areas of mutual interest to the three allies, other than discs. For example, another deal reached in 1947 between America, Britain and the major Commonwealth countries such as Canada, Australia and New Zealand was the so-called 'UKUSA' agreement, which followed in the footsteps of the wartime code-breaking set up at Bletchley Park and ensured a common intelligence protocol between these nations, under which intelligence acquired during the Cold War could now be shared. Two years later, in 1949, as the Control Commission in Berlin broke down as a result of the Soviets becoming unwilling to participate with the other occupying powers, the tensions that ensued led to the formation of NATO.

Whatever the history behind the TG, what's for certain is that from 1948 onwards, reported sightings of UFOs were increasing almost exponentially. Newspapers around the world were full of sensational reports from witnesses to the phenomenon, and it seemed as if new pulp paperbacks on the subject were appearing every month, purporting to reveal the truth behind the flying saucer mystery. Even Hollywood started getting in on the act, with several attempts at capturing the new global mood. Movies, such as 1951's *The Day the Earth Stood Still*, contain much potent imagery, with a large silver saucer landing on the White House lawn, and a kindly (though distinctly Aryan-looking) alien with a message to disarm the world's nuclear weapons, ultimately reinforced by his robotic minder. This is classic stuff, and it's no wonder that such pervasive material has entered our common psyche.

Whenever serious researchers have delved into the subject since then, they are always confronted by a dismissive, trite attitude of the public, typified by stories of 'little green men'. Naive it may all have been, yet the enduring imagery of the 1950s has done much to muddy the waters of the subject; which is perhaps what the CIA and other agencies were hoping it would do. After all, the last thing they needed then (as now) was to have the public get wind of an *actual* project of theirs; much better instead to let them focus their attention on something fantastical.

America, perhaps more than most other countries of the time, was becoming increasingly paranoid about its standing in the world and in particular about the threats – perceived or actual – coming from the other side of the Iron Curtain. With the McCarthy trials affecting everyone in the public eye who had ever been suspected of Communist leanings, this was the perfect time for some elements of the media to start considering whether or not these UFOs might in fact be Russian in origin. Yet when faced with such questions, the US Department of Defense issued a statement on 27 April 1949 in which it flatly refused to entertain this notion, and went on:

> The possibility that these flying objects may be foreign aircraft was taken into consideration, but the reported speeds are so much greater than those of any kind of airplane that we have technically approached to date, that only an accidental discovery so new *that it has only now been reached* could sufficiently explain them [author's italics].

In this classic statement, part of the answer is revealed, for in typically oblique language we see the ultimate military authority in the country hinting that they knew more than they were letting on and discounting rumours of Soviet intent, when on the face of it, it appeared an ideal opportunity to divert attention. Why let people believe these things to be Soviet, when alien origins were so much more alluring? This assumption is made all the more apparent when one examines the growing list of 'close encounters' also reported by civilian and military pilots alike at this time. One of the most notorious of the early cases occurred in 1948, and, like Roswell, it has never been satisfactorily explained.

Captain Philip Mantell was a seasoned air-force pilot and level-headed character, not prone to making easy mistakes. On 7 January 1948, he was on a training flight in his P-51 Mustang with two other aircraft when he encountered a UFO. His radio communication with the tower was occasionally blotted out by static, but the transcript released clearly records Mantell attempting to catch up with the strange object, in a bid to identify it more clearly. It's thought he then fired his machine guns on this unknown quarry; an act which succeeded in getting the UFO's attention, as it then appeared to change direction and head straight for him. As this retaliatory manoeuvre unfolded, Mantell reported the growing size of the approaching UFO as it filled his view from the cockpit, before he fell out of radio contact. His aircraft then plummeted earthwards out of control; for some reason unable to parachute to safety, he died on impact with the ground. If we discount the ridiculous official explanation – that Mantell was chasing the planet Venus – some researchers insist that he died in an act of self-defence by the UFO crewed by EBEs who, quite reasonably, didn't take kindly to being fired on. Not surprisingly, after this incident the standing order given to all US air-force pilots was altered so that if they should encounter a UFO, they should endeavour to intercept it but not open fire on it, unless faced with an obviously aggressive manoeuvre on the part of the

UFO. In other words, *look but don't touch*. The air force, then, not only believed in the phenomenon itself, but was issuing instructions to its pilots in the event of their encountering one of these craft. Overnight, the phenomenon could no longer be dismissed in Washington as tricks of the light.

Personally, as one who believes that the *real* history of UFOs does *not* involve visits from little grey or green men, my own interpretation of the Mantell case is that he was unfortunate to encounter one of the TG's discs. Given the extreme degree of secrecy afforded the project, no air-force officials at squadron level, let alone regular pilots, were being briefed on the truth, so when encountering the craft they naturally assumed it had alien origins – and thus a potentially aggressive intent, which led to them shooting first. After all, servicemen read newspapers and listened to radio reports too, and who is to say that, in the prevailing mood of the time, their assumption wasn't the truth as they believed it? Mantell chased and attacked the disc, but it's all-too-human crew could not afford to have their craft brought down to create another Roswell, so acting on their own standing orders they removed the immediate threat to the secret. Ultimately, Mantell was expendable. One life, one aircraft: sacrificed for the 'greater good'. He wasn't to be the last.

If we discount the Foo Fighters seen in the Second World War, the pattern of reported UFO sightings, with which we're still familiar today, began in 1947 with Kenneth Arnold's report of the nine silvery UFOs over the Rainier Mountains. But this was just the tip of the iceberg; the first public glimpse of something that would lead to the creation of the TG and a doctrine that placed the discs at the pinnacle of defence capability. Now that all three players had shown their hands, a new urgency was introduced into the TG's business, if it were to take advantage of the growing fears about the USSR's intentions.

Alaska and Canada, together with territory in the Antarctic, as we've seen, were now considered as suitable launching areas for the discs, should a third world war break out. The VTOL-capable discs could operate from any small clearing and be stored on site until needed, in camouflaged, isolated hangars. Once the first generation of American first strike ICBMs were developed, the TG would have planned to hold the discs in reserve in these isolated sites, as a perfect retaliatory weapon capable of delivering a second or third strike, in the event of the home countries succumbing to a nuclear onslaught. By choosing such remote areas, the USSR would have struggled just to find them and then knock them out, in a strange echo of the thinking that led to the Germans establishing Base 211 in the first place.

It was, I believe, as a result of this growing strategic realisation that disc development was accelerated in this arranged three-way marriage of convenience. This in turn would allow new military missions: for example, clandestine reconnaissance and covertly delivering and recovering TG personnel. New types of conventional military aircraft were of course still being developed, some of the more advanced of which, such as the U-2 spy plane, might very well have enjoyed spin-off technologies and ideas from the discs at a low level. Though aircraft such as the U-2 would have provided a better means of gathering intelligence than their antecedents, the TG knew all the while that one of their discs represented a degree of capability so far beyond any conventional aircraft as to be laughable. Capable of apparently effortless acceleration to speeds far beyond Mach 1, with unmatched manoeuvrability, the discs would have made for an unbeatable reconnaissance tool, and perhaps they were indeed used in this role at times. When UFO sightings were reported over certain Central and South American countries and over Eastern Europe during the 1950s, maybe people were simply seeing missions in progress. All of which rather begs the question as to why expensive aircraft such as the U-2 were even developed, when such advanced alternatives were available. As we shall see later, however, the development of unwitting 'red herrings', no matter how plausible they might have been in their own right (and the U-2 was certainly that), would appear to have been an integral part of the TG's strategy.

Intrinsically linked with the strategic aims of the project was the TG's fear of the possibility that similar projects might have already been under way in Soviet Russia. That the USSR was undergoing a technological revolution at this time is well known. With its acquisition of the atom bomb, the Sputnik satellite and, later, putting both the first man and woman in space, its rocket technologies had put the fear of God into the West – especially in the States – yet these technologies all owed as much to an inherited German legacy as did the American efforts then proceeding. At the time, the TG would have been concerned at these events and might easily have believed that a comparable Soviet disc project be under way. But aside from the capture of Habermohl at the end of the war, there is just no evidence, circumstantial or otherwise, to suggest that anything more of either the Haunebu or Foo Fighter projects surfaced in the USSR. Even if Habermohl's technical knowledge on the subject was indeed being exploited, little seems to have come from it. This author feels that once intelligence had come from Russia to confirm this situation, the TG's remit changed direction.

In the absence of an imminent Soviet disc project, the TG's activities could settle down and mature more naturally, as seems the pattern for the project from the late 1950s. Reported sightings had continued unabated, during several 'flaps' (concentrated bursts of sightings in a specific area), and the first few photographs of sightings were also beginning to appear, which confirmed many of the details and features described. Though many were later proved to be fakes, a few appeared genuine, which meant that the job of classifying the UFOs could finally begin.

Firstly, though, we should recap the likely state of the various original projects, as they would have been in 1947, starting with the scratch Haunebu built and/or test-flown at Base 211. In the more sophisticated Mark IV version originally envisaged by Miethe, the outer skin of the craft would have been formed from a Luftschwamm material, but the limitations of both time and the materials available would have precluded such an exotic mix and I suspect that Kammler's team reverted to the more basic and workmanlike Mark V – the design flown from Kahla before the end of the war. Similar in layout to the original compromised Mark IV version built by Schriever and Miethe, four turbojets would most likely have been mounted radially around the outer circumference of a disc planform; if this proved impractical, a simpler octagonal platform might have sufficed. As before, the air intakes would have been mounted close to the central hub of the craft, with the exhaust outlets channelled through a series of control vanes at the rim and using the Coanda effect for control. This, then, was the likely extent of the project that OHJ found in Antarctica.

The original Anglo-Canadian project, on the other hand, might well have been less compromised. After all, if its engineers had continued to make progress in refining their own Porosint material, along with other valuable spin-offs from the then-new British jet-fighter projects, such as the De Havilland Vampire, they might very well have got closer to the ideal shown in Miethe's ideas for the Mark IV. Certainly, if we go on the descriptions given by witnesses such as Kenneth Arnold, that he saw these craft flying at 'over 1,300 mph', then this might very well be the case.

Both projects, German and Anglo-Canadian, would certainly have had a dulled gunmetal-grey or brushed aluminium external appearance; aside from the obvious problems of increased conspicuousness, paint would have added extra weight and might also have been burned off through air friction at high speeds. Not only that, but the microscopic pores cratering the surface might have made Porosint simply unpaintable. We can also assume that both had simple retractable landing gear to facilitate ground handling. In the absence of hard information, some artists' impressions seem to show these Haunebu craft fitted with a complex series of semi-spherical 'inflatable cushions' on their underside, but these look too unwieldy and clumsy. Even if they *were* a genuine component of the project at this stage, I would prefer to view them as [possibly detachable] rubberised bladders filled either with fuel or simply water ballast to provide a lower centre of gravity. But inflatable landing cushions? I doubt it.

The main advantage enjoyed by the Anglo-Canadian disc team, however, was that, unlike the more isolated team in Base 211, it at least had access to the latest and more powerful turbojets. Units developed by BMW and others during the war had barely sufficient power at first. But with the war over, more powerful and reliable units from British and American firms became available and were in turn adapted for use in the discs. Perform-ance and agility increased as a result, but as long as exclusively air-breathing combustion engines were fitted, the ultimate perform-ance of these new craft could never be fully explored, restricting them to flights in the earth's atmosphere. Not that this was much of a drawback at first, as no other aircraft in service at the time were capable of matching them – and still aren't even now, several generations later. While their high speeds have since been reached by a few conventional aircraft, their incredible manoeuvrability remains unsurpassed. Remember, too, that all this was beginning at a time (1947) when Chuck Yeager officially broke the sound barrier in the experimental Bell X-1 rocket plane. With the advent of the TG in the same year, its own, very special technologies were to ensure that Yeager's efforts were like comparing those of a carthorse with a thoroughbred's. Yet imagine how frustrating it must have been for the development teams, in not being able to shout their achievements from the rooftops.

That some of the associated technologies first seen during the war were also still being developed, is outlined in one such 'close encounter' report mentioned in Vesco's book, which occurred in Iran during October 1954. A Tehran businessman came across a landed disc at rest in a yard adjoining to his own early one morning. He approached it, apparently without fear, after seeing a man's silhouette moving about beneath the central cockpit canopy. After putting his hand to the disc's surface, he immediately felt his hand being held down by suction, as if it were covering the nozzle of a giant vacuum cleaner. He shouted for help, but his cries caught only the pilot's attention, who then revved the engines harder to attain lift and escape. Luckily, the man pulled his hand free just as the craft shot up into the air, enveloping him in a blast of hot air in the process. This sounds remarkably similar to the effects one might expect from touching a material like Porosint or Luftschwamm. Even when idling, the jet engines would be taking in outside air through the material, causing the mild suction effect; as the pilot opened the throttles to achieve lift, so the suction increased, and, as the disc climbed, the hot air felt by the witness was simply the jet exhaust, vented back through another side of the outer skin to give thrust via the Coanda effect. This, in turn, might give rise to another effect that has often been reported – namely, the shimmering gleam that some UFOs exhibit in a certain light. If you've ever watched jet airliners at an airport, have you ever tried to look at objects through the heat haze from their engines? Everything looks distorted, and I would suggest that a similar effect occurs with a porous metal in this application. With the tremendous volume of cold air being sucked in and hot exhaust being vented out at various points around the disc, utilising the Coanda effect, might that very confluence of cold and hot air not create the optical effects reported?

When it began, the TG inherited the Anglo-Canadian discs and whatever had been found in Base 211 and, as it entered the 1950s, the best elements of both would have fused into the model most commonly reported by witnesses. This can best be described as their standard 'Jeep' disc model that varies between ten to twenty-five metres in diameter. This difference in size doubtless reflects its many variants and this basic configuration was seen in greater numbers simply because more of them were built. While the technologies were developed and shared out equally among the TG, the aerospace businesses in each country might have built their own native versions or contributed to the main production effort in, say, the USA. Whichever, discs were certainly built for different applications, and these variations are reflected in the different sizes reported.

With so many sightings of these first TG discs reported through-out the 1950s, the pressure was mounting on air forces and governments the world over to issue some form of official comment on proceedings. Independent investigators and the media were clamouring for answers, and the member governments of the TG in particular knew they couldn't put them off for ever, so decided to expand the complex policy of disinformation as previously explained. As well as instituting high-profile, though toothless, investigations [e.g. Project Blue Book], the TG members also embarked on a new round of expensive, superfluous (and, in comparison with craft such as the U-2, useless) 'red herring' projects, the existence of which they could safely allude to without drawing attention to the real agenda. As a convincing smokescreen, this worked brilliantly and, to one or two uninformed com-mentators, still does today. The most famous of these projects drew on experiences with the Chance-Vought 'flying pancake' for its inspiration and this, the most 'dumbed down' of all the red herrings, was publicly unveiled only in 1960, its job already done.

But for an illusion to work, you first have to set the scene, to show there's nothing up your sleeves before the sleight of hand plays out. This occurred on 11 February 1953 with a banner headline in the *Toronto Star*, which trumpeted that 'real flying saucers' were in fact under development at a plant in Malton, owned by the Canadian subsidiary of the British A. V. Roe aircraft company – AvroCanada. The as-yet nameless craft was said to be capable of speeds up to 1,500 mph and was seen as a new defensive weapon, to be used against possible Soviet attack from across the

Arctic Circle (no surprise there – it might just as well have been a TG or NATO press release). Convincingly, the scoop seemed to catch the authorities unawares, which may, of course, *not* have been the case at the most senior level. None the less, over the next few months officials in Ottawa and from Avro were careful, admitting only to evaluating such a project before tempering suggestions of success with the caveat that production would be at least six years away. That the TG might have already been in business for at *least* six years by this time remained airbrushed from the official story, and we can therefore see this admission in its true light – this was the sleight of hand to cover up the development of more advanced disc models.

In subsequent reports, the press duly noted the lack of denials of the existence of this decoy, which must have pleased the TG as it meant that, as long as the discs remained under cover, their continued research and development of the next generation of the craft could happily carry on behind the scenes, with no one any the wiser. Little more was heard that summer and press interest died away, only to be rekindled in October by more details of the project, by now publicly christened the 'Avro Omega'; doubtless the result of another tip-off to keep the illusion working. Incidentally, 'Omega' happens to be the last letter of the Greek alphabet, so if we think of it as the lowest rung in the project's ladder, perhaps the superior, 'real' project that was shielded behind it should be called 'Alpha' from hereon?

Readers learned that development of a single prototype to that point had cost Avro some '$200 million' and that the firm hoped eventually to sell production examples to the Royal Canadian Air Force. The RCAF were expected to deploy whole squadrons of them in the vast open wildernesses of northern Canada, once again deliberately echoing one of the aims of the 'real' project. A third report, in November 1953, spoke of presenting the Omega to 'a group of 25 Americans'. Perhaps as a result of this presentation, as 1954 dawned, the talk now revolved around moving the entire project to the States, where the craft's 'inefficient' design might be improved with 'elements from other projects' then being investigated by its original designer, one John Frost, an English aircraft designer previously employed by De Havilland in the UK, who later moved to New Zealand. Finally, in December 1954, the Canadian authorities announced that the Avro Omega would be abandoned, 'as it would have served no useful purpose'.

The statement sounds fair enough at first glance, but take a closer look and an entirely different picture emerges. For a start, $200 million in 1954, just to build *one* prototype, is an incredibly large figure. Even if the aircraft in question was experimental and wholly new, it would surely not have cost *that* much, so I challenge the reliability of that figure, unless, of course, it covers *more* than the Omega. Secondly, now consider the significance of showing the craft to the (unidentified) Americans. I would suggest that these were high-ranking members from the TG who were simply checking up on the progress of their red herring and, when the later announcement came that the project would be scrapped, it was *precisely* because the latest Alpha project was now in a position to start production – in the TG facility over the border. There was little point in building a whole fleet of Omegas merely as a spoiler. When the authorities stated that it would have served no purpose, they were right – it was, after all, the decoy, the red herring – and, unlike the successful U-2 spy plane, the Omega disc couldn't even *function* as intended, as the sole examples built were little more than mock-ups. But the basic strategic reasoning remained undimmed and was propelling the real agenda – the Alpha models. If limited manufacturing was now on the cards, the Americans were as well placed as any to take it on.

But the story doesn't end there. In October 1955 the US Air Force Secretary Donald Quarles released a statement, after much speculation, in which he stated:

We are now entering a period of aviation technology in which aircraft of unusual configuration and flight characteristics will begin to appear ... We have another project under contract with AVRO [sic] Ltd, of Canada, which could result in disc-shaped aircraft somewhat similar to the popular concept of a flying saucer ... [They are] direct-line descendants of conventional aircraft and should not be regarded as supra-natural or mysterious ...

The last phrase is particularly interesting, seeking as it does to end the muddled confusion over the very existence of the UFO phenomenon, although the allusion to continuing relations with Avro contradict the official Canadian view, perhaps a result of poor inter-governmental communications or more disinformation. With the Soviet threat still believed by everyone to be growing, so the Omega's mission continued to mask the TG's main Alpha project. For the next few years, all assumed that development was now moving ahead in America, until the first chinks began to appear in the project, when in 1959 Avro began to suffer a financial squeeze.

The almost hysterical paranoia that had been so prevalent in the USA during the early to mid-1950s now began to dissipate, as the realities of the imagined Soviet threat filtered through and were found wanting. The Soviets had many fewer long-range bombers, for example, than previously assumed and, as a result, many defence contracts across the industry were being scaled down. Avro was no exception, so as 1960 loomed the company laid off thousands of workers as contracts in other areas dried up. No official word was issued on Omega, however, apart from a statement from a USAF general in April, in which it was hoped that the first test-flight might take place soon, overcoming developmental problems in the process – obviously some projects live on regardless. Remember, though, that only five years previously, Donald Quarles was briefing journalists on what might be seen in the skies, and here we are being now told that a first test-flight was yet to occur. But let us not be confused, for what Quarles was obviously referring to was the Alpha – the Omega, by contrast, was the red herring and would therefore *never fly*. With hindsight, such problems were never likely – or required – to be overcome and, with the Alpha discs already flying, the USAF publicly threw in the Omega's towel by unveiling, in August 1960, a scaled-down variation on the original project, which followed a laughable technological blind alley.

Renamed the 'AvroCar', the single prototype shown sported a 'double-bubble' twin cockpit arrangement, each crewman sitting on opposite sides of a large central fan, which sucked in air from above and redirected it through to the ground by means of vents around the rim of the craft. The central fan was augmented by four smaller ones set around the circular fuselage, and even at first glance the AvroCar resembled a primitive and ungainly hovercraft without the rubber skirt around its bottom edge. Worse, it was incapable of achieving actual lift into the air much beyond hovering, and although tests into improving its horrendous low-speed handling persisted into 1961, it was too late: the red herring was no longer needed. To those ufologists who wholeheartedly believed in their quarry having alien origins, this deliberate public fiasco was simply ammunition for them to 'prove' that human technology 'couldn't match that of the EBEs'.

Which was, of course, exactly what the TG wanted to hear and, from that point of view, the Omega/AvroCar was a complete success. Eight years and untold millions had bought them time to develop the Alpha discs in complete secrecy; safe in the knowledge that any sightings could be passed off as the Omega – which, in its revealed form, had difficulty even leaving the ground, let alone performing the high-speed aerobatics of the new second-generation Alpha.

The AvroCar was pitched as the most visible of the red herrings, but AvroCanada were also busy developing other, more secret projects alongside (and not just TG's Alpha craft). Intended to represent a more feasible craft than the underachieving AvroCar, one such – Project Silver Bug – would not be declassified until 1995 – and only after a search under the American Freedom of Information Act – a full *forty years* after its time.

In essence, I prefer to think of Silver Bug as a 'halfway house', one step further on from the AvroCar and Omega, but one step back from the Alpha. If the AvroCar was ever exposed for the decoy it surely was, Silver Bug would have made an obvious second line of defence – even if it *still* didn't represent the state of the flying saucer art, it was none the less being developed with more serious intent. If the TG had ever been forced to admit to something more realistic than the Omega/AvroCar, this would have been it. Further, I would go as far as to suggest that, firstly, the development of the Silver Bug was covered by the inflated Omega budget and, secondly, that it may also have been a serious contender for production. In its own way it had merits that could have made for a believable red herring, like the U-2, masking the Alpha in ways the Omega never could. It flew for a start . . .

Significantly, Silver Bug (official title: 'Project Y' – 'Upsilon'?) was part-developed by none other than Dr Richard Miethe, lent as part of Operation Paperclip to Avro's facilities at Malton, Ontario. The craft's single cockpit sat ahead of a radial-flow turbojet within a circular platform of around 7 metres in diameter which, unlike the AvroCar, was fully enclosed. The jet took its air from a series of small vents at the leading, upper edge of the disc, exhausting its thrust through a variable system of vents on the underside. In so doing, the craft exploited the Coanda effect to channel the jet thrust to provide lift and propulsion, negating the need for additional control surfaces such as a rudder or flaps. The combined effect was to give Silver Bug an estimated performance of over Mach 3.5 at 80,000' – a tremendous feat back in 1955. This was only ten years since the end of the Second World War, so perhaps the old Haunebu Mark V might indeed have broken the sound barrier first as some claim.

A second model, Y-2, was also designed and incorporated a radial-flow, gas turbine motor, similar to that pioneered by Habermohl, though it's not known if this version actually flew or not. Impressive while these figures are, where Silver Bug fell short compared with the real Alpha project was its lack of a Porosint-type outer cover to defeat the boundary layer. It was also too small to incorporate more than one, possibly two jet units, and thus lacked the even higher performance gains already being exploited by Alpha. Nonetheless, its importance to the wider story today is immense, as its declassification was the first proof that projects other than either Omega or the AvroCar were being worked on by Avro at the time and casts our speculation on the Alpha project in a more realistic light. Silver Bug may have been a more serious decoy than AvroCar, but it's still a decoy. What is amazing is that it should have been admitted to at all. Officially, its test results were 'unpromising', but compared with the AvroCar they would still have looked spectacularly good, so where's the yardstick for comparison? Back in 1955, Silver Bug would have wiped the floor against any conventional aircraft, and yet it was cancelled. There-fore, we should turn our gaze once again to what these various red herrings were protecting – the Alpha discs. So much time has elapsed that perhaps the authorities are beginning the process of the slow drip, drip release of information that might yet yield the real story. Until then, the release of the hitherto completely secret Silver Bug shows us that there's probably more where that came from.

By 1960 the original 'Jeep' Alpha model would have become quite sophisticated – perhaps evolving into a third generation – but, as long as it used conventional jet engines, its performance was restricted to the earth's atmosphere. For it to progress, this handicap would need to be overcome, and in the Silver Bug project we see the first mention of a craft or technology that was intended to achieve precisely that – Project Winterhaven.

Modern Formula 1 racing drivers can sometimes be heard talking about the 'G-force load' which acts on their bodies during high-speed cornering. What they're describing is not just an increased force of gravity that effectively multiplies the weight of their bodies in those few seconds, but also the effect of that gravity on their *inertia*. You can experience the same feeling yourself on a fairground ride such as a roller coaster. When the cars tip gently over the edge of a precipitous drop, the body is accelerated from rest to speeds of up to 100 mph or more in a second or two, and in such moments you feel pinned down in the seat, seemingly unable to move or breathe. In sixteenth-century Italy, Galileo reputedly dropped two lead spheres from the Leaning Tower of Pisa – their weights (mass) were different, yet both accelerated and fell at the same speed, when under the same gravitational field (i.e. the earth's). According to Einstein's General Theory of Relativity and specifically its Principle of Equivalence, what Galileo and our roller coaster riders experience is the inseparable link between gravity and inertia – they are equal, to all intents.

Now translate this into a modern, high-performance (though conventional) fighter aircraft. Pilots have to wear special suits fitted with hydraulic pipes, which 'squeeze' down on their limbs and torsos in tight manoeuvres to ensure that their blood keeps circulating, stopping them from blacking out or worse. G-forces of up to three or four times 'normal' gravity can be routinely experienced in these aircraft, increasing the weight of a pilot from, say, 90 kilogrammes to over 300 in short bursts. Such fleeting weight increases are relative to the acceleration of the *mass* of the pilot. In other words, if the aircraft suddenly banks viciously to port, the pilot is momentarily still moving straight ahead, before his mass catches up with his aircraft: all as a result of his inertia – his body's 'reluctance to move'.

All this happens within a conventional aircraft designed with limitations to its manoeuvrability in order to preserve its crew. If it handled any faster, it would impose severe physiological effects on its pilots, causing something of a problem for aircraft designers at today's cutting edge. Back in the 1950s this was exactly the problem faced by the TG design teams looking to develop the disc technology and take it further forward.

Right from the first Alpha craft, the TG found itself having to cope with and learn the characteristics in flying and operating a craft that was effortlessly fast and could turn on a dime – and that was the problem. Most likely, the TG's test pilots weren't pushing the Alpha discs to their design limits because their own wellbeing was getting in the way and, quite reasonably, they weren't prepared to see themselves turned into strawberry jam in the course of investigating the extreme handling characteristics of their new craft. Something had to be done if the discs were to stay piloted by humans and not by electronic autopilots (the technology for which then existed but was still highly rudimentary).

To overcome these immovable hurdles, TG scientists looked at whether they might reduce the mass of the Alpha in relation to gravity. After all, if they could make a pilot weigh, say, 9 kilogrammes, instead of his usual 90 (or even less), wouldn't it be easier for him to cope with manoeuvres that took him to 30 kilogrammes instead of 300? Obviously, they couldn't start breeding a secret race of midget pilots (although some wags point to the grey EBEs so often reported as evidence that this is *exactly* what they've done), so instead they took to looking at the problem from the other side of the equation. If they could somehow 'trick' gravity into treating the pilot (and the disc too, for that matter) as being much lighter, it might be a solution. This is exactly what Project Winterhaven, together with a whole host of other projects, still classified, set out to do.

The answer came from examining the work of eminent scientists who had already studied gravity and its effects. Thomas T. Brown is said to be one of those consulted, as a result of his work into generating localised electrical fields, which had the side-effect of distorting the effects of gravity on objects within the field. His work, along with that of others, is thought to have been incorporated into Winterhaven, but the new generation of Alpha disc emerging in the 1950s still used turbojets for propulsion, so I would expect that on early Winterhaven prototypes the 'electro-gravitic' component was 'bolted on' to boost the performance of the jets, when what was actually required was a more holistic approach to the problem: in short, a disc that dispensed with the jets altogether, to rely solely on electrogravitic propulsion.

With at least nine other classified projects looking to develop the science of anti-gravity and inertia, as well as Winterhaven, it was only a matter of time before the preferred holistic solution presented itself. In essence, what all these projects were thought to have come up with, and which looks to have since been perfected, is a compact though highly powerful on-board electric alternator, which takes its primary power either from a small 'closed system' nuclear turbine or something as simple as a diesel generator. This alternator does three jobs.

Firstly, it powers all the electrical ancillary equipment on board, such as the avionics or air-conditioning. Secondly, it drives a suction fan(s) for removing and redirecting boundary layer air, through the (by-now perfected) porous outer covering of the disc (also useful for cooling). Lastly, it powers at least two coils, to a design originated by our old friend Nikola Tesla. Using a highly conductive material such as copper or a bespoke alloy, these 'Tesla coils' in turn generate huge voltages, which are then directed through one or more transformers to two more Tesla coils, one mounted centrally in the underside of the disc, the other perhaps mounted within the main body of the craft. These coils, in common with all this heavy-duty electrical equipment, are suspended within chambers filled with a non-conductive inert gas or vacuum, to prevent radiated heat from reaching the cockpit. While such specialised coils might be found throughout the actual discs, for this example I'll stick with these two. The coil mounted in the underside of the craft generates powerful laterally directed 'waves' of static electricity, while the other, mounted on board further up the superstructure, generates vertically directed waves. These forces are all channeled through conduits either to the rim of the disc or to the upper and under side, depending on whether they come from the vertical or lateral coil. These localised 'force fields', then, provide both vertical and lateral movement – propulsion and manoeuvrability – as they repel against the natural 'negative' gravity field of the earth and the positive polarity of the upper ionosphere. If you've ever seen the executive toy that suspends a ball bearing 'in space', using two opposed electromagnets, you've witnessed the principle at first hand. Increase the power to one magnet and the bearing is either repelled or attracted – just as the disc reacts to the skies, the earth or other worlds beyond.

These coils might also create a localised 'plasma field' around the fuselage, made up of 'disturbed' ionised air on its way either into or from the electrically charged Porosint, which might allow for even smoother passage through the atmosphere. Alternatively, with all the current flowing around the outer fuselage, perhaps such a *plasmatic* substance might somehow turn the 'sticky' boundary layer itself into a lubricant with the surrounding air, smoothing the disc's passage as it moves and entirely negating the need for a Porosint material – we don't know. The Northrop Corporation of America were supposedly looking at this tech-nology in the 1960s as a way of easing the passage of ICBM warheads as they re-entered the dense lower atmosphere, so perhaps this technology either superseded Porosint altogether or became complementary to it. The disc could still function without an air intake – the crew compartment could be made quite comfortable on a closed air recycling system, and the new engines would no longer require air for cooling; this requirement now reduced with the 'solid-state' nature of the main mechanisms and their insulated isolation.

Travel in the vacuum of outer space was now possible, thanks to Winterhaven and its sister projects. By 'focusing' or simply increasing the gravity force generated from the coils, the craft would then be able to 'bounce' off the gravity field of planets, transmitting either negatively or positively charged electromagnetic energy as required at the speed of light, to react with their natural gravity 'polarity', giving reactive 'repulsion' in the process and allowing craft to 'slingshot' from planet to planet – at speeds far in excess of the fastest moon-bound Apollo command module and all under completely safe control, compared with a rocket. In a rocket, remember, you need to apply reverse thrust if you wish to slow down in space, whereas in a disc you might merely need to redirect the gravity waves in your direction of travel, where they would react against your target planet, or lower the power being levelled to the planet at your back. Either way, the process would offer the same degree of control and manoeuvrability as if flying in the earth's atmosphere.

As far as the crew were concerned, a welcome by-product of Winterhaven would have been the generation of a localised 'microgravity' environment that affected both them and their craft. The 'electrogravitic' motor would cause the mass/inertia of the craft to be minimised, allowing near instantaneous acceleration/ deceleration and directional changes with no discernible effect on them. To the crew, looking through the portholes at the view outside would be like watching a past *recording* of their journey on TV; like a racing driver experiencing *less* G-force than the armchair viewer at home, *while he's actually driving*. Within a microgravity, a pilot would be as near weightless as practical – complete weightlessness would cause drinks to leave their cups and make bathroom breaks as challenging as existing astronauts have long reported, so I would suspect that perhaps lunar gravity – a sixth of the earth's – or similar, would have been adopted.

Whether or not this is *precisely* the system subsequently developed, no one in a position to know for sure is ever likely to confirm. But this writer, at least, is fairly certain that sometime in the early 1960s such a system was developed and gradually perfected. For example, in 1966, during government testimonies to the House Armed Services Committee hearings on UFOs, the noted ufologist Donald Keyhoe noted that forty-six projects involved in gravity research were acknowledged as then ongoing, of which thirty-three were being run by the USAF *and twenty-five of these were classified* (one of them presumably Winterhaven). And this, over thirty years ago! With the endless funds poured into such projects, it is surely an insult to our intelligence to interpret the official silence as suggesting little or no progress was ever achieved. *Of course it was achieved!* And the first recipient was the electrogravitic-equipped, second-generation Alpha series.

But a revolutionary propulsion system would have also transformed the basic design of the latest discs. With such high voltages zapping around, it would be safer to keep the crew within their own hermetically sealed, self-contained cupola, and this is what now happened. Observation portholes were removed and in their place came a clever system that would provide the pilot and his crew with the illusion of all-round visibility. The smooth interior walls, ceiling and floor of the cockpit would be made of a translucent material which would depict a 360-degree panoramic display of the exterior view – the pilot need only look in any one direction to gain his bearings. This sounds intuitive, though human nature being what it is, I can see that adopting this unusual approach would not have been easy for the crews to adapt to. The effect was achieved with the early (classified) development of optical glass fibres. Bundles of these fibres would be mounted flush with the exterior skin over the entire disc, their exposed tips picking up and thence carrying optical information to a magnifying projector behind the cockpit wall, which would in turn project these images on to the opaque wall, to be viewed by the crew on the other side. In this way, with sufficient projectors and fibres, a complete panoramic view could be constructed, in the same way as a fly's compound eye combines visual data from many lenses to form a complete composite. By 'back-projecting' the display, the crew could move about freely, without obscuring the projection of the display. An ability to view enhanced images in infrared would have allowed unhindered night operations, too, while ultraviolet screening would have facilitated safety in space from intense starlight and solar UV radiation.

The sophisticated avionic systems fitted to commercial and military aircraft today wouldn't have existed in the 1960s, but I believe that the systems adopted for the discs back then were still extremely advanced. The instrument panels and avionics would have had to be redesigned to allow pilots and crew to fly the discs and assimilate data quickly. Given the likely electronics then available, even at a classified level, I would suggest that many conventional dials and gauges would have been dispensed with, and in their place would have been cathode-ray tubes (mini-TVs) giving digital readouts, either in a panel of their own or projecting them on to the cockpit wall. Flight controls would have been handled by the pilot with a normal-looking joystick, but this would also have had a separate control for rise and descend and the pilot could blend these control inputs as required, similar to those of a helicopter. I don't believe these craft were flown by the pilot alone, as one or more flight engineers would have been needed to monitor the propulsion systems and navigation. Given the likely complexity of these sub-systems, the pilot could never have coped with so much data and would have required help.

The cockpit space in the smallest jet-powered Alpha would probably have been described as 'snug' for the two or three crew. But even replacing the bulky jet engines and their fuel tanks with the electrogravitic system wouldn't have liberated sufficient space for more than a few seats and perhaps storage lockers and a latrine – certainly not the most comfortable place for a long trip. With the electrostatic waves safely channelled to where they were needed, then leaving sufficient space for the view projectors on the inside of the cupola, the new generation of Alpha craft were probably just as cramped as before, once everything was plumbed in. However, with their incredible performance, flight times around the earth grew much shorter so crews weren't airborne for as long as they had been.

Up to now, we've spoken only of the utility Alpha disc: the 'Jeep' model. But because the new propulsion system allowed flights beyond the earth, much bigger craft were now required that would support larger crews for extended periods. The original Alpha discs stretched to something like 25 metres in diameter, but even this was now too small, so a new model evolved into the second type of disc reported: what I call the Beta disc. I see this craft as being the disc equivalent of any modern army's 'four-tonner' lorry: the go-anywhere load-lugger that can take any amount of abuse. While larger discs have been reported from the earliest days of the TG, we may assume these to have been one-off prototypes of other designs, such as a re-created Haunebu Mark IV, built to evaluate Miethe's principles (he might even have helped build it!). Such sightings were always rare, which would tend to support this notion. But with the requirement for larger craft of up to 100 metres in diameter, the Beta discs would have now entered the scene.

In a structure as large as this, round portholes are often reported (which would dissipate any swirling electrical plasma) at various elevations, throughout a distinctly domed superstructure at the disc's centre, leading observers to believe that these are observation windows from different decks, and I would agree. In the absence of hard data on the number of decks involved, it seems likely that for a craft of this size at least two or three levels would be needed for long voyages. The main cockpit might be on the upper deck, a small galley and crew quarters on the deck below, with any further lower decks given over to cargo. With the Beta models up and running and fitted with the powerful electrogravitic motors, I suspect that the TG then started looking at the next size of craft: what we might think of in the sci-fi age as the 'mothership'.

The mothership designs are invariably seen only at high altitude and are reportedly of gigantic size; some reports have suggested that they're over 1.5 kilometres in length, dwarfing the ship seen at the end of the film *Close Encounters of the Third Kind*. Smaller Alpha and Beta discs have also been reported as being launched from or entering their vast bulk.

In discounting any view that supports an alien origin for these craft, what might be the explanation? One answer might be that these are actually some form of large dirigible – an airship – constructed not here on earth but in space. This sounds an outlandish proposition, but allow me to explain. To build a self-supporting structure of this size, capable of flying through the earth's atmosphere, even at half the size, would be beyond any engineering discipline I can conceive of. To start with, its mass in the earth's gravity would be simply too great to overcome with conventional jets. Even with the electrogravitic power plant to help minimise its mass and so get it into the air, I can not accept that something as large and as secret as this could be built on the earth. It would simply be too big to be hidden anywhere other than in the middle of Antarctica or an Australian desert. Not *absolutely* inconceivable, then, but a bit too far-fetched. And as we know, Soviet spy satellites would surely notice something as big as this, even if steps were taken to conceal it.

But the new generation of Beta discs had the ability to leave the earth's gravity and, in turn, would have enabled some form of operation to be established – and I almost cringe when I say this – but established on the dark side of the moon. Why? For the simplest answer of all – that it's hidden from view. Without getting too involved, construction of such a huge mothership would have been more than possible in the depths of space and/or on the moon, where the gravity is only a sixth of that on the earth. This hidden location would have permitted such a huge construction effort to take place in secret, with materials either ferried up by the Beta discs or even extracted and refined on the moon itself – a proposition which isn't as far-fetched as it might sound, even back in the 1960s; especially if the Beta discs had been on hand. The behemoth of a ship that resulted would have been built as a massive dirigible, with a stressed metal exoskeleton, covered with an alloy or resin skin capable of resisting solar and other radiation. It would also need to be resistant to tearing and be self-sealing, after being hit by micro-meteorites – an ever-present hazard in space with a craft this big. Inside, decking would provide both lateral and vertical bracing, and the whole ship might have resembled the classic cylindrical shape for its strength and its efficient use of space. Once completed, one or more of these new motherships might then have provided forward bases for operations: carrying discs back and forth to the moon when required (perhaps to save fuel) and 'delivering' them just outside the upper reaches of the earth's upper atmosphere, where our gravity is weak enough to allow such a huge craft to manoeuvre safely under its own power. When 'docked' or 'anchored' at the dark side of the moon, either on the surface or in geo-stationary orbit, they might then have acted – or act still – as a *garage*, in which maintenance and so on is undertaken, the low gravity levels in the hangars liberating the mechanics inside, who would now be able to perform their duties without needing to be tethered down. As to the size of the craft, 1.5 kilometres in length still strikes me as a little adventurous, so I would plump for something maybe 400 to 600 metres long. What witnesses genuinely perceive as being 1.5 kilometres long might, in fact, simply be closer than they realise and so distorts their impressions.

Since the advent of the electrogravitic technology back in the 1960s, I believe the wares developed by the TG to have evolved gradually. As systems became more compact, efficient and reliable, a whole new wave of craft could then be built in all shapes and sizes – something that has certainly appeared to take place in the sightings of the past twenty years.

Talk of smaller craft leads me now to outline the possible

development of the original Foo Fighter project. Over many sightings, UFO witnesses have reported seeing discs accompanied by smaller craft seen only as multicoloured lights. This would be consistent with a small, unmanned 'drone' craft, operated either remotely from within the main disc or autonomously controlled but attached to one of the larger piloted craft, such as the Beta type.

Powered by a small electrogravitic system, their role would be to penetrate sensitive areas for reconnaissance, where the full-sized craft dare not go: monitoring ambient atmospheric conditions, acting as a discreet and passive observation platform or undertaking some other task. But what is certain is that they appear to be a direct descendant of the original German Foo Fighters. Fifty years of continual development has made them faster, lighter and more manoeuvrable, and instead of harassing Allied bombers their role now is far more sophisticated. Given the number of sightings in which witnesses have seen these smaller 'robotic' craft, they must be an integral component in the TG's activities.

What these mini-discs have in common with all their big brothers, though, is the variety of colours they've been known to display. Through every shade in the Pantone series, these coloured lights are central to the UFO phenomenon. Witnesses to UFOs of all sizes report seeing coloured lights from the size of a spotlamp through to huge coronas. What they are or what causes them, are subjects we perhaps should now focus on. For the spotlamp-type beams, there's no reason why these couldn't simply be actual spotlamps. Like any aircraft, lights would make it easier for a ground crew to recognise and orientate the craft at night. If a series of coloured filters were then applied over them during flight, they would confuse any observers lucky enough to see them. Of course, it would be just as effective to turn the lights off, but in creating and perpetuating the illusion, the lights are an integral psychological weapon, to prevent people from discerning more detail of the craft itself – as long as you're blinded by twinkling lights, it makes it hard to see beyond them.

For an explanation behind the all-over sheens of colour some-times reported to cover the entire craft, we should re-examine the propulsion system. In channelling waves of electromagnetic energy around the fuselage of a disc, there is bound to be a degree of corona discharge as the surrounding air is charged and ionised. It is known that this phenomenon can cause a glowing aura, and perhaps this is what observers see. The atmospheric conditions and ambient lighting, coupled with the angle at which you see the craft, all go to influence the colours seen.

Various noises have also been reported by witnesses, the most common form being a low vibratory hum, or rumble, which is most likely a side-effect of the energy waves as they pass over the listener. At one time it was thought that the human ear was incapable of such perception, but tests have shown that when modulated to a certain pattern, such electromagnetic radio waves (RF) can be 'heard' as a result of harmonic resonance – in exactly the same pattern as in these sightings. Before the electrogravitic systems were perfected, people would have heard the noise from the previously fitted jet engines as the discs passed by, modulated with the whistle from the air being sucked and expelled through the Porosint. Perhaps the porous fuselage coatings now used (if at all) still generate the whistle, but this is muffled out by the RF waves.

But as well as the bright lights and the basso profundo sound effects, what impact might the electrogravitic power plant have on its surroundings? Imagine a typical close encounter, where a person spots a real Beta disc, say, at rest in a forest glade. The pilot or some other crew member is seen outside taking measurements, but why? Perhaps he/she is measuring the effect of the power plant on the surrounding flora – after all, the vertical Tesla coil, which has brought the craft down to earth in something of a controlled free fall, has been pumping out standing waves of electromagnetic energy (not unlike a huge microwave transmitter dish used in telecommunications), and the waves have 'cooked' parts of the ground in the process. Whatever his job, the crewman is wearing the familiar silvery-metallic coverall – and why wouldn't he, when working in close proximity to such a powerful source of electrical and RF energy? The TG doesn't want our witness to recognise the crewman as a human for obvious reasons, so the protective suit and helmet also serve as a useful disguise. After a while and with the measurements over, the crewman returns to the craft through a hitherto unseen seamless doorway. The hatch is invisible only because, when shut, it forms part of the conductive surface over which the electromagnetic plasma is flowing. The optical effect this creates masks any sign of a door seal. Failing that, if the craft has a Porosint-type fuselage, perhaps the door is obscured by the turbulence of the airflow as it passes through. With a deep rumble that steadily increases in pitch and frequency, and which the witness feels throughout his bones, the craft gently lifts from the ground and rises to a height of around 50 metres before it zips from sight in the twinkle of an eye.

The rumble is caused by the vertical coils increasing their revs and their power output, from gently ticking over to something capable of generating sufficient lift to defeat the earth's gravity. As it climbs to a sufficiently safe height – above the tree line, for example, at 50 metres – the pilot then switches emphasis to the horizontal coils, which kick in with stupendous acceleration forwards. Remember, the mass, and thus inertia, will be a tiny fraction of what in reality it *should* be, so acceleration appears brutally fast to our witness, who therefore can't see where it's gone; the human eye is easily fooled by startling movement. With these vivid impressions tumbling over in his mind, the witness then rushes forwards to the spot where the craft had just been and sees small circles of grass, charred down to their roots, along with the soil, and is mystified. The cause behind what he sees is that these phenomena are conducive with having been *microwaved* –

which in essence is exactly what's happened to them. The electro-magnetic gravity waves emanating from the coils have caused these localised effects where they were most concentrated and most powerful, and this is what the crewman was measuring in all probability. This effect, as with all the others seen, is explainable, but because our witness is unable to comprehend what he's seen he therefore has no points of reference with which to compare it.

In centuries past, this would have been attributable to 'gods', but, to our modern witness, 'aliens' seems better to fit the bill. After all, thanks to the efforts of the TG over the past fifty years, he knows no better and as so many others – witnesses or sceptics – are fond of saying: 'If it were the work of a government, then we would know about it by now . . .'

Of course, the likelihood of either the TG or their projects ever coming out into the open is extremely remote – even in the wake of Silver Bug. Yet, even a project as secretive as this will have made its mark in various ways around the world. While there may never be a guided tour of the Canadian base on offer, nor a guidebook produced to outline the vast Area 51 Dreamland complex in New Mexico, there are a whole host of different sites about which we know very little and which, by implication, might be linked with our story. We shall be taking a closer look at some of them in the next chapter.

chapter nine

'To keep oneself safe does not mean to bury oneself.'
Seneca, *On Peace of Mind*.

'Do not speak of secret matters in a field that is full of little hills.'
Hebrew proverb.

As we've seen in past chapters, the level of secrecy covering the entire disc project is comparable to, if not exceeding, that given to the Manhattan Project – and *that* effort spawned the atom bomb. From the project's earliest days in wartime Germany, the various agencies charged with keeping the development of 'flying saucers' secret have spared no expense to ensure that it continues that way. Kammler's ambitious SS facility at Kahla and the one at Nordhausen were just two of many such sites in Nazi Germany capable of housing the project *and* keeping it safe from prying eyes. We know there were many others too – all playing their own, smaller role in the story: for example, the various Luftwaffe research centres involved in developing the technologies used.

If the assumption is correct that Britain acquired the blueprints of Schriever's and Miethe's discs, then a wholly new facility in which to develop them would have had to be constructed; a development that surely heralded the move to Canada and out of sight. The southern stretch of British Columbia stretches for many hundreds of square kilometres and is densely wooded, mountainous and sparsely populated: perfect conditions in which to hide an undertaking like this. As we've already seen, the Canadian Department of Mines would have been aware of the local topography, in greater detail than that available to the general public. As new editions of maps have since appeared of the area concerned, who can say whether all evidence of the existence of a base have simply been struck from the record? It would be easy enough to achieve. The Alaskan Highway has so many spur roads that missing off one or two on the maps might not be spotted.

I have already shown how and where such a base might have been built, so we should now focus on the form it might have taken. VTOL-capable discs do not require runways from which to operate so, as a result, no long and conspicuous runways are required. This drastically reduces the perimeter of the base and even allows for the use of special camouflaged hangars with shuttered apertures in the roof, allowing craft to fly direct from the hangar. Regular helicopters could also use a facility like this, like something out of a James Bond film in which the villain's secret lair is hidden inside a dormant volcano. One spin-off from taking such care over the camouflage is to ensure that operations can continue through the long winters experienced in this part of the world. Since the Second World War, Canadian military engineers have devised many tricks to keep conventional airfields open in adverse weather, and some of these techniques would surely have been incorporated into the design of the new Anglo-Canadian base. Within the camouflage, insulation for the roofs of hangars and other buildings would have ensured that both access doors and shutters continued working and that the infrared 'heat signature' that might be picked up by spy satellites was minimised.

I've already mentioned their combined efforts in establishing the uranium operation in Chalk River and the apparent efficiency and secrecy with which this was undertaken. But the discs were of a higher order of importance altogether, and while funding *did* ensure the start-up of the project and the creation of the base in British Columbia, at some point the British, if not also the Canadian government too, would have expected to see some return for their investment in plant and research and development. Both countries were coming out of the Second World War bruised and economically weakened, and, although they rightly believed themselves winners of the technological prize, they lacked the resources necessary to do it justice in the long term – even something as strategically critical and imperative as this.

While unfortunate, the crash at Roswell at least got the Americans interested and, with them on board and the TG under way, funding was no longer a problem. One can predict, perhaps somewhat accurately, that in return for contributing the lion's share of the budget, America would have demanded future manufacturing rights as a further boost to American industry. As the 1950s dawned, the Soviet Union began knocking on Western Europe's door with some of that same belligerence aimed at the USA itself, so it's not hard to see how and why the TG came together as it might have done. The generals and admirals who saw these discs, even red herrings such as Silver Bug, wouldn't have taken much persuasion to pump more resources into the TG, of that we can be *quite* sure.

And as the balance of power within the TG shifted, so the Canadian base would now act as a satellite to the main manufacturing and test effort in the USA; any British efforts would remain low key and geared to providing engineering expertise. Britain is a relatively small, crowded island, offering substantially less scope for building a secret facility in some deserted wilderness. Not only that, but any daylight flights of the discs over the UK in a regular test programme would be crazy, given the likely numbers of witnesses – even in the wilds of Wales or Scotland. This same stark choice was faced fifty years ago, which is why Britain's contribution to the TG's operational side has been to offer only occasional stopover facilities – remote air-force and private airfields geared up to providing temporary landing facilities. On the research and development side, British scientists have always had the TG base in Canada at their disposal, as well as access to the many sites in the USA believed to be linked to TG activity. This author would suggest that the British and Canadian input (if not joined by additional countries such as Australia) has been as valid and as influential as that of the USA. Each member is there on merit, after all.

Once the TG itself got going in around 1947–8, it would have needed an American HQ and so eyes turned to the south-west United States; an area that even today remains sparsely populated, in complete contrast to the UK. Las Vegas and Albuquerque were as villages compared with the cities that dominate the area now, and with wide stretches of desert, together with fine weather for much of the year, the area represented the ideal situation for the TG to set up operations. We've already learned of the close proximity to Roswell of the 509th bomber group, but that secluded base in New Mexico was just one of many in the neighbouring states of California, Arizona, Texas and Colorado. The Second World War had thrown up a need for such facilities, offering privacy for testing new aircraft, while the development of the atomic bomb, and the new levels of secrecy this had required, had given America's fledgling security services the means and expertise to develop them. From the forced purchase of land from ranchers and native Indians alike, to the sequestration and commandeering of land from other government departments, the air force, the Department of Defense and other unlikely agencies such as the Department of Agriculture were establishing themselves as the real power-brokers behind some of the region's largest land deals. As the Cold War raged on, no one individual dared to question these policies for fear of being branded a Communist sympathiser, so these federal agencies doggedly carried on with their 'land grabs' and various preparations for a third world war.

Some locations have since become familiar to those interested in aerospace history, such as White Sands proving ground and Edwards Air Force Base (formerly Muroc Field), to name but two. The American space agency NASA has itself enjoyed a long association with these bases and helped raise their profile. For example, when the space shuttle flies back to the earth, its second runway of choice is the 4.8-kilometre-long R-23 at Edwards. During the 1960s, NASA made a number of important research flights at the base and elsewhere with 'lifting body' aircraft – planes with fuselages carefully shaped to generate lift without the need for profiled wings; the shuttle is a direct descendant of this research. As a result of having these huge and secure open spaces at hand, it seems entirely possible that the TG would have been able to commandeer a small section of just such a site, with only a handful of people from the base in on the secret.

White Sands stretches for hundreds of square kilometres, and in the 1950s it was used as a missile test range, so it would have been relatively easy to hide a sizable base out of sight somewhere within the perimeter. While I'm being careful not to point the finger at White Sands as the location of the TG's first American base, we do know that Silver Bug was tested there, as well as at Edwards Air Force Base, which raises our suspicions. So, purely in a spirit of supposition, let's assume that the bigger White Sands site *was* chosen. Given the highly classified nature of Silver Bug, let alone the Alpha discs, compared with the 'conventional' rocketry experiments then being carried out at the base, it seems likely that some kind of 'semi-detached' arrangement with the air force would have been needed to keep it hidden, whereby the highest ranks know what's going on but lower-ranking personnel are none the wiser. That the White Sands radar controllers occasionally issued UFO reports lends further weight to the possibility that either they weren't informed and issued them in genuine belief or, once again, that such reports covertly marked Silver Bug and Alpha flights. Some observers might denounce either policy as misguided, if not plain irresponsible, given the potential for disaster with the discs sharing local airspace with missiles and jet fighters. But the simplest answer to such doubts is to bear in mind the likely resources used by the TG, wherever their base actually happened to be.

It seems highly probable that the Silver Bug and Alpha teams had their own radar and radio controllers, keeping a close watch on airspace and atmospheric conditions. But the Alpha's avionics were of a classified design, years ahead of anything then fitted in 'production' jet aircraft. With this degree of sophistication and their enhanced agility, Alphas and Silver Bugs would have enjoyed an overwhelming superiority, whenever in close quarters with conventional aircraft straying into their own airspace, intentionally or otherwise. Perhaps this advantage was actually tested on occasion, against unwitting fighter pilots, scrambled to confront 'alien spacecraft', which in reality were no more alien than they were. Perhaps Captain Mantell found himself in similar circum-stances back in 1948.

As for those who suggest it would be foolish for discs to operate from such a covert site, given the likelihood of being picked up by the radar of the 'host' base, such as White Sands (and thus have its origin publicly identified), I would offer two answers. Firstly, a disc could easily fly at low altitude over the desert floor, where radar could not detect it, until such time as it increased its altitude and thus suddenly appeared on screens, so keeping its point of origin secret. Secondly, the discs might even have incorporated some early form of stealth technology: for example, perhaps the electrogravitic propulsion system and the electrical plasma flowing over its fuselage might somehow have minimised its radar signature as a side-effect. This would have allowed discs to come and go freely, with local radar operators being none the wiser. Remember, too, that the radar equipment of forty or fifty years ago was much, much simpler and less effective than today's sophisticated devices.

Even if the TG's new base had been constructed along the same basic principles likely enshrined in the original Canadian site, it would still have been nearly invisible to observation from both ground and air, with no runways, large hangars, blockhouses etc. A visitor in the early 1950s would most likely have seen cars and trucks parked outside conventional-looking hangars and out-buildings, perhaps partially disguised with earth banking against the sides to disrupt the outline of the walls; a conspicuous radar array would have also been visible. But given the totally restricted nature of the site, none of this would have been visible from the nearest marked road on the air base, nor from the air and certainly not from a public road, which means it was at least 20 kilometres from the nearest signs of life – a distance easily swallowed in the White Sands complex. Given its inhospitable terrain, the site must have had its own water and electricity and been supplied with essential material, either from clandestine helicopter drops or nightly road convoys, taking lessons learned from the original Anglo-Canadian base. Roving swarms of security guards would watch all roads leading to the site and would use force where necessary to keep the secret safe. I wouldn't be at all surprised if, under free questioning, ex-employees of bases such as White Sands at least admitted to hearing rumours of strange things going on during the 1950s and 1960s.

The Soviets were known to be developing their own new generation of spy satellites during the 1960s and 1970s. This meant that the established sites at places such as White Sands were now under a degree of enhanced scrutiny, and this had implications for continuing operations, as it meant that the increasingly sophisti-cated Alpha discs might also now be show. Keeping them a secret from the numbers of other staff at the base, such as NASA personnel, was also going to be a difficult job, so a new location was sought.

Taking the base under ground, at another site, was by then a relatively easy task and would surely have been the preferred option when thoughts turned to its construction. Building an underground facility, while often hideously expensive initially, has several distinct advantages for the inevitable time when an enemy tries to locate it. To start with, unlike a base that's out in the open, the enemy first has to locate it. This might not be easy if the only outward signs of its existence visible from the air are a few discreet air vents and a camouflaged roadway; after all, Nordhausen stayed secret. Secondly, if it's built into a hillside or mountain, how would the enemy know in which direction the tunnels ran? They might target their bombs or missiles on one concentrated area, believing it to be at the hub of the complex, when in fact it might easily turn out to be an unused wing. Moreover, if the base itself is built deep enough, with masses of earth and bedrock above, then it becomes virtually impenetrable to conventional explosives, as was found during the Second World War when the Allies tried to bomb German U-boat pens and naval gun emplacements sunk into sheer cliffs. Even nuclear warheads must be considered futile in such cases – would an enemy have that many as to reduce a mountain range to dust?

An approach to coping with overkill has been subsequently adopted throughout the world when it comes to building secure sites. From huge (and recently extended) command bunkers under the Kremlin, to stockpiles of food and weapons hidden by survivalists in the backwoods of Montana, those looking to survive a future conflict view the ground beneath their feet as the answer and find unlimited room to manoeuvre once there. But we are less concerned with the architecture of a third world war than whether, in the isolated sites we know of, there are clues as to the existence of the TG and its continuing activities, fifty years since its inception.

But mention the notion that an entire air base could be sited underground and such a notion seems to skate glibly over the numerous technicalities and problems assumed to be inherent in creating such ambitious subterranean structures. The difficulties, however, have long since been ironed out and lessons learned.

From the time of the Roman occupation, British architects and builders with grand visions and large budgets have used limestone found in the hills surrounding the English city of Bath; taking it from open-cast quarries at first but later, as surface supplies dwindled, from sediments deep under ground. At its height, in the nineteenth century, the hills surrounding the city boasted over 8 kilometres of continual workings: and this at a time when the workings were literally blasted out by gunpowder and dynamite and the limestone carried out by legions of Irish navies. Brunel's London–Bristol Great Western Railway ran for 3 kilometres through the Box Tunnel, which runs parallel to the original mine workings and remains in daily use today. When considering the feasibility of such questions as whether or not an air base could be located under ground, we should remember such past achievements and conclude that it could – at a price. But with the almost bottomless TG budget, even such riders as the question of cost are irrelevant and, as we shall see, such resources buy structures that easily dwarf Brunel's accomplishments.

In the years leading up to the Second World War, techniques for underground construction revolved around two main pieces of equipment. The first, the labourer with a pickaxe and shovel, had been around since the dawn of time. The second was a relatively new machine called a stonecutter, which employed a large circular saw (with diamond-tipped cutting teeth) that would cut a rock face into manageable blocks, which could then be hauled away by conveyors, tractors or horses. Even with the other main tools of the trade, such as TNT for blasting and steel and concrete supports with which to shore up the roof, progress was often painfully slow, expensive and downright dangerous for those involved. Yet these trusted methods enabled the Germans to extend the Nordhausen workings and many others, and they allowed the British to convert the Bath stone quarries into ammunition stores and turn the Rock of Gibraltar into an anthill-like fortress.

After the war, private companies in the USA began looking at methods of speeding up the process, either as a result of their own initiative or from prompting by the American government, and their efforts were soon to bear fruit with the first TBM, or tunnel-boring machine. Many improvements have been made to the basic design in the decades since the machines first appeared, but the principle behind the TBM is essentially the same. In common with the earthworm, the typical TBM has a long, cylindrical shape of around 12 metres in diameter, with, at the 'mouth' end, either a single, large, rotating cutting head or a series of smaller heads of different materials, with which it bores through rock. In operation, a series of hydraulic grippers brace the body of the TBM to the walls of the tunnel to keep it level and on target, while more jacks keep the cutting head in contact with the rock face. The TBM moves forwards, as a result of these hydraulic jacks flexing in a synchronised fashion to drag it forwards, like the muscles in an earthworm or caterpillar. The spoil produced (known as 'muck') passes back through its 'body' all the while, to be emptied on to a conveyor or narrow-gauge rail waggons, which take it to the surface. In providing a safe environment for its operators, TBMs are generally electrically powered to prevent exhaust pollution, and the air-conditioned cabs in which the crew monitor progress are also mounted towards the rear.

But while a TBM can drill at a faster rate than ever achieved with conventional techniques, the resulting tunnel might still need to be strengthened to prevent falls of rock. These are still an operational hazard when tunnelling through unstable rock strata and might easily entomb both the TBM and its crew. To prevent such disasters, provision is usually made for inserting either concrete or steel sleeve supports into the walls of the tunnel as the TBM proceeds, though in structurally sound bedrock such reinforcement is often not required.

This, then, is the essence of the standard TBM first seen in the

1950s. Later models were used in the construction of the Anglo-French 'Chunnel', finally open for use in the 1990s. One of the TBMs used now sits in the railhead car-park at the side of the M20 motorway, giving a sense of just how big these machines can be.

But these 'conventional' TBMs are useful only in certain types of terrain, usually more or less horizontally, without descending down too steep a gradient, moving perpendicularly into the side of a hill or mountain from a plateau, or in a shape resembling a sagging length of spaghetti, as is the case with the English Chunnel, which is not flat and has to dip midway under the Channel to get below chalky strata on the seabed. But in order to maximise the use of space within a mountain, engineers need to bore out many levels – floors – and a TBM isn't flexible enough – or small enough for the job. So as well as developing new drills, which could bore vertical shafts wide enough for truck-sized lift cages, manufacturers also came up with a new generation of smaller machines, resembling armoured JCBs, called either roadheaders or mobile miners, which could be lowered into place down these shafts to a predetermined depth, before boring into the side of the shaft to open up a new gallery or workings. Their small size, compared with a TBM, gives the architects of these subterranean domains freedom to honeycomb the given mountain or stretch of land; crisscrossing it with spacious galleries, roadways, caverns and silos, and all at a faster speed than was ever achieved before and in a density that an unwieldy TBM would find hard to match.

The diamond-tipped drill bits on TBMs and roadheaders work as an abrasive, gnawing away at the rock. But this alone creates endless problems for those wishing to conceal the prime evidence of activity – the muck. Any satellite photograph of a site will show either endless truck or rail convoys leaving a tunnel, or nearby spoil tips. At first, the TG, along with other agencies in the US, would have had no choice but to put up with the muck. But new Soviet satellites would have detected this evidence, so new techniques for tunnelling were developed that would not create muck. Highly classified methods have been in operation for at least thirty years, ranging from high-pressure water cannon, in which small pellets are mixed with the water to jet-blast the rock surface and create a liquidised slurry which can be piped away out of sight, to perhaps the most intriguing idea of all – subterrenes.

The subterrene first appeared in patents granted to the Los Alamos National Laboratory and the US Atomic Energy Commission in 1972, but, after this, enthusiasm for the idea seems to have disappeared. The essence of the idea patented was of a nuclear-powered TBM that circulated super-heated, radioactive lithium to a rock face, liquefying it in the process. The molten muck is then forced, under pressure, into the fissures and cracks in the surrounding rock, as the subterrene passes by. The two main advantages are, firstly, there is no longer a need for roof supports as this vitrified tunnel lining is entirely self-supporting and, secondly, there is no muck to be dispersed. Due to the high temperatures and radioactivity involved, the crew compartment to the rear of the subterrene would need to be heavily insulated and shielded – assuming such devices even needed a human crew, as they might have been operated remotely.

A more prosaic design mentioned at the time involves adding to the cutting head of a more conventional TBM a series of industrial laser guns, which would blast the rock face, allowing the existing cutters to break it off more easily. Though this would certainly speed things up, compared with using a wholly conventional machine, it would still create muck and wouldn't be as cost-effective as a subterrene. Powered by a nuclear reactor, the subterrene would be almost self-sufficient in operation and could continue working with less maintenance, compared with a conventional TBM. If a crew was required, they could rotate shifts accordingly and keep the machine running continuously. In this manner, devices such as roadheaders and subterrenes could create huge, self-supporting open caverns by burrowing out a tunnel in a decreasing (or increasing) spiral from any given point.

While speculation on the existence of actual subterrenes continues, we should remember these apparently forgotten patents. Let it not go unsaid that such patents would not have been awarded in the first place had the design not been proven to work. After all, these are patents issued from one government agency to another, and this wouldn't happen if they were just 'going through the motions' to protect notional technology. Issuing patents – and therefore bringing this material into the public domain – could also be seen as part of the information management policy instigated by the TG as, once again, we're seeing things through a fog of asides and incidental material.

The official story has it that the US government first started using TBMs in the 1950s to construct a series of elaborate bomb shelters, for the evacuation of the government and military leaders in the event of nuclear war, along with the silos for America's various ICBMs. Most people are at least aware of such plans and have heard of sites such as NORAD (North American Aerospace Defense Command) – the 'super-command' bunker under Cheyenne Mountain, Colorado. In the 1980s, under President Reagan's policy of increased defence spending, this network was believed to have been further augmented with plans for an expanded chain of more missile silos.

Contract details, unearthed under the US Freedom of Information Act, were sent out to various companies involved in one such 'deep-basing' tunnel plan. The project, due for completion in 1990, involved excavating a deep tunnel of perhaps more than 915 metres deep and over *320 kilometres long*, along the length of a mountain range somewhere in the western USA. A few subterrenes would appear to be the most likely candidates to take on the task. For a tunnel of this length, the countless millions of tonnes of muck produced by conventional TBMs would be far too bulky to conceal and could easily show up on a satellite image, whereas that problem doesn't arise with a subterrene. If the main entrance is hidden under ground and reached only through other linking tunnels, then no one need know of the site's location. In the event of nuclear war, this tunnel would be permanently sealed, and from many dozens, if not hundreds, of offshoot spurs leading off the main 'road', autonomous TBMs (already in place and each towing a nuclear missile) would be readied by their now equally entombed crews. After judging that a suitable time had elapsed (which might even be years), these crews would start up the nuclear-powered TBMs, which would then bore their way to the surface along preprogrammed routes. The missiles would then be launched, turning a little bit more of the enemy to dust and giving the last laugh to America. Like the TG and its various projects, no one in a position to confirm or deny the rumours is saying anything about this tunnel – neither if or when it's been built, nor even if it's all a nonsensical red herring. To this author, such a tunnel seems not just possible, but probable. Furthermore, I would suggest that along its length are hangars for the long-term storage of certain TG production discs. After all, what better method of getting about an atomic wasteland or leaving the planet entirely than in a sealed flying saucer?

But all this was in the future when the TG first started relocating to the USA from British Columbia during the 1950s. We have already tried to guess at what form the original Anglo-Canadian site might have taken, but any base in America would need the same guaranteed concealment. During the 1950s, space technology hadn't yet advanced to building spy satellites, and with the Soviets unable to build either aircraft or discs capable of clandestine flights over the USA, aerial observation was the least concern. In choosing a site like White Sands, for example, the normal airspace restrictions in force on a military air base would have ensured that no one could 'accidentally' stray too close without meeting a concerted resistance. Even back then, this policy would also have dissuaded casual onlookers on the ground. But as the 1950s gave way to the 1960s, the TG would have begun to consider two issues: nuclear attack and possible Soviet spy satellites. All existing bases were doubtless already targeted for attack and, given the poor accuracy of the first generation of ICBMs on either side, even having a site on the periphery might end up receiving an accidental direct hit.

A new site, with the potential for underground development, was therefore sought. Happily, one such secret base already existed. Cloaked in mystery equivalent to that surrounding the F-117 stealth fighter-bomber before its announcement during the Gulf War, the U-2 spy plane was the most advanced conventional aircraft in the US air force during the 1950s and early 1960s, and every effort was made to keep its existence secret. To this end, a dry lake bed in the Nevada Desert, called Groom Lake was identified as a near-perfect area from which to operate the aircraft. It was close to a nuclear weapons range, so unauthorised ventures into its airspace were strictly forbidden, and it was many kilometres from the nearest habitation and roads. A scratch base was set up there in great haste in 1955, only a few months ahead of the arrival of the first U-2s. As no road entered the site, everything had to be flown in, and pilots were usually guided down on instructions issued from an anonymous control tower before seeing the almost unmarked runway at the last minute. During the 1950s, as this remote site became home to the U-2 training squadron, the flimsy prefab buildings gradually gave way to more permanent structures – but all the while Groom Lake stayed completely hidden and far from any prying eyes. As the 1960s arrived, I would suspect that the very remoteness of the site had already allowed some work on the discs to take place here and that plans for the relocation of the Alpha project here were already in train. The mountains surrounding Groom Lake, and in particular those surrounding the nearby Papoose Lake (24 kilometres to the south), offered a haven of peace and security and an environment in which production of the Alpha and Beta discs could begin. The U-2s operated only from Groom Lake, so I would hazard a guess that the TG then took over Papoose Lake, airlifting in tunnelling equipment, such as subterrenes, to create a more permanent home for the discs at the start of the 1960s – a location that at least one witness has named 'Es-4' (pronounced 'ess four'), though what the acronym translates to no one knows.

In recent years, the activities *known* to have been undertaken at Groom Lake itself have revolved around a unique air-force squadron that tests aircraft either captured or appropriated from various sources and manufacturers worldwide. Several Russian and Chinese jet fighters are stationed there, and mock dogfights have been conducted between pilots in the latest American and NATO fighters against colleagues in MIGs. As well as testing other once-secret American aircraft, such as the F-117, the B-2 stealth bomber and the U-2's successor, the SR-71 Blackbird, testing of 'alien' aircraft, to use the regular military jargon, seems to be its main activity. It all sounds innocent enough, until one learns that progressively through the 1990s the US government has grabbed more land surrounding Groom Lake to prevent any members of the public from seeing the base – even at a distance. At one time, onlookers could climb a ridge some 45 kilometres from the base to view it with telescopes, but, since Freedom Ridge was swallowed up in a land-grab, the legends surrounding the Groom Lake complex have grown almost exponentially. Observers have openly questioned why such steps should have been taken, if all that was flying there were old MIGs. Casual visitors to the open site cannot now trespass more than a few kilometres off the road before meeting camouflaged and armed guards (known locally as cammo dudes), who are authorised to shoot to kill persons who disregard their warnings to turn back.

If the name doesn't immediately ring any bells, perhaps its nickname of 'Dreamland' or 'Area 51' sounds more familiar? Technically, A 51 is the code attributed to the 'box' of airspace surrounding Groom Lake, but it seems to have been absorbed into the contemporary UFO culture, as in some way possessing the key to an Aladdin's cave of truly 'alien' technologies and mysteries.

Incidentally, the term 'Blue Fires', from which this book derives its title, is apparently the code given out by the Groom Lake air controllers when flight-testing is about to begin – whether of TG discs, the craft of visiting EBEs or F-16 fighters battling twenty-year-old MIGs.

Groom Lake and, more specifically, the apparent 'Es-4' facility at Papoose Lake have long been associated with tales of captured or donated EBE flying saucers being stripped down and retro-engineered by technicians eager to learn their engineering secrets. Some ufologists have also been keen to speculate on the extent of the ongoing collaboration between the US government and the various species of EBE perceived to have been visiting the earth all these years. EBEs are believed by some to be behind all sorts of exotic projects – from *X-Files*-style genetic engineering projects that will create a cloned human race, through to gradually inducting the world's population into the cosmological 'United Intergalactic Nations'. Such speculation has been rife for many years, since the public first learned of Area 51 and its apparent importance to the whole flying saucer story. But there is no concrete evidence – circumstantial or otherwise – that would support this view. Certainly, the base at Groom Lake exists – photographs taken before Freedom Ridge was put out of bounds clearly show some of its buildings and a large radar dish. Even today, airliners continue to ferry workers to the base, from Las Vegas' McCurran Airport. Before the withdrawal of access, buses could be seen ferrying personnel back and forth between the two dry lakes (the buses had blacked-out windows, so we have to assume they were carrying *human* workers).

Thus far, we have the evidence of only one witness to the 'Es-4' site at Papoose Lake – one Robert Lazar, whose wide-eyed testimony of what he saw when he apparently worked there remains the only clue as to what may or may not be actually going on. On the face of it, his eyewitness account of a series of up to nine underground hangars separated by shutters, each holding a *different* 'flying saucer', appears consistent with the TG's activities. For surely, if this really was – *is* – the main test site for the discs – if not a refurbishing plant (I wouldn't go as far as to suggest it was a manufacturing centre) – then might not the various past, present and future types that had been developed need to be stored and worked on? New technologies plumbed into older mule models, new prototypes being readied for their first flight programme, discs undergoing routine servicing – all a possible explanation for Lazar's claims. He also describes an oppressive security regime in which soldiers loom over the shoulders of all the civilian engineers and scientists working on the discs – a regime that might be expected at a facility as secret as this. It would certainly focus the mind and ensure silence was maintained. This author remembers hearing similar accounts from workmen and electricians employed to build and fit out the silos for American cruise missiles at Greenham Common, in Berkshire, England, during the early 1980s. They all reported similarly oppressive and intimidating working conditions and having guards assigned to them on virtually a one-to-one basis, even accompanying them to the lavatory. It sounds similar, then, but it's in more basic areas where Lazar's testimony starts to break down, not least because of the muddied waters of his past.

No creative engineering project can survive, let alone thrive, under such horrendously oppressive security as that described. It would stifle the creativity of the engineers present who, whether they were working on a stealth fighter or a flying disc, would all be equally committed to keeping the secret in any case. A well-motivated team works well on its own, without coercion. Just ask the operatives at the Lockheed 'skunk works' in Palmdale, California, who for decades have worked to build some of the most secretive 'conventional' aircraft ever built and flown. Security was maintained in every instance by people believing themselves to be working as an elite unit, so there is no reason to suspect that those working in Es-4 are experiencing more oppressive conditions. Lazar suggests that the guards are there as a result of the Es-4 project being run by the military authorities, but in reality there might well be roving guards who are there to ensure that no one snoops around outside their own areas, but not to the degree he reported. He was *meant* to see them being so oppressive because, in his (and therefore our own) view, this reinforces the notion that something of even greater cataclysmic importance is being developed there than 'just' flying saucers . . . something alien. That is precisely what he was meant to believe and subsequently report. And did so well. Just like the witnesses to the 'alien' corpses at Roswell forty years before: the illusion is still playing out.

It was probably for Lazar's benefit that the interconnecting doors between the hangars were opened, to give him a glimpse at the extent of the Es-4 base and what it actually held, even when this would not normally happen, in view of the air-conditioning problems it would create. But Lazar still saw things . . . They may not have been *real*, in the sense that they may not have reflected the day-to-day reality of those men and women who work there and who administer the TG, but he saw them none the less. To be fair, when pressed on one occasion to reveal more about the EBE he once glanced out of the corner of his eye while walking down a corridor, he admits that it could easily have been a manikin tailored to study the ergonomic implications in using the cramped craft he was working on.

But an organisation as efficient as the TG would, under normal circumstances, simply *never* have countenanced the employment of someone with Lazar's hazy credentials, regardless of what the man himself might say to the contrary, and his subsequent escapades and brushes with the law merely add weight to this argument. For example, he claims to have received two degrees, one from Cal-Tech university and the other from Massachusetts Institute of Technology, yet when a researcher in the early 1990s looked into the records around the relevant dates, no mention of Robert S. Lazar could be found as having attended either institution. The same went for those professors whom he had cited as having taught him. One figure, a Professor Duxler, turned out to have been a college lecturer in computing. Just to confuse matters even more, Lazar himself cannot remember how long he worked at Es-4, quoting between four and six months. This sounds odd, to say the least, given that his first revelations occurred shortly after he left his employment, and working on something like this would have been so momentous in his life as not to be easily forgotten. The fact that Lazar can't *prove* anything about his experiences there – even that he actually worked there – is worrying. He once produced a payslip with a security code 'attached to the Office of Naval Intelligence' but when researchers looked into it the code turned out to be listed as a dormant reserve code (perhaps activated as a front especially for him? It's possible).

While I don't want to get into character assassination, one or two points might account for Lazar's description of the layout of Es-4. Firstly, that he picked up odd snippets of information from workers there, whom he met socially or overheard, and strung them together to form his own interpretation of what was going on; credulous ufologists have taken these second-hand impressions and assumed them to be facts. Secondly, the most likely explanation is that Lazar *did* manage to gain employment at Es-4, but that he was chosen not for his technical brilliance in any particular field but deliberately *because* of his relative unsuitability for the post. He had worked for some time at the Los Alamos laboratory under the esteemed physicist Dr Edward Teller, and Lazar suggests that he used this connection as a reference for the opportunity at Es-4.

But I would argue that Teller suggested him because, having worked in whatever capacity with Lazar, he would have known the man and would therefore have been fully aware of his unsuitability for the post. Indeed, Teller might have even been asked by the TG to put forward the name of someone who could be relied on in the future to spill the beans. Lazar was to become merely a high-profile stool pigeon – part of the ongoing TG's disinformation campaign, which has been running since the earliest days of project Alpha. In the end, his employment was brought to an end, following an impromptu drive out to the site one evening with his wife, sister-in-law and a ufologist friend, after Lazar apparently had stated that a test-flight was to take place that night. They were apprehended, and during his next shift at the base Lazar was debriefed and later returned to Las Vegas, his employment over. Apparently, personal issues were also raised at the debriefing, having been unearthed through taps on his personal phone line. These were cited as the reasons for their dispensing with his contribution, though one might equally view the situation as being that Lazar had simply outlived his usefulness – he had learned enough.

At the time of Lazar's first revelations in 1989, the interest in Area 51 was building up to such a degree that a public statement was almost forced out of the air force. In the end, they admitted to no more than running the Groom Lake base, offering nothing about what they might have been doing there. After all, they could hardly come out and admit that for the past forty or so years an absolutely secret agency (which I've called the TG) had been developing its own flying saucers and that Groom and Papoose Lakes were being used expressly for their development . . . It's in the continued interests of member countries that the secret is kept, and the best tool for that is to have people believing in an alternative explanation – in this case, little green men.

But this book isn't about Es-4 or Bob Lazar. While Groom and Papoose Lakes play only a bit part in the TG's story, they manage to steal most of the glory on account of being the only chink in the armour hitherto impervious to outside gaze. In fact, over recent years the publicity surrounding the base is thought to have forced the authorities to move part of the operation to elsewhere within the site – to a place named Area 13, although to what extent this might be believed is open to question. No civilian unconnected with the site has ever conjured up photographs or visited the facility, so it might equally be a red herring – or a real part of the base. No one who knows is saying, and as long as sightseers still visit the nearby town of Rachel and buy 'alien' and 'A 51' souvenirs, they never will.

Aside from the one or two facilities within the Nevada Desert occupied by the TG today, there's also a good chance that the original Canadian facilities are still in use, simply because they're remote enough to remain useful. British engineers employed by companies such as Racal and BAe are probably also still involved in some way, as are facilities in the Australian outback. As well as the extensive test range at Woomera, over which discs would be considered safe to operate freely, the American NSA (National Security Agency) has a large listening post at a place near Alice Springs called Pine Gap, which might easily be used to track disc movements. It's because of this agency's extensive involvement behind the scenes, in eavesdropping on world communications, that it would seem an obvious partner in the activities of the TG. If the NSA weren't involved in some way, it would be impossible to keep the secret from them, as the Alpha discs need to use communications like any other airborne vehicle (albeit heavily encrypted). The NSA should therefore be assumed to be part of the project too, massaging and corrupting any data that leaks into commercial wavebands, thus further blurring the evidence of the TG's activities and/or existence.

The NSA is housed in a secure site at Fort George G. Meade, Maryland. As recently as 1982, it could boast a *ten-acre* underground computer site, which sprawled under several adjacent blocks and boasted perhaps the world's most concentrated array of computing power, with umpteen IBM mainframe machines and at least two CRAY supercomputers. One can only speculate as to what might lie beneath the fort today. As well as boasting its own college, the site has its own shops, hair salons, post office, medical facilities and many other amenities of a small town, on hand for its staff of many thousands. It is also completely self-sufficient with its own power-station, workshops and police force, which patrols the electrified and razor-wired perimeter fence.

The official role of the NSA is to eavesdrop on and decrypt electronic telecommunications traffic from around the world; interpreting it with a view to its importance on the country's national security. In addition to headquarters at Fort George G. Meade and the site at Pine Gap, the NSA occupies sundry other listening posts throughout the world, such as that at Menwith Hill in northern England; each of these sites acts as a relay station, passing the constant flow of data it intercepts and decrypts back to Maryland via satellite. However, with the rise of the Internet and mobile phone technology, its role is becoming harder to fulfil in this new information age, and it's anticipated that in the immediate years to come its activities and ambitions will need to be scaled back, in the face of such hard realities, perhaps to concentrate solely on data encryption and less on broadband eavesdropping.

During the 1950s and 1960s, many UFO witnesses reported visits from mysterious 'men in black', who would call on them in the days immediately following their 'close encounter' and threaten them with unspecified reprisals if they persisted in publicising their experiences. Many observers subsequently dismissed the claims of such visits as close to paranoia, yet they overlooked the relevance of the NSA in relation to the TG in favour of what they saw as the EBE origin of the UFOs/discs they'd seen and reported. I would argue that this huge and secretive agency – with a larger staff and greater intelligence assets at its disposal than even the CIA – might have been responsible for such visits. It would have been simple for the NSA to have tapped these witnesses' telephones and record conversations in which UFOs or flying saucers were mentioned. They would then send members of a particularly secretive, unaccountable and sinister team along to their homes to warn them off. While many such witnesses were doubtless articulate and intelligent, Orson Welles's *War of the Worlds* broadcast had, nonetheless, shown the authorities just how gullible and easily manipulated the public could be when faced with something as sinister and as inexplicable as an unidentified agent. As a result, the anonymous and somewhat faceless 'MiBs' were an ideal and effective silencing tool.

At the time of writing, the NSA continues to play a vital part in the global intelligence network and supporting the work of the TG who would be lost without it – yet there are other groups the TG could equally not be without. The main candidate is the NRO (National Reconnaissance Office) – an agency which provides visual data from its fleet of spy satellites and which occasionally checks on known TG locations to ensure their continued conceal-ment. Not forgetting the British equivalent to the NSA, the Cheltenham-based GCHQ, which receives a feed from Menwith Hill as part of the Operation Echelon eavesdropping programme. Background monitoring of voice and fax telephone traffic as it routes through exchanges or relay stations for key words (for example, 'UFO') would trigger a recording and perhaps even a translation into computer code – probably something only recently perfected. In this way, if a government, organisation or even an individual were embarking on a plan to uncover the secret of the TG and its activities, the NSA would be sure to know about it sooner than anyone else and, with this information, steps could be taken to nip such interest in the bud.

As well as the NSA and NRO, other American agencies have at one time or another been linked by paranoid ufologists with the imminent arrival of alien rule or the 'secret government'. The FEMA (Federal Emergency Management Agency) is one such, but as the agency charged with leading the USA through disasters large or small, one would expect it to have one or two impressive sites from where it might discharge its responsibilities. One can be found near Bluemont, Virginia. Dubbed 'Mount Weather', the 18,580-square-metre underground bunker employs around 900 civilians as part of its Continuity of Government contingency powers. It was built at a cost of over $1 billion during the 1950s and, in the event of an emergency, would provide a secure base for the President and up to 2,000 workers. It is expected that NORAD – being the most widely known base for just such an emergency – would be knocked out fairly quickly in the event of a massed nuclear attack, but Mount Weather, being less conspicuous, is expected to function for months following an attack. To ensure this, the site boasts its own crematoria, water reservoirs, radio and TV studio (part of the Emergency Broadcast System), emergency power plant and a computer centre; hardened against EMP attack, Mount Weather would be used to coordinate a response following FEMA's activation.

Another site is only 8 kilometres or so north of Camp David – the presidential weekend retreat. Known as Raven Rock or 'Site R', it was built by Truman in 1949 and functions as a shadow Pentagon whenever the President is in residence down the road. Staffed by 350 people, the centre is part of the same chain of command as Mount Weather; a seamless chain whose links are composed of up to fifty different bases across the USA. Each of these is always manned, either by military personnel or civilians, and all are funded by covert 'black budgets' – appropriations that fail to appear on any publicly accountable budget sheet. Funds are simply allocated from elsewhere in the awesomely large US defence budget – a figure which even in the comparatively lean years since the Cold War runs to hundreds of billions of dollars per year. The amount is large enough to hide not only the construction and continued maintenance of such bases but also stealth bomber projects, advanced nuclear submarines and, of course, the TG and its projects. While the TG might be a tiny part of the overall defence picture, it might possibly be *the* most secret.

Private industry is also integral to the TG, as it is to other projects such as the stealth bomber. Right from the start, industry's involvement has been critical in supplying skilled technicians; not just to build the bases, but also to develop the discs in the first place. The TG project would have been impossible without their involvement.

The military industrial complex, as this rough agglomeration of companies has sometimes been labelled, is undoubtedly powerful, with influence reaching across the world. Companies such as Northrop and Lockheed have been synonymous with the development of 'black' aircraft projects (those that have no official budget) since the Second World War. Their finances have flourished on the back of the Cold War, though things haven't been so easy following the break-up of the USSR. But those linked to the TG can still count on a highly lucrative dripping tap of funds, which will probably never stop.

By its nature, the disc project is one that must always be moving forwards with a sense of impetus, for if it were to stand still there is always the danger that the advantage gained over fifty years of continuous advancement might be lost, never to be regained if the core group of engineers at the heart of the project were let go. And just as the TG have been putting huge resources into the Alpha, Beta and other projects, so it seems that these military contractors have been following suit. For example, the company behind the billion-dollar B-2 stealth bomber, Northrop, is known to maintain an unusual-looking site near the Tehachapi Mountains in southern California, close to the town of Lancaster. Rumours among locals attest to the base having up to forty-two different underground levels and that it's linked in turn to many of the other underground facilities in the locality by a secret underground transportation system; some mention trams, others 'tunnel-saucers'. In any event, whatever is being developed there is of a highly secret nature, involving a long runway-like structure on the desert floor, at both ends of which are buildings sunk into culverts. In the middle of this runway appears to be a hydraulically powered iris which opens like a camera aperture and from out of which rises a weird-looking transmission tower topped off with a flat pentagonal aerial, thought to be used in the transmission and/or reception of radar signals bounced off remote targets. Both McDonnell-Douglas and Lockheed possess almost identical structures themselves (at Gray Butte airport and Hellendale respectively), and one must wonder what is going on between these firms that would make them collaborate in this fashion, for obviously the technology is being shared. The explanation I would offer is that these sites are actually owned by the American government in some manner and that these three companies are merely 'renting' them; leasing them as caretakers while they use them in a tripartite group of their own to develop a new form of radar or some other breakthrough. Witnesses living in the areas have all reported seeing strange lights emanating from these sites at night, which might have a lot more to do with the bases being also involved in the TG project, and less to do with their being part of an alien-dominated conspiracy.

But perhaps the last word on the subject of secret underground bases must lie with the Greenbrier Hotel in White Sulphur Springs, West Virginia. Dating from 1780, the Greenbrier developed in size and stature throughout the nineteenth and early twentieth centuries – even having its own airfield by 1930. During the Second World War it served as an army hospital for evacuated casualties before being remodelled and opened for business anew in 1948. In the hope of regaining its old reputation, in 1960 it added the extensive West Virginia wing. However, all was not as it seemed, for directly beneath the new wing the federal government constructed a huge bunker complex that would serve as home to 535 members of the US Congress and their staff in the event of nuclear war. At over 10,405 square metres, the bunker is one of the largest of its kind, yet during its construction into the rock beneath the hotel, *no one noticed* . . . For over thirty years until its decommissioning in 1992, the bunker was ready to start offering 'guests' facilities the equal of the hotel above – its own swimming-pool among the attractions. Just the thing to take one's mind off the nuclear winter raging above.

The 1979 Ryder Cup competition was held at the Greenbrier.

Thousands of golfing spectators and all their paraphernalia surrounded the site, yet no one noticed. If all that could be built back in the 1960s, imagine what might be achieved today. And then consider why the site was decommissioned . . . Could the powers-that-be have something newer and better on hand elsewhere? Surely, if the TG does exist, in whatever form, is it not conceivable that the bases it's been using for even longer are even more effectively concealed? I don't know if a 'super-tunnel' has been built, but it's a good guess to say it has. Likewise, the existence of Es-4 at Papoose Lake. But until the authorities are ready to announce them to the world, it's all just so much informed guesswork.

in conclusion

'Beware lest you lose the substance by grasping at the shadow.'
Aesop, *The Dog and the Shadow*.

'Realists do not fear the results of their study.'
Dostoevsky, *The Latest Literary Phenomenon*.

Throughout this book, I have endeavoured to present the facts and assumptions regarding the story of the discs in a stark and realistic light. At times, this stance has omitted several myths and rumours, which I have been more than once tempted to include. Therefore, for the sake of balance, this last chapter will concentrate on some of these less reliable fragments of 'evidence'. What I won't do, however, is offer a firm guarantee of their provenance. Instead, I leave readers to reach their own conclusions, though I'll offer a few opinions of my own along the way.

We can break these entries down into several distinct sub-groups, and, though we're going to view them in turn, there's no particular rank of credibility – they all claim part of the disc legend for themselves (some more convincingly than others, it has to be said).

First of all, let's look at the origins of the modern disc project in wartime Germany. I've spoken before of the various discs being developed there and documented their likely performance. But *some* observers claim that the Germans were not only building the one-or two-seater Haunebu craft as described, but also much larger craft of around 300 metres long, fitted with Schauberger-style engines, capable of taking Nazi astronauts to Mars. Further, I've seen reports of the 'official' German disc programme beginning as early as 1938, as well as photographs of mocked-up craft. In my opinion, this is just so much wishful thinking. Firstly, while the SS were more than capable of managing a disc project of a containable size, as we've seen, building a craft this big would have been beyond even *their* engineering resources. Moreover, the security involved in keeping a craft as big as this hidden all these years would also have been beyond the SS and Gestapo. The war was slowly coming to an end from the autumn of 1944 onwards and the SS knew it – hence the relocation of projects, in part to secure their future as much as on strategic grounds.

The disc project, as I've described, could be dispersed with a minimum of guards and labourers. But a craft 300 metres long? Consider the number of engineers, metallurgists etc. needed to work on it and whose tongues would need to be kept still. And what happened to the craft after the war? Did it land in Antarctica or South America from its sojourn in the outer reaches of our solar system? There to collect Hitler and a select few cronies and make for a Nazi moon base somewhere? This just doesn't add up.

With the exception of Dr Richard Miethe, I'm not even aware that any members of the German disc team have ever been conclusively *proved* to have existed, not that in the immediate post-war years this was a subject that many civilian ufologists were pursuing. An article that appeared in the German newspaper *Der Spiegel* in 1950 was attributed to Schriever, however, and went on to suggest that the discs had only ever reached the blueprint stage. But even this is somewhat discredited, when we bear in mind the most likely possibility that Schriever was probably working undercover as an Odessa agent, in the months and years immediately following the war, as a courier driver for *Stars & Stripes* magazine. Thus, assuming Schriever was a real figure and not the figment of a reporter or an intelligence agent's fevered imagination, who is to say that his article wasn't a deliberate plant? Consider the year of his article – 1950. The TG, if it had formed, would have been running for a couple of years by then, and Schriever might just as easily have been speaking for it, as much for his SS controllers, as part of a concerted disinformation campaign. The 'flying saucer' myth was beginning to get into gear around that time, and the authorities could see that if they let it develop naturally it might take the heat off their own project. Discounting the notion of the discs having a German origin would have switched focus to thoughts of aliens, and the illusion could then continue.

A few years later, in 1957 a book was published in Germany written by a Major Rudolf Lusar which claimed to offer the truth on many Nazi 'secret weapons', the discs among them. In discussing the discs, all that Lusar had apparently done was to take Schriever's original 1950 article and extrapolate from the hypothetical performance data shown to treat the discs as 'real'. He even gave the discs actual performance figures, which was like writing an in-depth road test of a new car without ever driving or seeing it. He also included an illustration which, though obviously an artist's whimsical impression, has since become part of the story's tapestry and includes for good measure what was to be an impressive-looking laser weapon on the under side. Lusar's book was translated into English two years later, and even prompted senior members of the National Advisory Committee for Aeronautics to comment on the claims it made. Hugh Dryden, director of the committee, said that there was no truth in Lusar's statement that the Germans had engineered a disc that could attain the speeds and altitudes claimed.

Note that he was careful not to rubbish the idea of German discs *per se* just the claims in the book. In any policy of *dis*information, one should always seed statements, rumours and announcements with at least *one* grain of the truth – wrapping a mystery inside an enigma. In a *mis*information campaign, no such elements are released; the story is all rubbish. When we look at the claims made by Rudolf Lusar, what we see is just so much blatant disinformation: for example, cameras with intensely high shutter speeds, discs that can fly at speeds seemingly plucked from the air. But what if, buried within his testimony, is at least one element of truth – in this case, that the German discs were real? This would contradict Schriever's earlier statement, in any case.

Now fast-forward thirty years to 1989 and the arrival of Robert Lazar on the scene, with his testimony of Es-4. Again, unlike a classic misinformation campaign, there are probable elements of truth to what he reputedly saw: the interconnected hangars and discs and so on. But what if there's another more subtle level to this case that's been eluding us to date? Consider their two names: Rudolf Lusar and Robert Lazar. Could not a mischievous case be made to show that the latter name is merely an anglicised version of the former? Is this merely an occurrence of coincidental serendipity, or a sign of something deeper? Is someone in the TG trying to tell us something about either man's testimony in the deliberate choice of names? We already know that certain elements of Lazar's past history don't add up, so can we view this apparent connection to a previous disinformant as further proof of Lazar's deeper role?

In looking at the issue of why we've never seen the discs, either German or TG models, some have suggested that this is *because they don't exist*. Yet such blind and simplistic sentiment doesn't stop with the discs. Take the German Hadubrand project, for example. Some have suggested that this death-ray project might have been a potential war-winner for the Reich, yet in the absence of proof (like the discs) a few observers question whether it even existed.

Personally, I veer towards scepticism on this particular project, though I would remind readers of the policy adopted by Hitler, when determining whether to deploy such Wunder Waffen. Following his gassing on the Western Front in the First World War, he had decided never to introduce a weapon that could either be quickly copied or bettered by the enemy. The V-1 and V-2 both fell within this category, as were the discs to a degree. But the death ray could easily be turned against German troops and civilians if an example were captured, as might the V-4 radiation bomb and nerve gases, such as VX or Sarin. For all his fanaticism, Hitler remained a patriot and had no interest in raising the stakes – even at such a late stage in the war – so the death ray was left on the shelf and, if it *did* exist, was either spirited away by the SS or captured by the Allies. Incidentally, the likely reason why the Allies never copied either the V-1 or V-2 is because they could see that, although technically intriguing, both weapons remained of essentially limited strategic value – although the V-2s used post-war for space research were invaluable.

None of the technologies eventually deployed were, by themselves, war winners, merely additional refinements to the art of waging war. Throughout history, this hasn't always been so, with previous armies enjoying decisive advantages in the form of longer swords, suits of armour, the longbow, the musket and cannon and finally, in the First World War, the machine gun, submarine and tank. Yet since the First World War and with the obvious exception of the A-bomb, warfare has settled into a pattern of refinements, with little innovation. Fighter planes became faster and more agile but remained essentially conventional. Tanks acquired heavier armour and larger guns, but were still lumbering and potentially vulnerable, unless supported. If the Second World War could be said to have ushered in anything, it was the extension of war to the home front. The trenches of the First World War had seen the attrition of the soldiers themselves; in the Second World War, this was to switch to the potential for direct attack on a country's home manufacturing base: witness the countless bomber raids carried out in Europe and Asia on industrial targets. Who could build the *most* aircraft, tanks and submarines, not necessarily the best . . . When the Americans dropped the A-bomb on Japan, it was only because its generals had realised that an assault on the Japanese home islands would see a First World War-style slaughter of their men. The Americans' technical superiority would mean little to a population that appeared willing to go to its collective death in support of its emperor. But in Germany, such a decision to commit national hara-kiri in support of Hitler was *never* required.

It's true to say that not *every* German civilian or serviceman was a member of the Nazi party. There weren't enough fanatics left at the tail end of 1944 to orchestrate a similar degree of resistance as in Japan, and with the capabilities of the armed forces draining away like air from a punctured football the fight was leaving the Reich. By contrast, the Allies had already discovered their advantage in the air and were exploiting the power this gave them to wreak daily havoc almost at will. The war was already lost and the discs now nothing more than an irrelevant sideshow, which is one reason why I suspect that Kammler packed the whole project up and shipped it off to pastures new. Commentators since, even surviving senior figures from within the Nazi hierarchy, have questioned whether Germany could ever have pursued a project such as the discs, but I would suggest that, even in the latter stages of the conflict, the capacity was there for limited production. Heinkel's He 162 Volksjäger jet fighter took just three months to leave the drawing board and make its first flight, entering mass production simultaneously, only to be stopped shortly after with the sudden end of the war. I would guess that the Haunebu employed barely more sophisticated engineering than the Volksjäger, so could easily have taken its place had things been different.

Further, here was a true war-winning device, so it's not hard to guess at what might have occurred if the Germans *had* put their discs into production before the end of the war. The first one to crash behind Allied lines would have been retro-engineered in double-quick time (with an urgency contrasting the efforts at copying a V-2), and pretty soon Allied pilots would have been flying discs over Germany, instead of P-51s, Spitfires and B-17s. Stalemate again. Germany would still have lost. Unfortunately, the Soviet Union might then have developed the technology too, so the ensuing Cold War might have become rather warm, rather quickly.

If the world had come through that period unscathed, it might have made worldwide travel a lot cheaper and more accessible, even more so than it is today, but the risks would have been far higher. Imagine a terrorist group or renegade dictator with a fleet of discs. Nowhere in the world could then consider itself safe, as attack could come at a moment's notice. So, assuming the British acquired the plans for the discs, should we then be surprised at the ensuing silence? The world of today is even more politically unstable than it was fifty years ago, leaving any such release or announcement as ill-advised. Look at the number of dirty little wars we've seen during the 1990s if any proof were needed that things are more unstable nowadays than they were during the Cold War, when at least each side could analyse and predict the intentions of the opposition.

But there's another side to all this. If a third world war broke out tomorrow and the TG discs were to appear in the open, imagine what a nuclear-equipped enemy might make of them. Without adequate measures itself, such an enemy might feel oppressed and backed into a corner, where the only action against its oppressor would be to carry out a pre-emptive first strike and to ask questions later. No shots might have been fired by the discs, but no matter; their presence would be enough for the red button to be pressed. A fear of escalation is one of the main reasons for the continued secrecy of all aspects of the project. Developments can continue as long as investigators and ufologists are willing to suspend disbelief and imagine there are EBEs flying the things. No one knows the whole picture, and those who claim to have inside knowledge are deluding themselves – and us.

But the discs are there – have no doubt. When Silver Bug was developed during the 1950s, its performance was nothing short of astounding – and that was almost forty-five years ago. Should we believe that development stopped at that level? Of course not. We're told about Silver Bug simply because it's now old enough to be no longer deemed a security risk. The likely truth is that there have already been several generations of discs following it.

A comparable example is the F-117 Nighthawk, the 'stealth fighter'. Actually more of an interceptor/bomber, this aircraft was first revealed during the Gulf War in 1990–91. Representing the state of the art as the world saw it, it was only in the footnotes that one discovered it had first flown in 1978–9 and entered operations in 1984 . . . Six years before Desert Storm. That's six whole years in which it had been flying operations, without a whisper to the outside world. Another example is the Northrop B-2 advanced technology bomber, first announced in 1988 yet stemming from a design programme begun in 1977.

Of a classic flying wing design, the B-2 was announced with plans for a limited production run – but at over $1 billion per aircraft it doesn't come cheap. The cost of these secret projects must be astronomical, as some of the published figures for the B-2 programme testify. The US spent $23 billion on the B-2 before a single plane took to the air. That was twenty times what the US had spent on AIDS research to that point in 1989. The B-2 was once considered too expensive ever to send into combat in case one were to be lost; the cost-per-kill ratio would never justify it. Senator William Cohen remarked of the B-2: 'It's the equivalent of saying we're going to send a Rolls-Royce down into a combat zone to pick up groceries.'

In other words, why blow up a $10 million bridge with a $1 billion aircraft, when a $200,000 missile will do the job just as effectively, fired from a $15 million fighter aircraft? And it's the same for the discs . . . These things are so expensive and precious that they can never be risked in operations where there might be the slightest chance that a $50,000 ground-to-air missile will bring one down. Imagine the adverse publicity something like *that* would cause. During the conflict in Kosovo, the USAF did indeed lose one of its B-2s in action, and I clearly recall the furore it garnered as a result. This is why we'll never see the discs publicly revealed. Can you imagine a government spokesperson – elected or otherwise – standing on a platform to announce the discs' existence and then having to defend them on cost grounds to reporters demanding to know why the TG (or whoever) has them but can't risk using them? And it's not just the discs that would fall under scrutiny, but also the support infrastructure: hangars, engineers, secret factories and test sites. Assume for a second that a B-2 and a 'basic' Alpha disc work out at roughly the same cost – $1 billion. I wonder what the comparative value is that justifies the disc? At least the B-2 is being used in combat, but with their many abilities I can't also believe that discs are just resting in their hangars . . .

Put simply, aircraft like the B-2 are built because designers are always looking to build a better mousetrap. Conveniently, this also means you have the ideal excuse to offer whenever people spot a disc in the skies . . . If you saw something that defied conventional explanation and was *obviously* a disc, in the past you'd have reported it as such and the official government response might have been something like 'atmospheric anomaly' or 'weather balloon'. Now, though, witnesses are offered explanations such as 'test-flying a B-2'. Not only does this sound convincing to the layman, but it immediately quells the interest of most people. If one were to persist in saying that the sighting was of a disc and not a flying wing-type aircraft such as the B-2, officials could think of any number of compelling reasons to explain away what you *think* you saw. To announce the discs publicly is to invite rival nations to copy the technology and then you'd be without the advantage. By keeping them locked away and using them selectively, you maintain their operational status and advantage, but also the mystique in the public's eye and the confusion in your opponents'.

Before we get too carried away on these themes, let us also remember that the F-117 is now a twenty-year-old programme. While the Gulf War heralded its emergence from the shadows, you can bet it was as much for Saddam Hussein's benefit as America's. If the additional propaganda hadn't been required, we may still not have been any the wiser but, given its age, is another reason for us knowing anything of it at all, down to the fact that its replacement is already flying? Similarly, the B-2. It was only political pressure from the American Senate over its budget which prompted the USAF to reveal the existence of the aircraft. Does that mean a replacement is already operational? At this point I should mention what little we know of this possibility and introduce the subject of Aurora.

The American Aurora programme is a top-secret, compartment-alised umbrella for advanced (though essentially conventional) aerospace vehicles, whose performance exceeds the previous high-speed record holder, the SR-71 Blackbird spy plane. One of the Aurora designs appears to carry the official designation TR-3B (an abbreviation of 'tier three', which might be interpreted as representing the third generation of such advanced craft following the U-2 and SR-71). Its prototype first flew in the mid-1980s, leading to at least three examples becoming operational in the early 1990s. Financed out of the vast black budget and diverted Space Defense Initiative funds, TR-3B uses a triangular flying wing platform (though dissimilar to the B-2) and is believed to be powered by a 'pulse-detonation wave engine'. This revolutionary engine works by detonating pellets of an unknown fuel in a blast chamber, the timed shock waves from which then propel the craft forwards. Rumours of other propulsion systems suggest they have been taken direct from the TG project: for example, a form of localised electrogravitic distortion to minimise the mass of the craft.

This is not seen as a primary source of propulsion, as in the discs, but merely a key to unlocking enhanced aerial performance through reducing mass.

Without wishing to get too deeply involved here, there have been many sightings in recent years of black-coloured aircraft resembling TR-3B, being escorted by helicopters or jet fighters. One that springs to mind was a weather satellite photograph of the English Channel published in the last few years which clearly shows a string of 'doughnut-rings' in the sky; these rings could be attributed to the passage of a high-flying aircraft using a pulse-detonation engine. Together with the unique vibratory and ear-splitting 'roaring thrum' that witnesses have reported hearing in its presence, there's clearly more to this story. The TR-3B and its apparently numerous sister aircraft within Aurora are all products of a culture of secrecy which was developed by the TG in the 1950s and which is still running today. I personally have no doubt whatsoever that Aurora actually exists, in one form or another, and is more than likely operating out of Groom Lake, or some other home base.

Given that the USA is the primary partner in the TG, we should also look at various aspects of its military chain of command to see the effectiveness of a policy of compartmentalisation in action. For many years the Presidents of both the USA and Russia have been shadowed wherever they go by unobtrusive agents carrying small black attache cases handcuffed to their wrists. Known as the 'football' in America, such cases contain the launch codes and authorisations for each country's entire nuclear arsenal, as well as strike options – set menus from which each President can order Armageddon. Yet the American President – believe it or not – is unaware of the contents of the case. The commander-in-chief doesn't know what's inside the football, so when the balloon goes up and he has at best thirty minutes in which to decide America's response; he has no previous briefing from which to draw a conclusion. It would be an understatement to suggest that this is a dangerous state of affairs, but if the President is in the dark, who does know? The answer lies with generals of SAC (Strategic Air Command) and others, to whom the President is merely a powerless figurehead. From opening the football, the President is more or less merely along for the ride, and one can only presume that a similar system operates in Russia.

But what does this have to do with the discs? I would suggest that very few civilians in the governments of both the US and its TG partners are even aware of the disc's existence, let alone aware of the huge logistical effort expended over the past fifty years to develop and build a fleet of the things and keep them secret. The civilian leaders might know of the existence of some projects, such as Aurora, but that's OK as long as the generals have one or two extra projects (like the discs) up their sleeves. Civilians work on the projects, of course, but the security measures surrounding them are likely to be exhaustive; they work under the tightest compartmented security conditions, under their shadowy military overseers. As a result, they, too, know little of the overall project. In reality, things may not be as oppressive as in Lazar's description of Es-4, but I would still expect a degree of frostiness in relations between guards and workers. Then there are considerations of the consequences involved in allowing the technology to spread out and ultimately end up in the hands of an enemy. This whole project has opened up Pandora's box, and, try as they sometimes might, the TG's overseers can't put their toys back inside, dis-invent them. They can merely hope to keep the lid tightly closed and prevent others from reaching inside, something that for the last fifty years they've been highly successful at doing.

While there's little doubt about the role played by the Soviet Union in all of this (very little), in the interests of fair play I should recount a story that cropped up in the 1950s regarding a German officer/engineer called Horst Pinkel. Long before the war and in the utmost secrecy, the USSR and Germany had embarked on a few military exchange programmes that covertly breached several clauses of the Treaty of Versailles, which had been brokered following the armistice in 1918 and dealt with restricting Germany's military rehabilitation. In 1928 Pinkel was involved in one such exchange and ended up in the Russian town of Kaluga, where he furthered the work of another German scientist, Walter Lewetzow, in generating certain energy beams that might be used as an energy source (in a manner similar to Tesla's 'transmitted electricity' idea). With the breakout of war with Germany, eleven years later, Pinkel was interned and he and his lab were moved to a remote district in the Urals, whereupon Stalin ordered him to turn his discovery into a weapon. It seems as though little progress was achieved during the war (after all, Pinkel's efforts would have been used against his own countrymen), but it was later reported, in 1948, that an American spy had come out of Russia, apparently bearing the formula for an exotic alloy that Pinkel had developed. The story has it that this metal was to be used to construct a craft that would use Pinkel's concentrated energy beams both for propulsion and weaponry. By the time the story broke, the Soviets were reputedly already in possession of five such craft and were testing them throughout the region, specifically in the Belaja district.

This all sounds impressive, but the story is not without its problems. Firstly, if Pinkel *had* been making such progress, surely his German controllers would have known about it, so why didn't they recall him long before the invasion of Russia in the summer of 1941? Furthermore, given that so much of Russian industry was completely obsolete and antiquated prior to the Second World War, what makes us think they had the capacity to work on something as complex as casting special alloys and had the engineering skills required in such an undertaking as complex as building one of these craft? I agree that even at the height of the German invasion the USSR's *potential* industrial output dwarfed that of Britain. But it was highly dependent on support from the West for its industrial infrastructure, and I simply cannot believe that somewhere deep in the Urals was a high-tech facility geared up to develop something like this. During the war, for instance, the Germans destroyed one of the huge dynamos at the Dneprostri generating plant and the Russians, unable to repair it and restore electricity to the surrounding area, had to wait until a replacement arrived from the USA. Stories such as this were occurring regularly at this time, making Pinkel's claims sound somewhat hollow.

I have suggested before that the extent of the Haunebu project that Kammler took down to Base 211 probably included blueprints from which engineers accompanying him were aiming to re-create the discs, from materials shipped in from Germany and South America. Following him a few months later were the U-boats U-977 and U-530, and the rumours of their cargoes have never eased. Did they take Hitler, Eva Braun, Bormann and other officials out of the Reich? There's not much connection with the discs themselves, but I think I ought to give the rest of the rumoured story, as I know it to be.

At the outset, I must say their escape *was* feasible. I have tried to be as sceptical as possible in reaching this conclusion, but the evidence of Hitler's suicide simply doesn't add up when examined closely, which must throw the subject out for further debate. Furthermore, while history accurately records Martin Bormann's escape from the bunker, what happened to him thereafter remains unconfirmed. Some reports have him being shot in a Berlin street by the Russians, but in the absence of any concrete evidence there's every chance that he, too, falsified his own death to rendezvous with the Führer later on. For a start, Bormann's body was never recovered (his 'skull' was reputedly found in an excavation of a Berlin playground during the 1970s, but this author is unaware of any DNA testing carried out to verify the claim); secondly, in any escape attempt, as Hitler's de facto deputy it would have been safer to have him travel separately from the Führer's party; thirdly, if we surmise that Hitler made his escape out of Berlin in a small aircraft, such as a Storch spotter plane before transferring to an Arado-234 jet bomber, there would not have been room for anyone else, other than the pilot, Hitler and Braun – and even then it would have been a squeeze. So what of the subsequent stories that have arisen over the years, which purport to revealing the truth behind the escape? A favourite, uncovered during the research for this book, involved Hitler's U-boat convoy, en route to Base 211, passing the island of South Georgia, where a secret base was then established, which was attacked and destroyed only during the Falklands conflict in 1982 . . . Amazing. As outlined previously, my own belief is that all these figures escaped and lived out their lives anonymously in South America, thanks to the efforts of groups such as Odessa and the Spider.

Rumours since the war have reported that secret Nazi bases have existed throughout Patagonia – southern Argentina and Chile. A 'secret SS legion' was once even believed to have established itself in the jungle bordering Peru and Brazil. This latter story was first publicised by the Swiss explorer and writer Karl Brugger in the 1960s, who also claimed to have found evidence of a secret underground realm and civilisation, called Akator, that extended under Argentina. Dwelling on this reminds me too much of the old Aryan legends of Vril, so let's move on to look at other secret bases and goings-on, which can be linked in some way with the pre-war UFO story.

Firstly, there are rumours of a UFO base in the waters of Tokyo Bay, Japan, which was apparently attacked sometime since the war by an American navy minesweeper equipped with special extremely low frequency radar that could pinpoint its position. Legend has it that this vessel was sunk by a UFO, although in the few enquiries I've made to corroborate this incident little progress has been forthcoming. Another base that definitely exists is situated on the tip of Long Island, New York, at a place called Montauk. Built during the 1920s, its original purpose was as a naval research centre, but its subsequent use is somewhat more mysterious, given that it's supposedly now disused. As well as the usual mysterious lights occasionally seen at night, residents have reported seeing trucks entering tumbledown shacks, never to emerge, which suggests that they're using elevators to take them down to perhaps an underground road . . . But where would such a facility lead to? The area is littered with various military installations, so there's plenty of material with which to speculate. The Montauk base itself is rumoured to be home to a sinister mind-control programme called Project Monarch, while across from Montauk Point is a nuclear submarine base in the nearby state of Connecticut, thirty-two kilometres to the west are the Brookhaven National Laboratories. This latter site has apparently been involved in accelerating nitrogen atoms as part of some kind of weapons experiment redolent of the death ray. Some commentators have even suggested that the nearby crash of TWA flight 800 is partly linked to these activities. Other, more paranoid commentators suggest that the FEMA agency is somehow involved, secretly readying itself to take over the American government, at which time it will install a military dictatorship, under which civil liberties such as the right to carry a gun would be removed. This is patent nonsense. While it is undisputed that the agency has certain statutory powers, which can be activated in the event of a national emergency, these are only to provide for centralised control; something of a structure which would coordinate recovery operations, from centres such as Mount Weather, for example. Are we really expected to believe that a country so wedded to democracy and free speech would be actively preparing to throw these all away for a virtual dictatorship? On a cynical note, American business wouldn't allow it, given the turmoil it would create in world markets.

In the introduction to this book I mentioned that in recent years the emphasis on UFO sightings had moved to talk of 'abductions' – *very* close encounters, in which the witness, to the best of his or her understanding, reports interaction with EBEs of various shapes and sizes.

What rubbish! While these contactees may wholeheartedly believe, with all their conscious mind, that such contact actually happened, what evidence do we or they have to go on that they met with EBEs? We have *no* photographs of such creatures that cannot be proven as anything other than fake. The 'Roswell autopsy film' of recent years, various smudged Polaroids of two-metre-tall creatures in Bacofoil suits, the old favourite of the supposed grey being holding the hand of what looks like a policeman in a mac and trilby . . . all these images and many, many more are all out there, laying in wait to befuddle the investigator and lead the unwary astray. Until we have *actual* proof – something we know for certain doesn't show a student or an airman dressed in a rubber suit – then taking these images or stories at face value is going to help no one wishing to uncover the truth.

Whenever contactees during the Cold War alleged that conversations had taken place with their alien hosts and/or abductors, the *one* message conveyed by our visiting space brethren was for us to abandon nuclear weapons. Funny how the people claiming to be contactees all shared the same message, even if the retelling varied time and again. As soon as the Cold War ended and imminent nuclear war seemed averted, what new message could our space brothers bring us? *Global warming . . . We must stop burning* CO_2 to avert a global catastrophe. No – it's all too trite, too convenient. I suspect that deep down what drives these people is either an unconscious or all-too-deliberate desire to publicise their own agendas, whatever these might be. The only problem is that, after a time, more and more people start to claim the same experience for themselves – which leads us to the present state of affairs, in which ten per cent of Americans – twenty-five million people – believe they've been abducted by aliens.

But there is another side to all this, for while many of these so-called abductees are surely deluded and have watched *The X-Files* once too often, there may be a small percentage who have had what they truly consider to be a genuine episode; something they can recall as well under regression as during full consciousness. But how do I square the circle between my innate disbelief in visiting EBEs and such cases?

Where the glib responses falter is in mentioning the little grey beings so often reported. Here, too, there may be a rational though distasteful explanation. Here we are at the turn of the twenty-first century. DNA and the genetic sequences of life were discovered fifty-odd years ago, yet authorities are only starting to talk openly about genetically modified crops and cloning. So are we being told, in a premise similar to Silver Bug, that it's taken five decades for such advances to have been made? I don't think so. No matter what we're told, who's not to say that scientists the world over have *already* cloned people and that their DNA sequences have long been manipulated for any number of illicit projects and experiments? I can guess at what some of you might be thinking, but remember that in this last chapter I'm simply throwing out ideas that have no provenance; ideas which I might not necessarily subscribe to either. But given that it's difficult not to mention the occupants of the discs, when so much has been spoken of their vehicles, I'll now outline *one* interpretation of what witnesses are reporting. It might not be at all accurate, but it's just as likely to be spot on – the one constant is that we'll never know for certain.

Let's start by looking at the height of the creatures reported, in three-quarters of all abduction cases. They are almost all uniformly put at between 0.7 and 1.3 metres tall, with the most common at around the metre mark. But such heights are already well known in humans. The malady known as infantile dwarfism produces very small individuals, usually by stunting the growth of the spine while the rest of the limbs grow normally (or near normally). The most famous case was that of Charles Sherwood Stratton. Billed as 'General Tom Thumb' by P. T. Barnum, he made his circus debut at the age of eighteen, standing only 0.83 metres tall. There have been many other documented cases of people even shorter than Stratton. For example, a Dutch female by the name of Pauline Masters was only 58.9 centimetres tall when she died aged nineteen. However, while I accept that these are rare enough cases, there are still native races of 'pygmies' found around the world displaying symptoms of 'bulldog syndrome' or achandroplastic dwarfism, in which those afflicted develop a disproportionately large head, short face with bulbous eyes and a broad nose. Shortened bones of the forearm and lower leg are also seen. African pygmies often have these characteristics, the smallest race being the North Twides of the Ituri forest, their average heights ranging from 1.37 metres for women to 1.44 metres for men.

Now compare these characteristics with those associated with the 'greys'. Large heads, almost out of proportion with the torso? Yes. Bulbous, prominent eyes? Yes. Where comparisons obviously differ is in the reported skin colour, though this might be as a result of many factors, from diet to conditions of habitation. It might even be that these 'greys' apply cosmetics to their faces in order to fool us into thinking they're genuine grey-green-skinned EBEs. However, an area that presents some difficulty with investigators looking to establish some kind of direct link between UFO crews and pygmies, is in the appearance of ears and mouths; EBEs reported as having mere slits, without ear lobes or lips.

As ever, I offer no claims for what follows, but this scenario does provide a solution of sorts. Imagine for a moment that the year is 1955 and that you've been placed in charge of a project by the TG to establish a 'captive breeding programme' that will provide your UFO project with crews tailored for smaller discs likely to be produced in the future, or for long-term voyages unsuitable for 'normal' human crews. You know that such figures mustn't exceed a certain height, but firstly you have to get your 'first generation' from somewhere. You hear of a race of pygmies that's just been discovered deep in the Amazonian forest and so set up a mission to locate them. With the help of TG-recruited anthropologists, you meet the tribe and gradually gain their trust over a series of meetings. During one such meeting – miles from anywhere and with no witnesses – you arrange for some Beta cargo discs to land in the clearing chosen for this meeting. The Indians – terrified at what is going on – are seemingly unable to respond or to escape, but perhaps this has more to do with the 'mind control', electromagnetic weapons aimed at them that induce temporary paralysis. Access doors in the discs open up, and from them emerge crewmen wearing protective clothing, who herd the entire population of the village aboard. The discs then depart, leaving the colluding anthropologists to report back to the nearest authorities that they had been unable to meet the tribe on that occasion and that they would have to depart for home immediately. So the cover story is sown. The discs, meanwhile, have taken the villagers to a remote site, far away from prying eyes – it could be anywhere, not necessarily at a main disc site development base such as Es-4 or White Sands.

The anthropologists join up with the confused and frightened villagers later. While some team members might be suppressing qualms over what they're going to attempt, there are sufficient security steps in place to ensure that in public at least the team presents a unified front to you, the project manager. Your next level of authority is the TG itself, and visiting officials from HQ are always around to ensure security.

Now let's consider this site. As well as the expected coterie of doctors and surgeons, there would also need to be a large though subtle military presence there, unless its location was so remote as to preclude escape for its new inmates or 'guests', with access only from the air via helicopters or discs, there being no need for a runway. In any case there would need to be hangars, where vehicles could be stored and worked on under cover, supply warehouses and barracks for the personnel and 'subjects'. A large hospital complex would also need to be constructed.

At first the team would take the opportunity to study the

physiological aspects of the pygmies during normal activities and perhaps teach the youngsters English and basic maths. Suitable candidates would then be picked for evaluation in a disc simulator, suitably altered to accommodate the frame of a small pilot. That would determine the eventual suitability of the subjects to the job for which they had been raised. As time passes, the elders of the village die; they're the lucky ones, as their offspring and those who follow will know of no other life than living solely to pilot the discs.

What you're really working towards is to integrate fully the new pilots with the discs in a cyborg-like relationship; a seamless fusion between humans and machines. Ultimately, your team is looking to see what basic organs and systems the human body can do without. Why? Because with fewer organs, subjects (they're no longer thought of as individuals) can function for longer, in more extreme environments at sustained high efficiency. They will tire less, require little sustenance and their brains do without sleep. One by one, the team develops a painstaking system, whereby the subjects' brains are cauterised in certain places, leaving them without memory or recall of their past life and extremely pliable and open to suggestion, through auditory nerve induction, via subcutaneous implants. No longer needing their ears for hearing in the regular sense, their lobes are removed. A sense of smell is no longer required either, so their noses are also removed, leaving behind two vestigial nostril holes for respiration. Finally, we come to the subject of eating and drinking. Subjects already possess a smaller frame than a regular human adult and will therefore need fewer calories. Flying a disc might also be a physically undemand-ing activity, so the stomach and bowels would also receive attention; shrinking the intestines through surgery would allow sustenance to occur only through a protein-rich liquid, which is all the reduced stomach and liver are now capable of processing.

No longer requiring solid food, all subjects have their teeth, gums and tongue removed, along with the vocal cords. Their jawbone is then broken and reset, with or without steel pins, to restrict movement and leave merely a slit through which they can both breathe and ingest this liquid. All, that is, apart from the more intelligent subjects, who retain their tongues and vocal capacity, to allow them to undertake aural contact with their handlers; perhaps they act as 'foremen', teaching the others by example, in addition to the auditory nerve induction used by the team.

Not surprisingly, in the earliest days of the project subjects often died of shock before their progress could be gauged, but this didn't deter your team; if anything, it merely spurred them on to perfect their techniques and procedures. Thoughts of morality or of simply questioning what they're doing are forgotten – after all, the TG was involved in a Cold War with the USSR, who for all we know were doing *exactly* the same sort of thing somewhere in Siberia. And anyway, where else are keen young scientists going to find such open-ended chequebooks and unfettered access, in the pursuit of goals which will ultimately – or so they believe – benefit humanity as a whole?

A decade passes and your project has reached 1965. The pygmy tribe is unrecognisable. All the original members have now died, but samples of their sperm and eggs are now being cross-matched, in the world's first test-tube conception project – a full eighteen years before Louise Brown, officially the world's first test-tube baby, is born in 1978. Occasional trips back to the jungle are still being made to collect samples from other tribes to provide bio-diversity; soon, even this will cease to be needed, as early results with cloning are looking good. Female pygmies are now used solely as 'child-vessels'; inserted with fertilised eggs at regular intervals, the terms of which are now prematurely ended at twenty-six weeks. The tiny babies are then altered at this stage with highly advanced microsurgery to ensure they grow to be perfect subjects. Further operations are required, but by the time these almost 'idiot savant' subjects reach only nine years old their flight training can begin, as by this age they're ready to begin assimilation of technical data and principles. Early exposure to the equipment in the simulator will only accelerate the learning process. Their lives are spent in harness, in communal dorms, with no free time as such – after all, with what could they fill it? There are no longer cases of violent behaviour – such tendencies were eliminated when their brains were cauterised, pacifying them.

Another decade passes and we're now in 1975 – twenty years after the first subject was captured. A lot has changed and been learned in that time. Since the cloning side of the project has been running for the past decade or so quite successfully, there are no longer any females in the project and little likelihood of their being born either. But then, the boys being produced are also sexless, hairless androgynes. Artificial wombs and placentas now nurture the foetus through to full term. With successive genetic advances, the number of operations required for each subject are also dwindling. The only operations still required are to cauterise the brain (with its complexity, genetic manipulation is still out of the question) and to address a few oddities in the torso and frame. As the years have gone by, the lungs have also been altered, to allow respiration at a lower rate than previously required – the normal heartbeat and rate of metabolism are now at half the regular human rate and are set to fall even further. This means that fewer supplies of oxygen need be carried on board the discs for long trips, and with the ingenious rebreather system, as seen in NASA's Apollo rockets, the discs now have a handy way of conserving and recycling supplies, further reducing weight and room. With advances in computer technology since the 1960s, command and control systems are also much improved. At first, voice commands in the native's own language were given, before early subjects learned English. But from the mid-1980s instructions are now issued direct by computers, via the implants inserted at the age of three, which straddle the auditory nerve and use a new rudimentary language comprised of odd sounds and notes, 'words' now deemed too unwieldy and difficult to assimilate quickly. Head-up displays mounted in goggles also project and present data clearly, using bespoke coloured symbols and icons.

Subjects are seldom exposed to sunlight and exist in a world where exposure to ultraviolet light is minimal. Out in space, however, radiation of this and other kinds is prevalent at all times, so their skin has changed to reflect that and is now comprised of a few more epidermatically optimised layers. The team has also long encouraged subjects habitually to apply a grey-green metallicised powder, which tinges the naturally pallid skin and helps seal it against solar burns.

And this brings us neatly to the present day. Thanks to advances in genetic science and gene inheritance, subjects are now almost completely ready on their emergence from the artificial wombs and require little in the way of additional operations, other than brain cauterisation. They are now 'batch-produced' to order; with a life-span of around a hundred years, some of the earliest completed subjects are still working; with fewer organs and external stimuli, senescence is paradoxically reduced. Life-threatening illnesses are virtually unheard of, because of the restricted, clean diet and lack of organs to become faulty, and while the oldest subjects no longer fly regularly, they are kept alive at another facility as part of an ongoing monitoring process to determine how long they can continue to function. As a result, they spend their days in the simulators there, flying endless imaginary missions, with their performance measured against operational crew. It's certainly a fantastical explanation for the 'grey' phenomena but what of the clothing such beings reportedly wear?

Witnesses almost always refer to the clothing worn by these EBEs, large or small, as one-piece coveralls. Either with or without a metallic finish, I would suggest these are another barrier to the radiation in space. On occasions, some 'humanoids' have been reported by witnesses as wearing shirts and trousers. One thing in common is that usually these uniforms are described as being devoid of fastenings of any kind. Such stories appeared in the days before the world had heard of Velcro – after all, although people like to believe it came from outer space, perhaps it really *was* developed as a result of the need to secure clothing in environments where conventional fastenings would be too awkward or liable to snag on controls.

Belts are also mentioned regularly, but whether or not the strange-looking buckles sometimes described are personal anti-gravity units, weapons or communications systems is never alluded to. Helmets are the other main feature seen by witnesses – from a glass fishbowl over the EBE's head, to an old-fashioned brass diving helmet. But on the bulk of sightings, helmets aren't used all that often and EBEs are able to breathe normally. So what can we deduce from that? Maybe, some crew members are primarily used out in space and breathe an unusual gas mixture, so that when they return to they earth they rely on a supply from a tank on their back.

On that note, my whistle-stop tour through the many speculative possibilities connected in some way with the TG and its EBE programme comes to an end. Personally, I would give my own view on the subject of EBEs as verging on the heavily sceptical. Not because I don't believe such schemes could ever have been undertaken, but simply because I have difficulty in believing that the TG's designers would need to reclaim space in the discs to such a degree that a crew of this nature would be the only viable option. When one considers how easy it would be to retain human pilots and crews compared with all this effort, it certainly does appear the rational and logical choice. With the electrogravitic propulsion system minimising the mass of even human crew members, why would designers feel the need to go to such an extreme? But so many witnesses report seeing the 'greys' in their accounts of abduction that, along with the assumed 'alien' origins of the discs mentioned in the introduction, I wanted to show that if *what* they see ever turns out to be real, then what you've just read might be one such explanation.

So what's stopping me from believing that the earth is being visited by little green Martians, or ambassadors from Zeta Reticuli? Why my unpopular insistence on trying to dismiss the possibility of little green men in favour of a distinctly home-grown option? In a nutshell, the easiest answer is why would any EBEs *want* to come here? I've no doubt that somewhere out there are probably countless millions of civilisations – the law of averages says there must be, and it's a wonderful thought.

But why would any EBEs in our celestial neighbourhood actually *want* to come to earth? This beautiful planet is burdened with a human race that's essentially still primitive – we pollute, kill, squabble, hate; that we're still around is all the more remarkable. Perhaps true EBEs are visiting us to see 'nature in the raw', as we might take an African safari . . . But I doubt it.

In wider terms our so-called modern age has only got going during the past hundred or so years – which is nothing; less than the blink of an eye in universal terms. The universe is so big – and we're just so small and insignificant.

In some ways it's to our credit that we should believe ourselves already members of a wider pan-galactic brotherhood, when in reality we're nowhere ready to even complete the application. We're sadly kidding ourselves as a race, if we continue to believe that the various UFOs seen in our skies since the Second World War are a sign of visitors from the heavens above, confirmation 'that we're not alone'.

Unfortunately, the truth, as I see it, has a distinctly *earthly* origin, and those guarding it from the rest of us know only too well what would happen to us – and them – if they were to open the lid on their secret for all to see.

afterword

'Nothing is more expensive than a start.'

Nietzsche, *The Will to Power*.

A secretive group of men met secretly to discuss what to do with a secret that had been passed to them by *another* secret group in secret – in other words, how best to keep this secret a secret. They decided the best thing to do would be to move the secret from its present, secret location and take it – in secret – to somewhere else that could be relied on to keep it *confidential*. But this new secret location was unfortunately discovered by other people who, while not officially in on the secrets, were keen to learn something of them. This forced the group to move the secret once again, to somewhere new. But before they had a chance to complete the move, some of those secrets leaked into the public domain. The loss of these secrets meant that the new location was missing a small fraction of the original number of secrets. After a short period of time had passed, this new site was itself compromised, so the secret group was forced to move those remaining secrets to yet another new site. This pattern continued for over fifty years, the original secret members of the secret groups by now long gone. But the groups they claimed membership of remained and continued their secret work all this time, adapting and perfecting the original secrets and even creating new ones, the existence of which they hoped future members of the groups would continue to protect. But all along some members have had their own secret agendas and have been secretly tipping off investigators with hints about some of the secrets, which directly led to each secret site being discovered in turn. They knew then as they know now that with the number of secrets growing all the time, continued overall secrecy becomes harder to maintain, so deliberately leaking a few now and again stops the bandwagon from becoming too heavy to move. As some new secrets seem to contradict old ones, the mystique is maintained as far as the general public is concerned, and business continues as normal.

What, who and where these groups are or what they've been doing all these years, I can't say.

It's a secret.

glossary

AFB   Air Force Base (USA)

ALSOS   American Intelligence Mission to Germany, which took its name from the Greek translation of the surname of Major-General Leslie R. Groves, who was in charge of the project. Its brief was to unearth secrets regarding Germany's nuclear programme. As a result of poor intelligence-gathering, the team failed to acknowledge or discover the reality of the German atomic programme, otherwise the contents of U-234 would not have been so much of a shock

Aryan physics   A Nazi doctrine inspired by the physicists Lenard and Stark, which refuted all twentieth-century developments in atomic science, including Einstein's Theory of Relativity, labelling them 'Jewish pseudo-science'

BdM   Bund Deutscher Mädchen (German Girls' League)

CIA   Central Intelligence Agency (USA)

DAP   Deutsche Arbeiterpartei (German Workers' Party); forerunner of NSDAP

ELF   Extreme low frequency

EMP   Electromagnetic pulse. The aftermath of a nuclear explosion sends out a blast wave of electromagnetism which will disable any electric circuit not hardened to withstand it

GCHQ   General Communications Headquarters (UK)

Gestapo   Geheime Staatspolizei (Secret State Police)

HJ   Hitlerjügend (Hitler Youth)

ICBM   Inter-Continental Ballistic Missile

LUFTWAFFE   German airforce

NASA   National Aeronautical Space Administration – the official American space agency

NATO   North Atlantic Treaty Organisation

Neu Schwabenland   Literally 'New Swabia', an area of Germany which lent its name to the Antarctic territorial claim. The ship used in the first expedition was also called 'MS Schwabenland'

NRO   National Reconnaissance Office (USA)

NSA   National Security Agency (USA)

NSDAP   National Sozialistisches Deutsche Arbeiter Partei (National Socialist German Workers' Party)

Odessa   Organisation der SS Abteilung (Organisation of SS Members) – the organisation dedicated to the resettlement and reintegration into post-war society of SS men, usually those with something to hide, like a record of war crimes. Odessa laundered money raised through the illegal sale of art and other treasures looted throughout the war from the conquered territories of the Reich and used it to fund new business enterprises which had legitimate faces and could employ its members

OT   Organisation Toot (German Paramilitary Construction Corps)

RAF   Royal Air Force (UK)

RCAF   Royal Canadian Air Force

RF   Radio frequency

RLM   German air ministry

SA   Sturmabteilung. Group that organised political militia and rival of the SS before Himmler orchestrated its end

SDI   Space Defense Initiative (USA)

The Spider   (Der Spinne) A companion organisation to Odessa, but without the economic benefits. Ran more like an extended social club – another secret society, like the Germanenorden or Thule

SS   (SchutzStaffel) The 'Black Order' founded by Himmler and spun off from an elite bodyguard unit assigned to Hitler. Later spawned military wing, Waffen SS

STOL   Short TakeOff and Landing

TBM   Tunnel boring machine

TG   Tripartite Group, the supposed backbone of post-war disc development

TNT   A variant of high explosive

UFO   Unidentified Flying Object

Uranium   A lustrous metal with the appearance of iron. It is the heaviest known natural metallic element with a density of 19.04 g/ml as compared to lead with 11.34 g/ml

USAAF   United States Army Air Force, forerunner of the USAF

USAF   United States Air Force

USSR   Union of Soviet Socialist Republics

Völkisch   Originally a Germanisation of 'nationalist', it acquired racialist and almost mystical overtones which the English word fails to convey. Hence the attempt to convey them by 'folkish', a neologism when used in this context

VTOL   Vertical TakeOff and Landing

Waffen SS   Military wing of SS. Fanatical troops loyal to Hitler and the Nazi party unto death

Wehrmacht   Regular German army of the Second World War

bibliography

Tom Agoston, *Blunder!* Dodd, Mead, 1985

Olaf Alexandersson, *Living Water: Viktor Schauberger & the secrets of natural energy*, Gateway Books, 1982

Ken Anderson, *Hitler and the Occult*, Prometheus Books, 1995

Ash/Hewitt, *The Vortex*, Gateway Books, 1995

Baigent, Leigh & Lincoln, *Holy Blood, Holy Grail*, Dell/Jonathan Cape, 1982

Michael Baigent & Richard Leigh, *Secret Germany*, Jonathan Cape, 1994

James Bamford, *The Puzzle Palace*, Houghton Miffin/Penguin, 1982/3

Michel Bar-Zohar, *The Hunt for German Scientists*, Arthur Barker, 1967

Gray Barker, *They knew too much about flying saucers*, University Books, NY, 1956

Hans Peter Bleuel, *Strength Through Joy*, Secker & Warburg, 1974

Tom Bower, *The Paperclip Conspiracy*, Michael Joseph, 1987

Geoffrey Brooks, *Hitler's Nuclear Weapons*, Leo Cooper, 1992

Col. Philip J. Corso (ret.), *The Day After Roswell*, Simon & Schuster, 1997

267

Edward Crankshaw, *Gestapo*, Putnam, 1956

David Darlington, *The Dreamland Chronicles*, Little, Brown, 1997

Frank Edwards, *Flying Saucers – Serious Business*, Bantam Books, NY, 1967

Joachim C. Fest, *The Face of the Third Reich*, Penguin, 1979

Stanton Friedman, *Top Secret/MAJIC*, Michael O'Mara, 1997

General Adolf Galland, *The First and the Last*, Ballantine, NY, 1967

Joscelyn Godwin, *Arktos – the Polar myth in science, symbolism & Nazi survival*, Thames & Hudson, 1993

Dr Nicholas Goodrick-Clarke, *The Occult Roots of Nazism*, New York University Press, 1985

Samuel A. Goudsmit, *ALSOS*, Schuman, NY, 1947

Gerald Heard, *The Riddle of the Fying Saucers*, Caroll & Nicholson, 1950

I. V. Hogg, *German Secret Weapons of World War II*, London Press, 1970

Hyland/Gill, *Last Talons of the Eagle*, Headline, 1998

David Irving, *The Mare's Nest*, William Kimber, Granada, 1964

Kaufmann/Jurga, *Fortress Europe*, Greenhill Books, 1999

Jim Keith, *Casebook on Alternative 3*, Illuminet Press, 1994

Donald H. Keyhoe, *The Flying Saucers Are Real*, Fawcett, NY, 1950

Donald H. Keyhoe, *Flying Saucers from Outer Space*, Henry Holt, NY, 1953

Lawrence P. Kirwan, *A History of Polar Exploration*, Penguin, 1959

David Langford, *War in 2080*, William Morrow, 1979

Stan Lauryssens, *The Man Who Invented the Third Reich*, Sutton, 1999

Asher Lee, *The Soviet Air & Rocket Forces*, Weidenfeld & Nicholson, 1959

Stephen J. Lee, *The Weimar Republic*, Routledge, 1998

R. Lomas, *The Man Who Invented the Twentieth Century*, Headline, 1999

Rudolf Lusar, *German Secret Weapons of World War 2*, Neville Spearman, 1959

Robin Lumsden, *Himmler's Black Order*, Sutton, 1997

N. J. McCamley, *Secret Underground Cities*, Leo Cooper, 1999

James M. McCampbell, *UFOlogy*, Celestial Arts, 1976

Alec Maclellan, *The Lost World of Agharti*, Souvenir Press, 1982

Mallory/Ottar, *The Architecture of War*, Pantheon, 1973

Mattern/Friedrich, *UFOs, Secret Nazi Weapon?*, Samisdat Publications, Toronto, 1974

Tim Matthews, *UFO Cover-Up*, Blandford, 1999

H. Montgomery-Hyde, *The Atom Bomb Spies*, Hamish Hamilton 1980

Richard O'Neill, *The Suicide Squads*, Salamander, 1981

Peter Padfield, *War Beneath the Sea*, John Wiley & Sons, 1995

Louis Pauwels & Jacques Bergier, *The Dawn of Magic or The Morning of the Magicians*, Panther, 1969

Nigel Pennick, *Hitler's Secret Sciences*, Neville Spearman, 1981

John Pilger, *A Secret Country*, Jonathan Cape, Sydney, 1989

David Pritchard, *The Radar War*, Patrick Stephens, 1989

Richard Sauder, *Underground Bases and Tunnels*, Adventures Unlimited Press, 1995

Heinz Schaeffer, *U-Boat 977*, William Kimber, 1953

Leslie E. Simon, *Secret Weapons of the Third Reich*, WE Inc., 1971

Smith/Kay, *German Aircraft of the Second World War*, Purnell, 1976

Viktor Schauberger (Callum Coats, trans.), *The Water Wizard*, Gateway Books, 1998

P. W. Stahl, *KG 200*, Book Club Associates, 1981

William Stevenson, *The Bormann Brotherhood*, Weidenfeld & Nicolson, 1973

Walter Sullivan, *Quest for a Continent*, McGraw-Hill, 1957

Vajda/Dancey, *German Aircraft Industry & Production*, Airlife, 1998

Renato Vesco, *Intercettateli Senza Sparare*, E. Murzia, Milan, 1968 (English-language versions: *Intercept – But Don't Shoot*, Grove Press, 1971; *Intercept UFO*, Zebra Publications, NY, 1974)

Leslie Watkins, *'Alternative 3'*, BBC/Sphere, 1977

Tim Weiner, *Blank Cheque – The Pentagon's Black Budget*, Warner
  Books, 1990
John F. White, *U-Boat Tankers, 1941–1945*, USNI, 1998

index

271